KINGDOM
COMMUNITIES

What leaders are saying about *Kingdom Communities: Shining the light of Christ through faith, hope and love.*

"Kingdom Communities offers all those interested in building Christian communities of faith, hope and love, imaginative ways forward that are deeply connected to the heart of the gospel. At a time in our life when people are retreating within circles of like-mindedness, Kingdom Communities points the way to inclusive, open, and affirming communities that reflect the confidence of faith in the God revealed in Jesus Christ."

Rev David Baker,
Moderator, Uniting Church in Australia, Queensland Synod.

"Andrew and Dean have Kingdom hearts and so speak from this perspective. *Kingdom Communities* is not about them but about Christ! With sharp theological insight, examples and ample reflection, they share in an engaging and challenging way to stimulate us to personally think about life, ministry, leadership, mission and the models that will promote advance. This book is not theory but rather is laced with fresh perspective and practical application tailored for the 21st century. I am sure this book will enrich your ministry and your understanding of the Kingdom with method that matters."

John Bond, Chairperson, Compassion Australia Board, Minister at Large, Lifestreams Christian Church and Asia & South East Pacific World Zone Leader of Dynamic Church Planting International.

"Invite a theological college principal and a denominational executive to write about the future hope of the church and what do you get? Not what you might expect. Andrew and Dean offer thoughtful social analysis, inspiring case studies and grassroots leadership principles for re-focusing the work of the church where it belongs: loving and serving local neigbourhoods. With hopeful implications for congregational transformation, denominational resourcing, theological education and especially the mission of the whole people of God, *Kingdom Communities* is essential reading for anyone concerned about the complacency and decline of the church as we know it."

Rev Professor Darren Cronshaw, Head of Research and Professor Missional Leadership with Australian College of Ministries (Sydney College of Divinity) and Pastor of AuburnLife Baptist Church.

"Andrew and Dean are panning for gold as they skilfully sift through the often murky waters of church history. With a keen eye across the globe as well as insightful analysis of the Australian mission scene, the writers provide denominational and local church leaders with a treasure house of ideas for advancing local mission. What emerges is a clear pathway for developing people on mission with God in their local context. A must read for those concerned with developing local mission. Highly recommended."

Rev Dean Eaton, Church Planting Mentor and Mission Facilitator, Lutheran Church of Australia and New Zealand and Author of *Lighthouses: Christian Coaching in a Post-Christian World*.

"I am so pleased this story has been well documented with real world, current examples and provides excellent keys and ideas to release God's power within an organisation and across a whole system. I have been privileged to be part of the leadership and have learnt much about my own Christian walk. The stories of *Kingdom Communities* are a constant source of encouragement."

Gary Edwards, Chair of Churches of Christ in Queensland Board.

"What a privilege to commend such a profound and captivating book. My deepest response is that I believe it expresses the *heart* of God. The combination of sound theology and biblical principles, innovative ideas and a significant case study, communicated with both sensitivity and courage, provides a significant contribution to the deep challenge facing Christian faith in Australia and beyond."

Rev Dr Keith Farmer, Former Principal of Australian College of Ministries and mentor to leaders.

"*Kingdom Communities* is different for all the right reasons. It gives a sophisticated yet clear analysis of the missional situation we are in today but rather than suggesting that we need to do more of the same in better ways, it points to a Biblical model of ministry, ecclesiology and method that deals with the core issues we need to address. It is a wonderful read and highly recommended."

Rev Darryl Gardiner, St Luke's Anglican Waikanae New Zealand and Urban Neighbours of Hope Commissioner.

"Andrew and Dean love Jesus and his church and mission. They see the struggles of the contemporary church, but also signs of hope and renewal. They call the church to join with Jesus in proclaiming and embodying the kingdom of God, through new and transforming approaches to discipleship, mission, reconciliation, community, loving neighbours, and embracing fresh practices. Andrew and Dean show how churches can draw on the power of stories and language and practices to become kingdom communities that glorify and serve Jesus Christ. This is one of the most important books I've read for many years."

Rev Dr Graham Hill, Founder & Director The Global Church Project, Author of *Healing our Broken Humanity* and *Salt, Light and a City*.

"In *Kingdom Communities*, my friends Dean and Andrew present something of a missional analysis of the Australian Church, one that exposes some of the inherent flaws in our thinking. They go on to present an approach to ecclesiogenesis based on the working model fleshed out in Queensland and beyond. A worthy read."

> **Alan Hirsch**, author of *The Forgotten Ways*, *The Shaping of Things to Come*, 5Q, among others. Founder of *Forge Missional Training Network*, *100movements*, and *The 5Q Collective*.

"Based on their leadership and experience in local, state, national and international church and business contexts, Andrew and Dean offer a depiction of the challenges facing the church today. Using data, stories of change and neighbourhood engagement, backed by theological and biblical reflection, hope springs up as Kingdom Communities emerge. Rather than focusing on despair, the book has a practical application to churches of all sizes and models, to individuals, and to creative neighbourhood experiments where the light of Christ is shining through faith, hope, love and compassion. I found it an inspiring book which hopefully will spark imagination for the sake of Kingdom possibilities."

> **Rev Lynette Leach**, Former CEO, Churches of Christ in Victoria & Tasmania, Chair of Stirling College Board.

"*Kingdom Communities* serves as tour guide and theological primer. As tour guides, Andrew and Dean skilfully transport the reader to all manner of delightful places where kingdom communities are flourishing. In so doing, the authors point out what new expressions of God's work look like in a myriad of local contexts. But just as important, Andrew and Dean ground their touring in solid but accessible theological frameworks. Readers not only experience the pleasure of new places visited, but they will have biblical and theological resources to imagine what God might be up to in their own context. *Kingdom Communities* possesses catalytic possibilities for Christian leaders and communities who are willing to imagine anew God's kingdom."

> **Dr Carson E Reed**, Vice President for Church Relations and Executive Director, Siburt Institute for Church Ministry and Frazer Chair for Church Enrichment, Graduate School of Theology, Abilene Christian University, USA.

"Andrew and Dean are undoubtedly successful *insiders* in terms of church life. Their experience is enhanced with the fresh eye of the 'practitioner/ theorist'. Their combination of clear thought and practitioner engagement offers the reader practical insights for the future emergence of a church deeply devoted to mission in our immediate contexts. This is a must read for all Christians passionate about mission in their neighbourhood."

> **Rev Dr Martin Robinson**, Principal ForMission College, UK, Author of several books including *Faith of the Unbeliever* and *Invading Secular Space*.

"I am so pleased that Dean and Andrew have put down in print, the amazing Jesus journey possible when we prayerfully seek His will for growing His Kingdom, and step out in faith to the leading of the Holy Spirit. As a Christian in Australian business and industry for more than forty years I have learnt that we just need to always strive to be Christ where we are, bringing the light of Christ into our communities. *Kingdom Communities* is an easy but challenging must read for all Christians in leadership, and a great encouragement to all those who earnestly seek to grow Christ's Kingdom on earth."

Greg Runge, Former Managing Director David Mitchell Limited and Chair of Council 2013-16 Churches of Christ in Queensland.

"Let me be straightforward with you. You cannot wait any longer. This book is the best survival guide you can get to cross the desert from the old world to the new! Gather those you love. Step into the practices of *Kingdom Communities* together. The future is filled with hope for those who do."

Paul Sparks, Co-Author of the award-winning book *The New Parish: How Neighborhood Churches Are Transforming Mission, Discipleship, and Community.*

"All Australian church leaders are right to be concerned about the Body of Christ in this Country and in our time. Andrew and Dean rightly call for mutual discernment that must include deep listening to what the Spirit is saying. Mutual discernment must also include, as they have done, an embrace of the discipline to write down deep reflections based on insight and experience. This book is a brave contribution to the Australian Church discernment process and I hope that it inspires two responses: considered engagement and more considered writing by Australian Christian leaders and thinkers."

Rev Tania Watson, Executive Minister, Churches of Christ in Western Australia.

"Drawing on informed empirical research, wide theological reading and reflections on active contextually relevant examples, Andrew and Dean have provided an honest, engaging, reflective and empowering work that will assist all leaders who are involved in seeking to articulate living expressions of communities of Christ-followers for the 21st century. I commend this book to leaders of denominations, networks, local churches and their local leaders, along with key influencers within theological colleges to read, reflect, digest and inculcate the needed change that is being considered in this vital and timely work. Perhaps by learning to live and tell new stories from a transformed imagination, the future will have the kind of church that is keenly attentive to the life-empowering Spirit of God who continues to challenge, provoke and lead us into the *missio Dei* for our generation and the ones to come."

Rev Dan Yarnell, National Co-ordinator, the Fellowship of Churches of Christ in Great Britain and Ireland, Senior Lecturer at ForMission College.

"Andrew and Dean offer a sober yet refreshing portrayal of the challenges facing the contemporary church in a rapidly changing, disrupted world. Drawing richly on scripture, history and scholarship, they search out signs of what God is already doing in this world. The result is a book filled with hope. It tells the stories of dozens of Christian communities around the world who seek to follow Jesus step-by-step. Crucially, it sets out a paradigm for action and concludes with a manual of practical advice. Kingdom Communities makes the seemingly impossible possible, and offers a new way to connect with God's mission of justice and love."

Professor Peter Sherlock, Vice-Chancellor, University of Divinity

Kingdom Communities

Shining the Light of Christ through Faith, Hope and Love

Andrew Menzies *and* Dean Phelan

Published by Acorn Press
An imprint of Bible Society Australia
ACN 148 058 306 | Charity licence 19 000 528
GPO Box 4161
Sydney NSW 2001
Australia
www.acornpress.net.au | www.biblesociety.org.au

© Andrew Menzies and Dean Phelan, 2024. All rights reserved.

ISBN 978-0-647-53340-6

First published by Morning Star Publishing in 2018,
ISBN 978-0-648-37652-1

Andrew Menzies and Dean Phelan assert their right under section 193 of the *Copyright Act 1968* (Cth) to be identified as the author of this work.

Unless otherwise noted, Scripture quotations are from taken from the Holy Bible, New International Version ™, NIV ™ Copyright © 1973, 1978, 1984, 2011 by Biblica, Inc. Used with permission. All rights reserved worldwide.

Scripture quotations marked (ESV) are the ESV® Bible (The Holy Bible,English Standard Version®) Copyright © 2001 by Crossway, a publishing ministry of Good News Publishers. Used with permission. All rights reserved worldwide.

Apart from any fair dealing for the purposes of private study, research, criticism or review, no part of this work may be reproduced by electronic or other means without the permission of the publisher.

 A catalogue record for this work is available from the National Library of Australia

Cover and text design and layout by John Healy

Contents

FOREWORD 11

INTRODUCTION 15

CHAPTER ONE 39
    Stuck

CHAPTER TWO 63
    Back and Forth

CHAPTER THREE 97
    Base Ecclesial Communities

CHAPTER FOUR 127
    Into the Neighbourhood

CHAPTER FIVE 153
    Kingdom Communities in Queensland

CHAPTER SIX 181
    From Silos to Kingdom Communities

CHAPTER SEVEN 207
    Leadershifts

CHAPTER EIGHT 241
    Practises of Kingdom Communities

CHAPTER NINE 263
    Frequently Asked Questions.

CONCLUSION 275
    And Finally…

BIBLIOGRAPHY 285

ACKNOWLEDGEMENTS 291

Foreword

I love this book!

There's so much that is good and helpful about Andrew and Dean's writing in these pages. More than anything else I read here the story of two leaders, each with years of grounded experience in the local and everyday, sharing with us some critical learning about being God's people today. I have worked with denominational and congregational leaders for many years. As Dean and Andrew discuss here, these leaders are facing huge challenges in terms of their future and the ways in which they address the massive culture shifts that have made most current forms of church untenable. They describe this well in the early part of the book. What is happening in Australia parallels what's happening across many parts of North America.

In these pages, Andrew and Dean share both the dilemmas confronting the churches and, rather than up in the sky proposals from people who have never been on the ground, they tell stories about the powerful ways God's Spirit has been quietly at work in unexpected ways. You are going to be taken on a journey that introduces you to ways of being the church that will surprise you. You are not going to get a rant about how wrong things are in the churches and what they ought to do to change. You will read the heart of practitioners who have done the work on the ground, who see the challenges for what they are and who continue, as followers of Christ, to believe deeply that the Spirit of God still has much for these old, dry bones to do.

You will read about method and technique. In the stories of challenge, resistance, imagination and change in Queensland's Churches of Christ I was encouraged and heartened by the wisdom that underlies the work of transformation that has been going on. These pages contain huge clues to the ways the Spirit is already about the task of making all things new. Here you will read about how the Spirit has been taking those wonderful, old wineskins and filling them with fresh imagination. That's one of the brilliant points of this book. Churches and organisations (we euphemistically call them *denominational systems*) that have been in existence for a long time, that had calcified and forgotten their own past stories of being a movement of God's people (language which Churches of Christ love to use to describe themselves) discovered again that movement of God. Rather than being focused on getting "church" right (identity) they learned to ask a different kind of question about what God was doing ahead of them. The stories make it clear that this wasn't an easy journey but, when there was a willingness to step out of boxes and risk with God, they rediscovered the powerful movement of the Spirit in their communities. The Spirit doesn't throw us away but breathes new life into the old bones. That is what is being described in this book.

I would underline an important theme Andrew and Dean make in the first part of this book. While these stories describe how an existing system rediscovered life and mission, it wasn't because they set out to rescue their denomination or churches. On the contrary, if I am reading what they are proposing here correctly, they are proposing that the forms and notions of being church that have shaped the denominations don't have much of a future. Beneath the surface of what appear to be simple stories of people discovering fresh ways of being God's people in their communities is a recognition that the denominational systems and forms of ministry leadership that currently shape these systems cannot carry the ferment of the Spirit described in these pages. This is a journey that calls for a huge transformation of imagination for ministers (leaders) and the systems they serve. The introduction of Boff's *base Christian communities* into this conversation is critical and should not be passed over as a bit of theory that has been thrown in to write a book. On the contrary, this is a critical discussion about the ways of being God's people in a time of unravelling; of being a people who are able to discern the bubbling and ferment of the Spirit out of the usual "church" forms and in the communities that are all around us.

One final observation that I was aware of all through this book – it's about leadership. Both Dean and Andrew are skilled, experienced leaders with lots of miles travelled. They will describe for you here some important methods for listening with one another, discerning the Spirit's movement and creating ways of joining with God. Within these practices something else stands out. If we look at the ministry of Jesus we discover

Foreword

that the vast majority of his time was spent in a particular kind of way. Jesus was hardly ever "doing for" people (coming up with plans to change, to create the next best "church" if people would just follow; putting into place the discipleship program that will make Christians vital, getting churches to develop a new vision and so on). On the contrary, almost all of Jesus' time came from "being with" people (participation, presence, listening to them). That's what I read most of all in this book, it's the clue about what drives everything else in these pages. That is why I loved reading it. It's why I encourage you to read it too.

Alan J Roxburgh
Vancouver, Canada

Introduction

> *"Jesus was announcing the coming of a new reality that only some would be able to see and hear. In the midst of our great unravelling, the Spirit is calling the church toward a new way of being. The call is for us to have the eyes and ears to see and hear what God is doing in front of us. Can we see it?"*
>
> Alan Roxburgh[1]
>
> *"Then Jesus asked, 'What is the kingdom of God like? What shall I compare it to? It is like a mustard seed, which a gardener took and planted in the garden. It grew and became a tree, and the birds of the air perched in its branches'. Again he asked, 'What shall I compare the kingdom of God to? It is like yeast that a baker mixes into a large amount of flour until it is worked all through the dough.'"*
>
> Luke 13:18-21

A mustard seed is one of the smaller seeds in the plant world. Yet Jesus said that the kingdom of God was like a tiny mustard seed (Lk 13:18-19). It is extraordinary that something about the size of a grain of sand was selected as a metaphor for God's kingdom. Kingdoms are meant to be mighty. They have armies and structures that cannot be penetrated. They enforce. They have defences and strongholds to ensure the prominence and supremacy of their ruler, the monarch. Everyone serves the monarch so that the kingdom might prosper and hopefully each subject will get by okay (with their head on!). Power comes from the top and dissipates downwards. Those at the bottom usually are last and least.

We know that God's kingdom is very different to a human kingdom. But comparing the kingdom of God to a mustard seed? Really? How could something so small and common possibly be an appropriate metaphor? Jesus said that the kingdom of God was like a person who took a small mustard seed and planted it in a garden. It grew and became a tree where all the birds enjoyed perching in its branches.

---

[1] Alan Roxburgh, Joining God, *Remaking Church, Changing the World: The New Shape of the Church in our time*, New York: Morehouse Publishing, 2015, x.

We know that a mustard seed is tiny but, in this parable, we see that when it is planted it becomes a tree. Not just any tree – a mighty garden tree in which the birds can perch. We think we get it; it's not really about the seed but the tree it becomes. Our cultural imagination encourages vision of a big, powerful tree. Large trees like oak trees and mighty eucalypts seem suitable imagery for a biblical kingdom. Eugene Peterson even borrows the metaphor of a pine nut growing into a mighty pine tree in his translation in *The Message*.[2] So, we form an appropriate image of God's kingdom because the parable seems to make sense to our prevailing cultural worldview. Except that if we are reading the parable this way we are reading it incorrectly and imposing our values and worldview. It's not what Jesus implied.

By reading the text this way, we miss a core part of message that Jesus communicated. We have placed our Western cultural perspective onto a text written for an ancient world. Thus, we force the text to affirm the top-down power structures and corporate imagery that are familiar to so many of us. In doing so, we sweep away part of Jesus' message and deny the humble and local imagery where God is often found. Too often those in positions of power (yes, Dean and Andrew are educated, white males) take over this parable and the real, deeper message is missed.

So, let's look again at this parable and try to understand it in its context. Yes, Jesus meant it when he said that the kingdom of God was like a mustard seed and he meant it when he said it was like that a seed that grows into a large garden tree. But a garden tree that is not particularly grand. Actually, it isn't even officially a tree – it is a shrub! Mustard shrubs only grow to about five metres in height and are not even ranked by botanists as trees. In a garden, they provide wonderful perches for birds over the fruit, vegetables and herbs. However, they are just shrubs. We have to let go of the kingdom imagery of mighty trees and understand Jesus' parable in this new light. More closely, the kingdom of God is like a hardy, scraggy shrub!

The parable of the mustard seed goes further. Besides being very hardy, a healthy mustard shrub produces up to eight thousand seeds. They reproduce other mustard shrubs very well. If you left a mustard

---

2 Eugene Peterson, *The Message: The Bible in Contemporary Language*, Colorado Springs: NavPress, 2002.

shrub alone in your yard for a few years you might come back to find the area taken over by them. And 'the birds that perch in its branches', will probably transport mustard seeds all around the neighbourhood too!

The kingdom of God is like a mustard seed, which when planted grows into a mustard shrub that grows and spreads, often to the most unexpected of places. This small seed represents things that are ordinary, overlooked and unremarkable yet, which bear fruit in all sorts of unpredictable places. Jesus did not choose the Temple, a mighty tree of the forest or a powerful monarch for this kingdom metaphor. He did not choose an image of a vast forest either, but rather a simple garden. The kingdom of God seeks to bring about shalom where it is needed most: the everyday, the commonplace, markets, workplaces, prisons, slums, schools and communities. This is the nature of God's kingdom.

Over the last generation, there has been an immense amount of literature written to assist the technical improvement and growth of the church. Every area of social sciences has been drawn upon as technicians and consultants have tried to develop churches that are better in a whole range of categories: evangelism, pastoral care, worship, preaching and teaching, leadership development, corporate governance, therapy, community engagement and among specific generations, for example. Some church growth and health technicians focus primarily on specific quantitative areas that directly help a church enlarge (for example: car parking, leadership, seating, integration programs, etc.) Others draw our attention to the qualitative aspects of church life. The popular Natural Church Development (NCD) tool for example argues that through continual testing and improvement in the quality of eight specific criteria in church life, that church will grow.[3] The NCD website states, "Churches that have done three or more NCD Surveys, have increased their average growth rate by 51% between the first and the third survey. We plant, we water. God gives the increase."[4]

---

[3] Christian Schwartz, *Natural Church Development: Eight essential qualities of healthy churches*, Mt Gravatt East: Direction Ministry Resources, 1996. The eight areas for quality improvement are: Loving Relationships, Empowering Leadership, Need-Oriented Evangelism, Functional Structures, Holistic Small Groups, Inspiring Worship Service, Passionate Spirituality and Gift Oriented Ministry.
[4] http://www.ncd-international.org/public/what-is-ncd.html

A focus on technical improvement is important in any endeavour. Hard-nosed realists tell us that metrics are what count and we must aim towards church growth. We often hear it said that if a church is not growing then something in it is ill. Yet if it is this simple we are compelled to ask, why are the vast majority of the churches in Australia in plateau or decline? And why are healthy, growing churches usually situated in certain middle-class suburbs? We suspect that there are wider issues like cultural change and demographics at stake in an all too easy prognosis.

In the next chapter, we will explore current data that shows us that the model and expression of church is losing ground in Australian society on every measure available, despite all of the available, technical tools. We accept that there are isolated exceptions, but the census data shows that the current church life is not successful with Australians. It seems Australians do not want to come to what we have made church into. Dean and Andrew are strongly convinced that we are living in a cultural moment that is calling followers of Christ to be more biblical, flexible, creative and meaningful in the birth and support of what we will call 'Kingdom Communities'.

As two people who love and are vitally invested in church life, but with a higher commitment to the kingdom of God, we are challenged by the apparent fruitlessness in the continual focus and refinement on the improvement of the modern church. It is after all a model that does not appear in the New Testament or throughout early church expansion. As important and precious as the current, modern church might be to those who have a vested interest, it cannot be the only model in which we invest and build, particularly when the vast majority of Australians have already voted with their feet. All is not gloom though (really, it isn't). We aim to show that each church still has a valuable contribution to the kingdom. We might first have to metaphorically strip off a bit of paint and sand things back a bit to get the preparation work done but we will get there!

We are challenged by the difference between the ancient parable of a mustard seed (or of yeast, which will come next) and what the modern Australian church has become. Too much activity for ourselves seems to have become the preoccupation of too many modern church leaders,

Introduction

rather than the in-breaking of the kingdom of God in the world, as taught in Jesus' sermon in Matthew (chapters five to seven) and emphasised in the parable of the mustard seed.

Jesus continued on after this parable and for reinforcement used another insightful metaphor in Luke's gospel. Jesus spoke of the kingdom being like yeast that is worked through a large quantity of dough. Yeast is a biological agent that causes bread to rise. So, as members of the kingdom, we are also to help contribute to a rise in the quality, ethical standards and life of our local communities as well as wider society. Wherever 'kingdom of God people' go, so go potential, 'kingdom-raising' agents.

Contrary to what the reader might be perceiving from the trajectory of our discussion so far, the purpose in this book is not the deconstruction of the modern church nor the discouragement of those who find themselves in leadership of it. Rather, we too are a part of the problem and so choose to be a part of the solution. We will propose in this book a transition of what we find ourselves in stewardship over towards greater alignment with what we read of Christianity's first expressions. We will present a model that we believe any church, small or large, from any tradition, is capable of expressing and show that it is already possible and thriving in many places, like mustard shrubs. Indeed, we will argue that the two expressions – new and old – can flourish best, if in partnership.

Our aim is to help you, your church (and the denominational system in which it lives and identifies) as well the many Christians who have walked away from modern church life, to be introduced to the biblical idea of Kingdom Communities which we describe as two or more followers of Christ who are committed to the regular pursuit of basic practices for the purpose of shining the light of Christ through faith, hope and love. We hope you will find this book as a sort of blueprint that offers new possibilities for being God's people in communities.

***

There is a particular place Andrew can take you where, if it is the right time of the year, he guarantees you will catch a fish. To be even more specific, you will catch a beautiful eight-pound Black Bream. Literally, he guarantees you the fish – the spot is that good! This particular spot has never let him down and he is not even very good at fishing.

The spot being described is several hours drive east of Melbourne and at the end of a river and lake system that flows from the Snowy Mountains. It is beautiful, wild and most importantly filled with fish. You might try fishing other places in the lake system with mixed success, but he knows exactly where to go and how far up which inlet. He was shown by a local and sworn to secrecy. If he took you there, he would have to blindfold you! Is there anything better, after a day of fishing in the wilderness than cooking the fish you caught on a campfire with salt, pepper, butter, soy sauce, Chinese cooking wine, ginger and some Asian spices? Perfect!

The art of fishing is similar to sowing seeds. Jesus told a famous parable about seed sowing to a crowd of listeners in Matthew chapter thirteen. You can scatter seeds on the ground anywhere, just as you can fish any place there is water, but only certain areas and certain methods yield a good harvest. Knowledge (especially the local variety) is very valuable with fishing, as with sowing seeds. The only way to become a good grower of seeds or a good catcher of fish is through listening, learning and practice.

Jesus was very clear that seed, which landed on pathways, rocky ground, shallow soil or among thorns had little chance of growth to maturity. Yet, Jesus continued, "Still other seed fell on good soil, where it produced a crop—a hundred, sixty or thirty times what was sown" (Matt 13:8). There is nothing wrong with a poor harvest the first time you sow seeds or go fishing. We all have to start somewhere. Problems arise however if you keep doing the same activity over and over, without improving through learning or listening to knowledgeable advice. Albert Einstein has been famously attributed as the author of the saying that, "The purest form of insanity is to leave everything the same and at the same time hope that things will change." So it is with fishing, planting seeds or the current practice of too many in the church in Australia.

As we examine some of the harvest parables used by Jesus it might occur to you that the language of harvest is not something readily experienced in your church. Indeed, harvest is not a common experience in many Western churches. Currently, churches that are growing do so predominantly because of transfer growth (people moving from other churches) or through biological growth – when the children of Christians confirm the faith that was passed onto them. Statistically, very few Australians enter the church through conversion these days. In fact, far more people are leaving than joining churches and every year the average age of church attendees gets a little older and greyer. The average age of an Australian church attendee is now 53 years of age and a quarter of church attendees are over 70 years of age.[5] Churches are spending increasing amounts of time and money on themselves (on websites, signage, services, specialist staff, buildings, programs and media), yet there is no harvest. Certainly, there is no harvest like the multitudes that Jesus alluded to, which the early church did experience.[6] Yet John records Jesus as saying, "I tell you, open your eyes and look at the fields! They are ripe for harvest" (John 4:35).

Luke also recorded a similar statement by Jesus when he sent his closest followers into villages on a mission trip. Jesus sent about seventy followers with the words, "The harvest is plentiful, but the workers are few. Ask the Lord of the harvest, therefore, to send out workers into his harvest field" (Luke 10:2). If there is no perceivable harvest in most of the Australian church, we must also ask if the language of harvest still applies in the Australian context or can we shrink away from this promise/challenge? Typical of much that Jesus said, these harvest statements seem to combine challenge and promise.

If you follow the trajectory of the New Testament and the global mission of the church, it is clear that harvest language still applies today. Across the Majority World there is a dramatically different story compared to the data about the Australian church (and the West in general). In the Majority world, when Christians hear these words they put them into practice and the harvest is seen. The Christian church is now a majority world faith. In the West, most local churches and their denominations tinker away at technical improvements, intellectualise or

---

[5] *The McCrindle Blog*, "A Demographic snapshot of Christianity and church attenders in Australia", April 18th 2014.
[6] See: Acts 2:41; 4:4; 5:14 & 16:5.

simply ignore the promise/challenge of harvest parables. Yet something is afoot. Humbly and quietly there is a movement going on in Australia. We hope that the following stories help to introduce you to the movement of Kingdom Communities that is advancing the kingdom of God.

This following handful of stories introduces this phenomenon. Allow us to take you on a journey around communities in Australia and beyond. We will start to our north in neighbouring Indonesia.

***

The island of Java, Indonesia is populated by over 141 million people. It has a landmass approximately equal to England's or double the size of Tasmania's. The Javanese population includes the 10 million plus people who inhabit the hot, crowded, smoggy, mega-city, capital of Jakarta as well as the tens of millions who live in the many thousands of rural villages and islands. When you fly over Java, wherever you look you see the scattering of roofs of small villages. Underneath the dominance of Islam (above 86 percent) it is a fascinating religious melting pot with Animist, Buddhist, Hindu, Catholic, Protestant and other religious influences.

Christianity had a tough start in Java when the Portuguese clashed with Malaccan Muslims over the taking of cities. Dutch colonisation gave Reformed Christianity a minor foothold, but it was always very much the religion of the oppressor. The Dutch gave the Roman Catholic Church permission to missionalise some areas of Indonesia and, in the case of Kalimantan, they were permitted anywhere except along rivers, which were reserved for Protestant missionaries. There have been periods of direct violence against Christians by elements of radical Islam, particularly between 1999 and 2002. Today, the majority of obstacles and persecution comes through bureaucratic and local abuses of power or personally through Muslim families who reject and disinherit family members who convert to Christianity.

In the mountains and on the fertile plains of Java, if you know where to look, there is a growing movement of Kingdom Communities. Often these Christians are too poor to afford a building, so they meet in a home or they are simply denied permission by a local governing authority, so it can be easy for a visitor to miss the Christian presence. One of the major differences between Indonesian and Western Christianity is the venue of ministry. For many Australians, ministry is conducted inside a church building. Australian Christians complain that it is persecution when a church building is covered in graffiti. Many in the global church don't even have a building.

Javanese Christians love to sing and worship joyfully and often for hours, but their theology and practice is not centred in a building. God is in the street, the home, the market and (if there is one) the church building. God has gone ahead, and they understand that their task is to participate in what God is already doing. So partly because of their minority status and partly because of a big, biblical theology, the result is that Indonesian Christians go in the name of Christ to serve their neighbours and their community. They are 'sent' people day and night and bring uplift (yeast) to their neighbourhood 24/7. That is a reason why their Christian training colleges teach courses like: hairdressing, child care, first-aid, teaching and hygiene, as well as the traditional fields of theology and ministry.

Graduating from many Indonesian Christian colleges requires that the student has started an intentional Christian community (what we term a Kingdom Community) in a neighbourhood that is self-sustaining, multiplying and ongoing. Students often spend each weekend of their studies in a village putting what they are learning into practice by serving and being 'yeast' among their neighbours. Three-year degree programs are paced over five years to allow solid praxis. Classroom discussion is therefore rigorous and more advanced compared to the typical Australian seminary, due to the student's understanding of ministry in a particular context.

The result is that many thousands of Christian communities have sprung up all over Indonesia like mustard seeds. These churches are typically small and reflect the village structure in Indonesian life. Villages have between 70 and 140 families and are situated in a specific geographical area marked by city gates. Churches therefore reflect this and function like what was once the case in Europe, where people work, play and worship together. When asked about their *raison d'être*

Christians will often say, "I want to bless my community and share the love of Christ with my neighbours."

There are other notable aspects within this growing movement that we observe. *Firstly*, these Kingdom Communities stay small and contextual to village life.[7] Each community requires its own Christian presence where the good news can be lived and contextualised through relationship and sensitivity to the Spirit's activity. Much of this activity is outside the walls of a church building, which gives us insight into the missional activity of God and explains why these Christian movements are growing and active.

Secondly, the leadership in these systems are nationals. Foreign missionaries wisely and sensitively stepped back decades ago and handed over leadership to local people completely. Having planted seeds, the local church grew and is now in its second and third generations of apostolic leadership.

Thirdly, there is a beautiful spirit of unity across the movement. When a Kingdom Community is under stress or persecution, all suffer, and when there is success, all rejoice. The idea of competition between Christians is absent and abhorrent. Recently, one of the community centres run by a Kingdom Community was felled in a landslide. Within days of hearing this news many other communities were sending donations and resources to rebuild the centre. Some people just turned up and started the rebuilding. This organised generosity was a wonderful witness to the Muslim neighbours in the village as they saw the power of organised and unified Christians.

Finally, these Kingdom Communities are multiplying exponentially, and because of the spirit of unity, they are working together to plant new communities and form the planters and leaders who serve there. New Kingdom Communities are fuelled by leaders and planters who receive the benefits of excellent quality training colleges, made possible only through generosity and unity. These communities also identify people with potential leadership qualities and support them through college

---

[7] There are large and mega churches in some areas of Indonesia. However, the predominant model of faith community/church has been local, indigenous and contextual at a size appropriate to villages.

studies so that more leaders and planters are sent across Indonesia's many islands and language groups.

Things are changing inside Christianity. Movements such as those we have described have made Indonesia the second largest Christian nation in South-East Asia (after the Philippines), while the Western churches in the region (including Australia) continue to decline. There are at least triple the number of active and passionate disciples of Christ in Java alone compared to Australia, largely because of the spread of Kingdom Communities. The vast number of Indonesians are still Muslim but there is a growing, multiplying, indigenous church with gifted apostolic leadership that understands its context and it is rewriting the playbook for the churches in Australia to witness.

***

A couple of thousand kilometres south (but still in the same time zone) Busselton, Western Australia is known as a beautiful, beachside town and a gateway to the famous Margaret River Region. Situated under three hours' drive south of Perth on beautiful Geographe Bay, one of life's great joys is having a gelato ice-cream while walking along the two-kilometre wooden jetty on a sunny afternoon. Among its population of just over 20 thousand permanent residents are the usual garden-variety array of denominational churches, each trying to keep their head above water.

One of those churches, Busselton Church of Christ, aware of their need to educate and disciple their young people assessed the local community and identified a specific area of need: a quality, reasonably-priced community school that supported families to raise their children in a safe and nurturing environment. Thus started a dream and then reality of a local school. In 1986, the Cornerstone Christian School began in the church manse with seventeen students. Initially the school was open only to children from Christian families. However, as the school reviewed their aims they realised that an open admission policy would enable benefits: greater resources, better socialisation for all children and an opportunity to introduce more young people and their families to Jesus. Today there are over five hundred students across a program that runs from pre-school to year twelve. The facilities are very impressive for a young school, which has very reasonable fees and all the students are from the local area.

Operating with an open enrolment policy means that anyone can enrol and attend the college regardless of gender, religious belief, and socio-economic, ethnic and/or cultural background as long as they understand the nature and mission of the school community. It operates very much like a 'Christian local community in the community'. Anyone who joins is welcomed with warm hospitality and offered the best of what is available. The school website states that,

"Students achieve excellent ATAR and/or vocational outcomes with well-developed life skills … We are other-centred, serving our College and community with integrity. We see ourselves as researchers, developing reputable projects that will benefit Cornerstone and others."[8]

As the school has grown, the church, which started it, also adopted the school name of 'Cornerstone' and continues to be a very active supporter through personnel, governance and shared facilities. Having such a strong local footprint has opened many doors for student participation in local community events and projects. The school has also become an active initiator of local church unity and, so far, has partnerships with twelve local churches from a range of denominations.

This is not a church school like so many elite private schools across Australia, which charge exorbitant fees and admit the nation's elite into a network of power and privilege. As a Kingdom Community it is embedded in a local, regional community and very much an agent of yeast, uplifting students and families. To come near the kingdom of God in Busselton it is not necessary to go to church on a Sunday – just go to school.

***

Across east, the middle ring of Melbourne's eastern suburbs is about as close to a 'bible-belt' as you will find. Many of Melbourne's large and megachurches are located within a twenty-minute drive in these

---

[8] www.cornerstone.education/about/vision-mission/educational-philosophy/

suburbs. In one of the larger churches in this area, a newly retired couple, Jan and Graeme, expected their next years to be peaceful as they cared for grandchildren, travelled and helped around the church. Graeme was a recently retired senior executive from an ASX top 200 company and Jan was a retired nurse.

Graeme and Jan led a small group in their church and soon the leadership invited Graeme onto the church Board given his corporate experience and extra time available. Couples like Graeme and Jan are typically great blessings to churches and help underpin them. As is quite common, this couple found retirement action-packed with busy schedules unfolding for them both. Yet, as happy as they were, they were about to be jolted from the comfort of leading a church small group, serving on the Board and being a part of the busy social networks that underpin church life.

A strange experience happened to this couple. They had recently scaled down from their family home to a smaller and more manageable apartment. In doing so they changed phone numbers, however to their great distress the new phone number was the old number of a local brothel. Not only were they receiving calls from heavy-breathing unpleasant characters, but most calls came late in the evening and throughout the night. Initially, this became a simple dispute with the telephone company, which for various reasons could not be resolved. However, over time as the disturbances continued, Graeme and Jan felt that God was getting their attention.

They both concluded that God was using this disturbance to draw their attention to the women who worked at the brothel. Jan, being a grandmother, decided to take around a basket of cupcakes! No one had ever done this for the women at the brothel before and they eagerly received the cupcakes from her. Most of the women were very young and often from Asia. Very few even had decent English language ability.

Jan started visiting the women regularly, each time with her fresh baked cupcakes. Over time she got to know some of the girls more closely. Being migrant workers, they had no family support and Jan quickly became a grandmother figure to them. She started helping them with reading tasks. She also started reflecting on the reality that their church, being very straight-laced and middle-class, was not really a suitable community to take the women to. As Graeme and Jan started talking about this situation they realised that their extensive church involvement had a language of concern for mission but that rarely translated into action. The church activities and busyness were actually hindering them from fully engaging in mission. Everything was centred around and inside the church and not outside in the community.

They met with the pastor and discussed the situation. He was very understanding and naturally quite surprised about this new opportunity. Jan and Graeme were definitely not the sort of people you would expect this sort of initiative to come from. However, their pastor was a wise person and could see the importance of this connection into an area of the local community that their church programs had no hope of connecting with. He released and blessed them from their other leadership roles and enabled them to develop their small, quiet ministry to prostitutes under the supervision and support of the church. They recruited a few other women to join them in the ministry and today run a vital ministry of shining light and love into three local brothels. The kingdom of God is shining light in a dark place through Graeme and Jan's bold and caring openness to start a Kingdom Community.

***

Heading north, on Queensland's Sunshine Coast, ministers from three churches were in conversation about planting a new church. They were all from the same growing region, north of Brisbane, and realised the natural thing to do was to plant another church. There was an exciting level of cooperation as they began to meet and identify new suburbs where a church could be started. As the conversation developed, Gerry (a member of Dean's executive) asked them a simple question, "Have you asked the community what it needs?"

Those present rubbed their chins and scratched their heads as this novel question was floated. Asking about community needs was not a common method of church planting. Community needs are usually assumed because the aim of most church plants, in coarse language, is to extend the franchise model of the denomination through opening another church. The group pursued Gerry's question a little further and sought further help from their denominational colleagues at Churches of Christ in Queensland. Together the group formed a Strategic Action Learning Team (SALT) to guide the project forward. We will explain SALTs in more detail in chapter six.

The SALT conducted widespread research about local needs, especially from local government leaders. One well respected leader commented, "Please don't build another church building. We already have more than enough churches that are less than half-full on Sundays – there is enough capacity for that already." So, the group identified areas of social need without service delivery. On the Sunshine Coast it emerged that there was a significant problem area of men's mental health with accompanying high levels of isolation, depression and suicide. After further research the group identified that a 'Men's Shed' offered a safe community for relationships, conversations and ultimately the improvement of men's health and wellbeing. Dean has written about this,

> "So, the idea of a men's shed was born, and collectively the SALT, with other Church of Christ staff, together looked at how we could get this off the ground. Our retirement village manager identified some land adjacent to our retirement village. A large company donated a shed that had been written off during floods when they heard about the local community goal. A large Hardware chain got on board and donated equipment. Men from our local churches and retirement village got on board and worked together to build benches and shelving ... and so forth. The new men's shed was born."[9]

Local men now have access to a community of other men who build needed things for community groups, talk in a friendly and open environment, and holistically improve men's health.[10] By creating a Men's Shed, the group really desired that the place would become a Kingdom Community; a place where men could access all that the kingdom had

---

[9] Dean Phelan, *Journal of Missional Practice*, Issue 7, 2016, "The light of Christ in Queensland". http://journalofmissionalpractice.com/light-of-christ-in-queensland/
[10] For further details about this story see: http://journalofmissionalpractice.com/light-of-christ-in-queensland

to offer. Together the SALT not only initiated a Men's Shed but they appointed a coordinator. This person was a trained Christian minister with a passion for ministry to men.

Within six months there were over one hundred men coming regularly. Men's health sessions were held; unofficial counselling and spiritual guidance were provided; mate-ship and a sense of belonging grew. A number started filtering back into our local churches. There were new commitments of faith and some decisions to be baptised. It was a remarkable success. More SALTs were formed in other regions.

***

Sixteen hundred kilometres up the road in beautiful Far North Queensland (FNQ) a unique set of events aligned. Cairns is the regional capital of FNQ. Phil Bignill, the Senior Pastor of one of the area's larger regional churches (The Lakes Church) being apostolic in vision, was always looking more widely for opportunities to advance the kingdom. Through his leadership, the church had already planted another church in nearby areas and the country town of Atherton was next on his list.

Atherton is a rural, country town on pastoral tableland, about ninety minutes up the mountains that skirt the tropical FNQ coast. Its economy is heavily dependent on agriculture and the seasonal workers who come through to pick fruit. It also has a sizeable population of people who live in affordable accommodation often through government support. There were already a few traditional churches in the town but Phil started investigating options. He was greeted with initial resistance from some local pastors who were threatened by the possibility of a new church coming to town.

Phil was discussing this when Gerry asked what were his dreams and visions for the area? Gerry dug deeper and suggested that Phil should ask the people who lived in Atherton what the area's needs were. Gerry then said something that brought clarity to what had been playing with Phil's mind, "You have to find out where the needs are and what is God up to in the community. God might not be calling you to plant a church. It might be something different, where people can access the kingdom of God."

Phil and the leadership of his church, joined with Churches of Christ in Queensland in pursuing possibilities in Atherton. Their highest priority was to advance the kingdom of God rather than any particular model of church. The mission of Churches of Christ in Queensland was to 'Shine the light of Christ' and they already did this through community human services, aged care and churches and they saw no reason to limit their operations to just those areas.

In order to understand the needs of the Atherton community they decided to start a coffee shop in the main street, which would be served by volunteers from the local churches. It was a means of gaining a local presence and therefore being able to become more incarnational in the community in order to hear and see what God was up to. They also met with local community and church leaders, always asking, "What are the needs?" While suspicious of Phil's motives (old suspicions die slowly) the local churches agreed to participate on the condition that he wouldn't turn the coffee shop into another church. Reciprocally, Phil insisted that all volunteers agreed to a basic rule that once someone entered the coffee shop there would be no recruiting people to any particular church. The coffee shop was named 'The Access Place' because the kingdom of God could be accessed there.

As the coffee shop was established the team looked for others in the community who were people of peace in this new Kingdom Community. Coffee, cake and friendship enabled many local people to drop-in. Many people never visited a church but were very interested in The Access Place. A community chaplain (Kerry), funded by Churches of Christ in Queensland was employed. She started a poet's corner, which looked at a different style of poetry each week. Attendees were encouraged to write their own poems. A colouring-in group was started. Craft groups commenced.

One day it emerged that one of The Access Place regulars had no social life. She spent every night alone in her caravan. Upon this discovery, Kerry found that there were many isolated people in this situation. So, a one-off social night was organised, which was a raging success. Those in attendance wanted to know when the next one was on. It is now a part of The Access Place calendar. The volunteer base from the local churches has expanded significantly, there is greater unity across the churches and other combined initiatives like BBQ's in the local caravan park have commenced, all because of a Kingdom Community.

***

We could tell many more stories like these few. What is common in each of these very diverse situations is that without any set rulebook, groups of Christians have been drawn together with specific attention upon the needs of a local area, which are outside the walls of organised church life. Their focus is from the grassroots and usually not the result of a church strategic plan. They actively listen to the needs of their community and seek to bring the blessing of God's kingdom into that context through what we term a Kingdom Community.

In some stories there is a central building, which is used for worship, prayer, programs, conversations and coffee but sometimes there is nothing, at least initially. Each of these local Kingdom Communities shine the light of Christ and demonstrate the good news of the gospel, but they do not necessarily aim to draw people to a traditional church service. Something deep, authentic and fruitful is going on as these groups, prompted by the Spirit, attend to their local community. Each group seeks to serve and bless their neighbourhood and community, not to draw people out of it. Some groups are tiny, and some are large with extensive budgets. Each are what we call in this book, Kingdom Communities.

The future of faith

In The Future of Faith[11], Harvey Cox presents a helpful framework of three 'ages', which explains the trajectory of Christianity over its 2000 years of growth. Christianity (which didn't carry the name in its initial decades) started as a movement initiated and commissioned by Jesus and pursued by his disciples and followers after the extraordinary scenes at Pentecost. We read in the book of Acts some of the amazing events and defining moments of the infant church and see several milestones eventuate, thanks to the account provided by Luke. None of the earliest

---

[11] Harvey Cox, *The Future of Faith*, New York: Harper One, 2009.

Introduction

followers expected the movement to last for 2000 years, choosing to face each day as it came while they waited for the return of their Lord. Scenes like Acts 2:42-47 and Acts 4:32-37 capture their expectation. However, Jesus did not return as quickly as expected and over time the movement developed into more predictable rhythms and practices.

It is recorded through the records of history that there were times when the movement was under severe pressure as it negotiated a place with Judaism, while under the rule of the Roman Empire. During this period of trials, persecution and extraordinary growth, the followers of Jesus were united together by the Spirit of Christ. Cox notes, "To be a Christian meant to live in his Spirit, embrace his hope and follow him in the work that he had begun."[12] Cox identifies these beginnings as the first of his three ages, the Age of Faith. He describes faith as a sense of deep-seated confidence.

Towards the end of its first century, Christianity had formed layers of hierarchy, which changed the structure and nature of the movement. Presbyters, bishops and deacons all started to emerge as the apostles and others of their generation died. The change was subtle and well-meaning, driven by the necessity for theological interpretation and reflection but set a trajectory gradually towards a more institutionalised structure and approach. Perhaps this was inevitable over a couple of hundred years of development. However, a growing distance emerged between the nature and method of leadership that Jesus and his earliest followers practised and what the church became. An organisational psychologist would describe this as a transition from a movement to an institution. The whole development is a story of transition from unregulated church organisation to a more close-knit arrangement."[13]

A result of this gradual development was that by the time of Constantine, an "elite class of Christians"[14] had emerged. These were

---

[12] Cox, *The Future of Faith*, 5.
[13] Henry Chadwick, *The Early Church: The Story of Emergent Christianity from the Apostolic Age to the Dividing of the ways between the Greek East and the Latin West*, London: Penguin, 1993, 51-52. Chadwick provides a useful summary of the shift in faith and order in the early church from a loose, missionary movement to a structured church throughout the second and third centuries.
[14] Cox, *The Future of Faith*, 5.

the ones who started developing initiation and orientation programs for new recruits who were new to the movement. As these new forms of catechesis were developed, the emphasis was placed less on faith and more on belief. Cox describes belief as an opinion that is used especially when one is not fully certain. For example, people may say, 'I'm not sure about that, but I believe it is probably true.' This form of belief is more cerebral and less connected to the heart.

The rise of these elites, in effect, produced a wrestle for the nature of movement of Christ followers. Would they stay as a grassroots, local movement as modelled and lived by Jesus, the apostles and early followers or would they become a top-down religion with layers of hierarchy? The movement was increasingly led by the elites in what Cox describes as an 'ominous direction'. At its core, Christianity's early practices, "varied widely from place to place, and as the fourth century began there was still no single creed. The various, scattered congregations were united by a common Spirit. A wide range of different theologies thrived."[15]

History shows us that there were significant issues for the early church to resolve concerning identity and the essence of what it meant to be the church, interwoven with pastoral concerns and challenges. However, these matters did not necessitate the radical shift that occurred. The radical shift came when Constantine became Emperor and the elites brokered the future of what was now known as the church, right into the centre of the Roman Empire. Cox offers a historically orthodox perspective to confirm the arrival of Christianity's second age, the *Age of Belief*,

> "Constantine also imposed a muscular leadership over the churches, appointing and dismissing bishops, paying salaries, funding buildings, and distributing largesse. He and not the Pope was the real head of the church. For Christianity it proved to be a disaster: its enthronement actually degraded it. From an energetic movement of faith, it coagulated into a phalanx of required beliefs. Thereby laying the foundation for every succeeding Christian fundamentalism for centuries to come."[16]

---

[15] Cox, *The Future of Faith*, 5.
[16] Cox, *The Future of Faith*, 5-6.

It was after these events that synods were organised to establish creeds where followers were 'in' or 'out' of fellowship based on confession of beliefs determined by the hierarchy, with the emperor at the top, with whom no one could really disagree. Gifts, character and godly fruit were reduced in importance. Cox comments,

> "Creeds are clusters of beliefs. But the history of Christianity is not a history of creeds. It is the story of a people of faith who sometimes cobbled together creeds out of beliefs. It is also the history of equally faithful people who questioned, alerted, and discarded those same creeds."[17]

While there were ebbs and flows, this second age was to last for the next 1500 years and still is a significant force upon the Western church today. Despite the negative overlay, there were many great individuals and groups who resisted and disputed the church hierarchy, within and outside of the church. After one and a half millennium the tectonic plates began to shift. The *Age of Belief* found itself in retreat, which brings us to today.

Two historic milestones occurred in 2005. First, the European Union decided not to mention the word Christianity in its new constitution. No longer was the foundational document that united Europe, Christian in orientation. The decision of Constantine and his church elites had finally been unwound from the centre of European culture and power. Paradoxically, the other milestone was also passed in the same year (with less fanfare). Christianity became a Majority World movement. More Christians and churches existed in the global South (Africa, Asia, Central and South America and the Pacific) than in the global West. Importantly, this new wave of Christianity was not built on belief but on the Spirit. This is what Cox suggests is the new phase in the Christian story. He calls it the *Age of the Spirit*.

---

[17] Cox, *The Future of Faith*, 4.

For Cox, the *Age of the Spirit* is represented by the thriving majority world church[18], experiences of the Holy Spirit and a growing interest in spirituality. The fastest growth in the church of the global south is through Pentecostal and Charismatic churches where discernment of the Spirit is the preferred method of hearing and being touched by God. Cox notes also that many women are coming into leadership and they also prefer the language of the Spirit. This third age is often stimulated by wonder or protest. It usually has porous borders between different traditions. People freely move where they find truth or experience.

This typology, provided by Cox, provides us with a useful tool as we begin our journey. It helps us understand why some local churches, imprisoned in the *Age of Belief*, feel shipwrecked and actively prepare for their generation to be the last one. These churches seem unable to move on from the constraints of clericalism, denominationalism and creeds, in order to participate with freedom and vitality where the Spirit now appears to be leading. Their medieval structures seem unable to accommodate what God is doing and where people are going. This helps explain, why so many Christians are leaving churches yet keeping a degree of personal faith. They are no longer able to restrict their faith to within the parameters allowed by their church.[19]

It helps us also understand the rigidity at the heart of some churches as they proclaim what is right, wrong, orthodox or heresy. Locally and across our region, there are thriving Kingdom Communities and Christian movements freed of such rigid boundaries, creeds and constraints. They thrive in varying cultures and adapt as context requires.

---

[18] Graham Hill, *GlobalChurch: Reshaping Our Conversations, Renewing Our Mission, Revitalising Our Churches.* Downers Grove: IVP Academic, 2016. The growing majority world church has been well documented by many scholars and missiologists in recent years, however the recent work by Graham Hill is worthy of note. Hill has sought to make accessible the many voices and messages of the global Church. See also theglobalchurchproject.com

[19] Alan Jamieson, *A Churchless Faith: Faith Journeys beyond Churches, London*: SPCK, 2000. This important research by Kiwi researcher and pastor, Alan Jamieson, listens to the accounts of people who have left Pentecostal, Charismatic and Evangelical churches and yet have kept their faith. It has relevant findings for the wider Western Church and provides helpful examples to Cox's second *Age of Belief.* See also Alan Jamieson, Jenny MacIntosh, Adrienne Thompson, *Five years on: Continuing Faith Journeys of those who left the Church,* Wellington: Portland Research Trust, 2006.

Introduction

This is the hope and grace-filled future of the Australian church and what this book investigates.

This book is written to support leaders, teachers, community developers, activists, agents of the kingdom, pastors who yearn for more and people who don't quite fit into the traditional church but who feel the pursuit of Jesus in their bones. We (Andrew and Dean) both love the church. We have both given many years of leadership and prayerful service and are personally and theologically committed to the Body of Christ. It is not our intention to simplistically deconstruct and criticise the church (something others seem free to engage in). We are both indebted to the many wonderful people across several churches that have invested in us and given us opportunities when wisdom might have suggested otherwise.

However, like a conversation with your local mechanic who tells you that the well-used family car has finally passed its use-by date, we both see too much unrealised opportunity and resistance to change in too many expressions of church. We see signs all around us of the gentle, renewing work of the Spirit in the *missio Dei* (mission of God) in what Cox now calls the *Age of the Spirit*. For this to be realised, the kingdom must come before the complacency and comfort of the church. There are clear and visible signs of the Spirit's leading in healing, reconciling, recreating, revaluing, re-orientating, re-hoping and renewing people and communities all about us. Jesus' kingdom is indeed advancing in extraordinary ways. Mustard-seed-like Kingdom Communities are growing in the most common places as Jesus promised they would.

CHAPTER ONE

Stuck

"The challenge for us as evangelical communities is to reconsider our practices and methods and remember why we do them. Preaching, praying, sharing communion, building community - these should not be an empty ritual... Will we allow God to raise up new methods of reaching people and changing the life of our neighbourhood and society?"
Ash Barker[1]

"I thank my God in all my remembrance of you, always in every prayer of mine for you all making my prayer with joy, because of your partnership in the gospel from the first day until now. And I am sure of this, that he who began a good work in you will bring it to completion at the day of Jesus Christ."
Philippians 1: 3-6 (ESV)

There are two types of people in the world: those who like cricket and those who don't. For well over one hundred years the game of cricket has had a reasonably standard structure. If you were good enough as a player for your club you would be selected for the premier league. If you were the best in that league you would be selected for your state. Then, if you were the best in your state you would be selected for the national team. Everyone knew the pathway. Everyone could see how selection might progress to higher levels. Importantly, everyone also knew which region they were representing.

Things lasted like that for well over a century. Then in one generation, the game of cricket changed remarkably. Now there are three forms of cricket (go figure?): twenty overs; fifty overs and four or five days – this is where people who don't like cricket ask how can you possibly enjoy watching a game for so many days that ends in a draw? The modern international fixture is incredibly busy with these different forms of cricket and the various competitions at each level. It is not possible for

---

[1] Ash Barker, *Making Poverty Personal: Taking the poor as seriously as the Bible does*, Grand Rapids: Baker Books, 2009.

top players to compete in every game and they are often rotated. And, because cricket is an international sport, players are often flying around the world to participate in various competitions. Some competitions are commercially run where teams are owned privately and not representative, while others are still run by the cricket authorities.

Recently, Andrew's father was trying to understand how the local twenty over competition is structured and players are selected. He had followed cricket for his whole life with one structure and suddenly there were new and unusual competitions and players. For his generation, modern cricket is now a somewhat incomprehensible activity. So, he asked his twelve-year-old grandchildren to explain. For young students of the game, fluidity is all they know. One of the sticking points that Andrew's father pressed them on was what region, state or country the teams were representing. For someone of his generation, cricket was not just entertainment but also about representation. He couldn't understand the point of meaningless entertainment in a private competition when it came to cricket. His grandchildren had a completely different perspective and struggled to understand the nature of his question. Both generations needed to make a paradigm shift to understand the other's world.

Most of us have experiences like this from time to time, when the way we understand things no longer makes sense. Modern life is filled with this form of disruption. It is in these moments of disruption that we are forced to develop new understanding in order to move forward. Andrew can remember purchasing his first smart phone and seeing all the little squares (apps) on the screen and wondering what they were. Shifting to a smart phone required a paradigm shift.

In this book, we propose that a significant paradigm shift is required for effective ministry in the world around us. This paradigm shift is described with concern for the alignment of the church to God's activity in the world. The church is called to embody Christ's good news in the world. We have written this book because as we read the data we have come to the conclusion that in too many places in the Western world, the church is deeply stuck. Sometimes it feels more than stuck. It feels like we are in quicksand and don't know how to get out of the mire. But this is firstly a story of hope. We have written this book because we see wonderful signs of hope and growth in places where the kingdom of God is prioritised over the structure, shape, arguments, particularities or plans of the church.

Let's play with the metaphor of quicksand for a moment. Every time you move in quicksand you risk sinking deeper into the mire. So, in an attempt to do something, churches are investing in technical changes, which may just be getting themselves more stuck[2]. The situation is like an older generation who love cricket in its traditional forms and are now perplexed about how to adapt to new realities while their grandchildren don't understand all the fuss. Their struggle is whether they are loyal to what they have been trained to believe is right, or whether they take a leap and adapt to where there is life and a future.[3]

The paradigm shift that is explored in this book will be difficult for some in church leadership to negotiate, while for others it will be a breath of fresh air. So much is invested in what are now our traditional and institutional systems, practices and hierarchies. Every minister in a local church setting has been trained and moulded into a suitable model of what the old world required. The paradigm explored in this book jeopardises that skill-set and possibly its whole economy.

Many local churches have been doing the same things for years and have forced young ministers into a shape that suits the church. Too often, if the minister has agitated for change, things will have turned on them. Too many churches are resistant to necessary change in response to the world around them and are dying as a consequence. It is a point well illustrated in an old Leadership Journal cartoon set in a church foyer. Along a wall there are a series of heads set on plaques – like hunters used to mount with their prize game. The chair of the Elders is standing with the new minister explaining the meaning, "Each of these are former ministers who tried to change things around here." It is a not so subtle reminder that change in many churches ends badly.

---

[2] See http://tosavealife.com/faith/12-reasons-millennials-church/
[3] The absence of an emerging generation is obvious in most churches. According to the Barna Group in the USA only 20% of under 30s believe attending church is worthwhile; 59% of under 30s who were raised in a church have dropped out; and 35% believe that church does more harm than good (see www.barna.com/research-americans-divided-on-the-importance-of-church/). The statistics are similar in Australia.

We seek to demonstrate in this chapter that continued resistance to change is no longer a sustainable option. Yet, too many in church leadership stubbornly refuse to acknowledge the situation. We know too many people who have been badly hurt by a well-intentioned change in a resistant church. Remember, the church is responsible for discerning what God is up to in the world and responding to that. The kingdom of God must come first, not the comfort of the church.

From the outset, we want to clearly say that many local churches have been wonderful communities, often for generations, where individuals and families have together worshipped, shared life, baptised, broken bread, married, buried and grown in the Christian faith. Some local churches have taken the lead on important social justice matters and helped create a better world. Andrew remembers the church of his childhood taking an active role in settling Vietnamese 'boatpeople' through the provision of homes, education, friendship and language. Dean has similar stories and memories. Many people who are reading this book have grown up in and benefit greatly from a traditional local church. But it wasn't all good though. We also add that too many people have been harmed by sinful leadership, bad judgement and toxic cultures in some of these very same churches and we acknowledge that.

As difficult as it might be to openly acknowledge, the twenty-first century local church model in the West is faced with a tremendous paradigm shift if it is to survive. If we desire to see local Christian communities faithfully continue a presence in a world that is filled with rapid, discontinuous change, then they are going to have to begin a huge series of transitions. It is not possible to continue to tinker around the edges. The changes required will challenge every aspect of church life. Businesses have to do this regularly when the environment changes, but churches often choose a softer, pastoral path and back away from hard change, until they run out of money. Former Executive Officer of Churches of Christ in Victoria and Tasmania, Lynette Leach, recently commented to Andrew that most church closures occur because tough decisions were not made a decade before the closure.

Some people point to large and mega-churches as a source of hope for church life. This book will argue that large and mega-churches face the same challenges and are not immune from the changes going on in society.[4] This is because most of the numerical growth for megachurches has been transfer growth from smaller churches and the supply line is running out. The particular challenge for the large and mega-church will be that their size, busyness and success may disguise the coming challenge, thus making it harder to see until it is too late.

The Palo Alto Research Centre (PARC) was founded by Xerox in 1970. Located on a campus of Stanford University, PARC developed some staggering technological advancements including the world's first personal computer, the mouse, icons and pull-down menus, laser printing and a local area network of computers. Xerox invested $150 million dollars into PARC, which in the 1970s was a huge amount for research and development.

The problem for PARC was that it was founded to develop the 'office of the future' and the Xerox executives could not see the genius of the inventions. Being a paper copying company, Xerox only took commercial advantage of the development of laser printing. The other four significant developments were given away and seized by others who could see the future. Among these others, famously, was Steve Jobs who hired several PARC employees in order to eventually develop the Apple Macintosh.[5]

> **Learning:** There are enormous cultural and structural changes occurring throughout Western society and the attraction of a local congregation is lacking in meaning and need for the majority of people. Churches do not have the luxury of resisting change.

---

[4] This book is not a commentary on church size. All churches, of all sizes are valued expressions of the Body of Christ. We argue that all need to engage with the paradigm shift identified in this book for missiological reasons and all should be concerned and prayerful in regard to the welfare of other churches going through struggles. Churches of various sizes and cultures will have challenges with adapting to the required paradigm shift, but they will also find abilities, resources and possibilities for the shifts required within and about them – if they are open, self-reflective and imaginative.
[5] Everett M Rogers, *Diffusion of Innovations*, New York: Free Press, 2003, 153-155.

The Problem

Most of us see the church through the lens of congregations, denominations and/or buildings. However, it has not always been like this. The structures and models that we have inherited are simply ones that have endured or developed over recent centuries. The model of the contemporary local congregation developed through a series of continuous adaptations from what was the village or parish. Once, people lived, worked and worshipped within a village area. Over time as people migrated, cities grew and added suburbs, so the village church model was adapted. Even today, many churches still employ this model when they plant churches in new suburbs. However, the modern local church context where the same people might be at the same service once a month is a very different community to a village in times past where people worked, lived and played together.

Sustaining this model has also become very expensive. For example, church planting is so expensive and cumbersome that few churches are planted today. Also, the number of failures further contributes to the risk of investing in this strategy alone today. The next time you drive past a new suburb or sub-division, count how many church buildings are being constructed—usually none. The cost of buying land, constructing a new building and employing a minister is massive if measured by the number of people it reaches.[6] In a denominational newsletter, Joel Plotnek, Head of Operations and Financial Services for Churches of Christ in Victoria and Tasmania commented that they were,

> "Exploring ways in which we can support new church planting and church development in getting new churches on the map. This has been central to our mission and something we are very passionate about. However, it is also a big challenge as the cost of land and construction for new churches has proved to be highly capital intensive."[7]

This challenge is for all of us who are concerned with the advance of God's kingdom. We should not be content to continue to sustain a dying model through the exhaustion of diminishing resources. We follow a

---

[6] In chapter two, we will examine the original New Testament model and nature of the Body of Christ and compare it with our modern, declining hybrid.
[7] Joel Plotnek, *The Edition*, "What's New: Operations and CCFS", Fairfield: CCVT, 2018, 24.

creative missional God who is always leading his people, as co-heirs, towards a path of renewal, restoration and redemption. We are living in a changing culture where key participants who share a desire for the expansion of God's kingdom need to expend vision, energy and faith in what God is up to in our world today and in the future, not in what the church used to be. This challenge calls local churches, denominations, church agencies and seminaries together, to work towards a shared future in service of the kingdom of God, rather than existing and ageing church structures.

Denominations are synchronous products of the traditional local church. Most denominational executives are selected because they are successful and competent local church ministers. They are appointed to their role to maintain the system, fix any roadblocks and help local churches grow in fairly traditional ways. It is a tough job as they manage a constant stream of scandals, politics, disputes, divisions, silos, ructions, administration, breakdowns and burnouts as the existing system strains onward looking for release, an outlet or someone to blame. They spend huge amounts of time and resource managing and troubleshooting for local churches. Sometimes they build leadership programs to produce more leaders because they are not satisfied with their seminary graduates, but significant issues are raised in this methodology.[8] Working towards a shared future is a challenge for the whole church inclusive of size, function, tradition and role. Our strongest resource is prayerful unity as we negotiate together the quicksand we are in. Together we are all the Body of Christ and when any part suffers we all suffer (1 Cor 12:26) and when any part has success we all rejoice.

A key point of resistance to change is a mentality that sees the traditional model of local church as tied to denominational identity. Denominations are required to administer areas like ordination, accreditation, annual conferences, church planting and professional development all in servitude to a traditional model of church. These programs are usually geared towards the health and continuity of that

---

[8] See: Robert J. Nyhuis, *Pentecostal Ministry Formation within Christian Revival Churches (CRC) in Australia: a History, Case Study and Vision, Melbourne*: University of Divinity - Doctor of Philosophy, 2018.

traditional model and its paid, professional ministers. The typical denominational office functions somewhat like a franchise head office (think fast food chains and car dealerships). It is all keeping people busy but as the data suggests not growing or engaging most Australians.

While there is so much investment in the traditional model of local church from ministers, local churches, denominations and seminaries, it has significant and obvious challenges for its continued existence. It is costly, the model is in general decline and it is not the totality of the kingdom of God. It is, in effect, an endangered species because the world about it has changed.

Local churches are getting older and greyer with many doubting the possibility of another generation emerging. Some have not had a baptism for many years. Modes of communication and liturgy (usually packed with meaning) are not engaged or understood by younger generations. Budgets continue to increase for stipends and buildings. Increasing property values also raise an ethical issue of how can a church community of a few dozen people tie up multi-millions of dollars of assets just for themselves? There are many more challenges like these as church and society change.

Seminaries by and large are still designed to prepare ministers within a traditional model of church. Typically, the 'bulls-eye' for a seminary is still a well-prepared candidate for ordination and a life of service in a traditional local church. As a seminary Principal, Andrew remembers a retired denominational executive telling him that his effectiveness as Principal would be directly determined by the number of ministers the seminary produced for local churches. And, to be fair, this was the primary reason denominational seminaries were set up generations ago – to train ministers for local church service.

The general problem for seminaries is that by and large, compared to other vocational areas, far fewer people are presenting for a traditional life-long ministry career. It is a touchy subject for seminaries to discuss because this usually is their assumed *raison d'être*. Dean and Andrew are convinced that the issue is not about a lack of resources, personnel, or the relevance of theological education, which we believe is needed more than ever. It is that the culture has changed, and younger people expect that they will have several careers. For them, ministry is no different, and in fact ministry is being seen as possible across all areas of their lives. They also often don't want to risk being trapped inside the church for life via a traditional ministry pathway. They want a more seamless transitional pathway between their faith community and other networks. In many cases people who feel the strong call of God on their lives want to be associated with a movement or cause that has 'fire in the belly' and, rightly or wrongly, they are not seeing this is in the traditional ministry pathway any more.

Seminaries hold wonderful reserves of wisdom that are not just for traditional ministry trainees. Increasingly, seminaries must equip wider cohorts of people with wisdom for life and ministry. They must become more easily accessible in the formation of all of God's people as complex life, culture and ethical issues are negotiated.

Australian society has changed through various factors including mobility, technology, education, travel, migration, scandal, urbanisation, secularisation and increased awareness of human rights and the equality of all people. Local churches have been overwhelmed by wave after wave of these challenges.

Many thoughtful people who care for the future of Christ's church are raising these sorts of questions. Dr Keith Suter (well known and respected scholar and media commentator) was a member of the founding generation of the Uniting Church in Australia (UCA) in 1977. The creation of the UCA was a signal moment in ecumenism in Australia, when the majority of three denominations (Presbyterian, Methodist and Congregational) chose to unite as one, new church.[9] There was great hope and optimism. Forty years on, Suter has produced his third doctorate on scenario planning for the decline of the UCA.[10]

He is not alone. As an example, the number of Uniting churches in Queensland has dropped by 36% over the last two decades, going

---

9 Regardless of what path the UCA takes, its establishment was a highpoint in ecumenism and its founding document, The Basis of Union is a wonderful piece of theology.
10 Keith D. Suter, *The future of the Uniting Church in Australia: The application of scenario planning to the creation of four 'futures' for the Uniting Church in Australia*, Sydney: University of Sydney – Doctor of Philosophy, 2013, see churchfutures.com.au

from 518 to 333 congregations and faith communities in that time. This represents closure or merger of 185 churches in Queensland; and nationally the Uniting Church has experienced a loss of 60,000 attendees since 1991. At the 31st Queensland Synod in October 2014, Dean heard the following question was openly asked, "If the UCA keeps declining at the same rate as we have over the past few decades, we may have just forty years left until there are no congregations remaining."

The church in Australia today: The data

We might sound alarmist, but our argument is based on the data we will now expand. In this section we will look at four different and respected sources that each address aspects of current church participation, societal expectations and perceptions for the ongoing future of the church in Australian society.

The key sources we will examine are the Christian Research Association's analysis of the 2011 Australian Census, *Australia's Religious Communities: Facts and Figures from the 2011 Australian Census and other Sources*[11], current data from Roy Morgan research and findings by well respected social researchers Hugh Mackay and Mark McCrindle. Additionally, we will introduce some wider observations from two well respected international voices – Alan Roxburgh (missiologist) and Phyllis Tickle (journalist) – who use similar helpful metaphors to describe the moment in which we find ourselves.

The Australian Census

Since its inception in 1985, the Christian Research Association has produced many publications on trends in the church and in Australian society. Philip Hughes, Margaret Fraser and Stephen Reid in *Australia's Religious Communities* argue that denominations in Australia today are under great threat if they do not adapt to changing demographics across the nation. These trends have been forecast for many years, but, they argue, are now pressing upon us. Some denominations are in stubborn denial. Others, like the Uniting Church in Australia, as cited above, have

---

11 Philip J. Hughes, Margaret Fraser and Stephen Reid, *Australia's Religious Communities: Facts and Figures from the 2011 Australian Census and other Sources*, Nunawading: CRA, 2012.

been honest about their future, and their struggle to coalesce around an overall strategy to improve things. Hughes et al identify many important trends about each denomination, taken directly from the Australian 2011 Census. Through the many facts and distillations of information, three clear trends and warnings emerge.

First, the only real church growth that is occurring is not through anything to do with a certain model(s) employed by local churches but through migration. Actually, most of the growth occurring in religious communities, whatever the religion or denomination, is related to migration. The general pattern is that the more 'Anglo' the context, the fewer the adherents who seem to stick. Conversely, the closer the religion or tradition is to a new migrant's background, the higher the level of adherence and growth. Hughes et al argue that the motives for growing religious, migrant, communities include factors like desire for a sense of connection and community in Australia; shared language; shared values; and confirmation of identity through ethno-religious association combined with a sense of duty to attend. These patterns have continued in Australian immigration since 1788.

The data demonstrates that religious groups do better among new Australians and that 'immigrant-friendly' denominations are more likely to grow. Denominations that are growing have each received high proportions of immigrants (Baptists, Seventh-Day Adventists and Asian Christians). Denominations, which have declined, have attracted small numbers of immigrants (Salvation Army, Churches of Christ and Brethren).

Second, there is a big back door in churches. One of the prevailing messages from this research is that Australia's religious communities have big back doors. A back door is a metaphor for where people slip out and are lost from a church or religious community. Data presented in *Australia's Religious Communities* suggests that religious organisations that are concerned with and have a reputation for growth are in fact, not growing. There is a widespread plateau across many religious organisations that have been assumed to be growing while others are in well-established decline. It gets worse. Across all of this, the research reveals a very serious trend, which should concern all who care for the church's future. The biggest 'back door' issue for religious communities in Australia concerned 10-34-year olds. Somewhere between 300,000 to 500,000 Australian young people disengaged from any level of participation in or identification with religious life between the 2006 and 2011 censuses. There is almost no next generation coming through the pipeline.

Third, 'no religion' is a growing movement. *Australia's Religious Communities* also identifies movement in the census towards the 'no religion' category. The statistical research shows that the emerging church conversation, methods and programs of evangelism, church growth, church health, missional church ideas and Pentecostalism have not made a discernible difference to the growth of Australian religious life. If religious organisations had simply been a little better at holding onto their own flock – closed their back doors – they might have had better success. This trend is increasing. In the 2016 Australian census, more than seven million people ticked 'no religion', up three point seven million in 2006.[12]

> **Learning:** Successive Australian Censuses tell us that two or three generations after migration, Australians are leaving the church. All church denominations are in plateau or decline except those with many first and second-generation migrants.

Roy Morgan Research

Roy Morgan Research is one of the best-known market research companies in Australia. Founded in 1941, Roy Morgan has been taking national surveys on just about every imaginable aspect of Australian life. One of the interesting annual surveys that they take is the Image of Professions Survey.[13] In 1997, ministers of religion were rated at an all-time high of 59 percent for ethics and honesty. However, in only twenty years that has fallen to its all-time lowest level of 34 percent. Said another way, two-thirds of Australian society now rate Minsters low on

---

[12] https://cra.org.au/pointers-december-2017/
[13] http://www.roymorgan.com/findings/7244-roy-morgan-image-of-professions-may-2017-201706051543

ethics and integrity, and in the last twenty years one third of Australians have lowered their view of clergy. Even lawyers are rated above clergy. This is a telling and tragic survey, for if church leaders are not perceived to be people of good ethics and honesty, what chance do they have?

Observations from Australian Social Researchers

Hugh Mackay and Mark McCrindle are social researchers who employ very different methodologies, yet there are common themes in what can be distilled from their data. Mackay is more widely known as a commentator and social researcher. He has been sitting with Australians for decades through focused listening groups in living rooms across the country and is widely respected. He has published many insightful and popular books on various aspects of Australian life as thoughtful précis of his deep listening. He is widely sought as an authority in many forms of popular media. Three of his most recent books are directly relevant to church life and we recommend they sit on every church leader's bookshelf.[14]

Mackay notes that,

"Around 61 percent of Australians and almost 50 percent of New Zealanders still tick 'Christian' in the national census, only about 15 percent attend church once a month or more often, and regular weekly attenders are down to about 8 percent of the population – a very similar picture to that of the UK, Germany, France and Belgium."[15]

As a social researcher, he makes an ironic and telling comment in his introduction to the decline of church attendance,

"Given the steady fifty-year decline in church attendance, it's not hard to find people who can tell you why they stopped going to church. Nor, these days, is it hard to find younger people who have never been churchgoers and can't imagine taking it up."[16]

---

[14] Hugh Mackay, *The Good Life: What makes a life worth living?* Sydney: Pan Macmillan, 2013; *The Art of Belonging: it's not where you live, it's how you live*, Sydney: Pan Macmillan, 2014; and *Beyond Belief: How we find meaning, with or without Religion*, Sydney: Pan Macmillan, 2016.
[15] Mackay, *Beyond Belief*, 9.
[16] Mackay, *Beyond Belief*, 51.

Mackay notes the reasons why people still go to church, in no particular order, as: desire for nurturing of faith; a community to belong to; access to pastoral care; a sense of duty; 'it keeps me on the straight and narrow'; peace and quiet; aesthetics; engagement with ritual; interesting sermons; erotic stimulation[17]; faithfulness; being forced to go; and to qualify the children for a church school.[18] He then comments on why people stop going to church, which given the Australian Census data and associated anecdotes is of great interest here.

There is an important point at the start of Mackay's observations about why people stop going to church. He observes two of the big pull factors in Western society away from faith communities,

"Any analysis of why people have stopped going to church needs to take account of the massive bombardment of Western society over the past thirty years by propaganda in two directions – both antithetical to the messages of religion and spirituality. The first barrage has come from the world of consumer mass marketing ... The unambiguous message embedded in all this consumerist frenzy is that 'it's all about me'... The second bombardment has been from the merchants of happiness. Marshalling their considerable forces, they have also been telling us exactly what we want to hear: your entitlement isn't confined to material prosperity; you're entitled to happiness as well, and the pursuit of personal happiness is a perfectly suitable goal for your life."[19]

Following these relevant observations about serious impediments to Australian societal receptiveness to the message of Christianity, Mackay then identifies the reasons he hears from people in his focus groups about why people stop going to church: boring and irrelevant; alien; 'I could no longer go along with it'[20]; 'I felt too exposed'; too rigid,

---

[17] Mackay, *Beyond Belief*, 63-64. The category of 'erotic stimulation' refers to the adolescent blend of the spiritual and the sexual and also the transference that can occur between a minister/priest and a church attendee.
[18] Mackay, *Beyond Belief*, 52-65.
[19] Mackay, *Beyond Belief*, 65-67.
[20] Mackay, *Beyond Belief*, 75. "When a churchgoer reaches a point of feeling uncomfortable with the whole structure of the church and its teachings, it's easy to understand why they might feel it's time to leave. Sometimes the tipping point is over their resistance to a specific piece of doctrine... Sometimes, the repetitiveness of a service that had once seemed reassuringly familiar may come to feel tedious or uninspiring, particularly if the clergy

exclusive or insulting; the treatment of women; being too busy; loss of respect for the integrity of the institution; and, choosing not to go to church but to access a church school for the kids as a compromise.[21]

Mackay summarises,

"All this creates a conundrum for local churches. While they generally receive a strong tick of approval from their neighbourhood, and while declining church attendance is often associated in people's minds with a general loss of moral clarity and 'shared values' and with the evolution of a less sharing, more self-interested society, those attitudes rarely translate into a desire to support the local church by actually going to it. Even in the case of weddings and funerals, the trend is away from church based ceremonies: 70 percent of Australian weddings are now conducted by civil celebrants."[22]

Mark McCrindle is a futurist, demographer and social researcher. Through regular surveys to a wide sample of Australians, over several years, he has developed an important database that helps us understand, among many other domains, the church in Australian society. As a general overview McCrindle observes that since 1976 Christianity has reduced by 22 percent and church attendance has dropped by 48 percent while the number of Australians describing themselves of 'no religion' has increased by 269 percent.[23] Citing similar figures to Mackay, McCrindle also notes that in 1998, 50 percent of weddings were conducted by religious celebrants and 50 percent were conducted by civil celebrants. By 2011, those numbers had changed to 30 percent conducted by religious celebrants and 70 percent conducted by civil celebrants.[24] By any account, this is a huge shift in a relatively short period and reflects the changing preferences of society.

One of the most alarming statistics that McCrindle identifies is the ageing of the church. The average age of church attendees in 2014 was 53 years of age. 44 percent of church attendees are over 60 years of age

---

conducting the service are themselves perceived to be merely going through the motions."
[21] Mackay, *Beyond Belief*, 65-89.
[22] Mackay, *Beyond Belief*, 91.
[23] *The McCrindle Blog*, "A Demographic snapshot of Christianity and church attenders in Australia", April 18th 2014.
[24] *The McCrindle Blog*, "Going to the chapel... or the park!" October 12th, 2012.

and 25 percent of church attendees are 70 years of age or older.[25] Data such as this suggests that things are going to only get worse for church attendance in Australia as the most senior quartile pass away.

McCrindle's surveys identify the top six reasons why Australians don't go to church: irrelevant to my life (46 percent); don't accept how it's taught (26 percent); outdated style (24 percent); issues with clergy/ministers (22 percent); don't believe the Bible (19 percent); and too busy to attend (18 percent). Again, there are clear points of agreement and alignment with Mackay's analysis, although McCrindle quantifies the data.[26]

Asking what the greatest areas of priority for Australians were, McCrindle identified the following, commencing with the highest priority: relationships & family; physical health; emotional/mental wellbeing; finances/earnings; career/vocation; social connections and spiritual/religious. This research suggests that generally, Australians seem to be a long way away from existential crisis, yet this is what most church programs are geared towards. McCrindle also noted that among the things that Australians would most like to see in their community, a church is rated thirteenth, behind – among other needs – a park with play equipment and a leash-free dog park!

Whether using the Australian Census or the analyses of respected social researchers, the data is consistent. There is a major tsunami about to hit the local church. Some say it is already upon us, but the data suggests that there is worse to come. In a few, short years as the oldest generation passes away there will be very few younger people to replace them. While churches are busy with meaningful and important activities like pastoral care, funerals and programs, few people are preparing for real change.

There tends to be four reactions to this data when we disclose it. The first and obvious response is denial and even anger that it is published. Some people try to reshape it, so it doesn't look so bad. Some people don't want to think about it and many older ministers simply put it in the 'too hard basket' and leave it for the next generation. The second response is

---

[25] *The McCrindle Blog*, "A Demographic snapshot of Christianity and church attenders in Australia", April 18th 2014.
[26] *The McCrindle Blog*, "Church attendance in Australia". March 23rd 2013.

a shrug of the shoulders followed by statements like, 'What can you do about it', or *'Que Sara, Sara'*. The third response is that this sort of thing falls into head office's responsibility. They comment, "The denomination will figure things out." The problem is that the denominations are just as stuck as everyone else and are too busy just keeping things going. Many are surviving on proceeds from the sale of properties of closed down churches. Finally, some people put their heads down and focus on what they can control in their own church. They say, "Other churches may sink but we will weatherproof our own church." This attitude results in more pressure on the minister, concerted attempts to attract people from other churches or a tightening of the budget.

None of these responses are appropriate, adequate or reflective of a movement filled with purpose and growth. We are faced with a task that requires significant theological reflection as well as creative and imaginative thinking and experimentation. We cannot be like the religious leaders who observed what Jesus was up to two thousand years ago. In chapter nine of John's gospel, Jesus was confronted by the appearance of a blind man. The disciples suggested his blindness was a product of his or his parents' sin. Jesus taught that it was neither but simply an opportunity for the work of God to be displayed in his life. In the midst of our challenges we must ask, what is God up to and where are the opportunities for partnering with the Spirit? We must wonder why, after all these years, are our inherited frameworks, vision and imagination insufficient? As Mark Twain famously said, "You can't depend on your eyes when your imagination is out of focus!"

John then records the story of the healing of this man where the gift of sight is given to him by Jesus. Sadly, having been healed, this humble man and his parents were accosted by the religious authorities. It seems crazy to us today, but the authorities were not happy that this man now had sight. They abused their authority and the man's parents didn't want to explain what had occurred except to say that he was their son, who had been blind, and he could now see. His parents did not want to be excluded from the synagogue and the community life it opened. When a religious climate, created and nurtured by leaders, stops testimony and attention on what the Spirit is up to, we hinder truth and alignment with God.

The story continues and the man who could now see was brought before the authorities. The parents replied, 'Yes he can see' and, 'Yes he was blind.' The questions went on and on because the leaders did not want to face the truth. So, they then turned the debate onto their area of strength and intellectualised away the situation and made it an either-or situation. Ultimately, because the man would not deny his testimony, they threw him out of the synagogue. Jesus was told about the incident subsequent of the healing and how because of it the man had been thrown out of the synagogue, so he went to him. The man, who could now see, confessed his faith in Jesus and worshipped him. His sight was now physical and spiritual, whereas Jesus admonished that the religious leaders were the ones who were really blind.

It is easy for us to be blind too. We can dig into our known worlds of comfort and patterns of security. We can attack change and blame others. Church life can justify itself because of the theological meaning we pile onto it. Meanwhile, the data suggests the rest of society is getting on with life without us. Society wants the church less and less for counselling, weddings or funerals or for building of community, while many Christian leaders justify the way things are and just keep busy and preoccupied. Like the religious leaders in the story, they are trapped in their own ways of seeing things. Just as a fish can't describe the water it lives in; too often church leaders are not able to articulate the reign of God outside of church life. Spiritual blindness in religious leadership is an age-old problem and as is written in the Jewish Talmud, "We don't see things the way they are, we see things the way we are." Fortunately, we have friends on the journey who speak with intelligence and insight.

Unravelling and recalibrating

Phyllis Tickle and Alan Roxburgh share a deep concern for the Body of Christ and its engagement within culture. Their ability to explain complex issues and to translate them in accessible form is a valuable resource for us. Both have written extensively on the wider challenges the church faces in Western culture. Both articulate the challenge through helpful metaphors which speak to our problem. Tickle writes as a journalist who articulates both the centre and the breadth of the issue. Similarly, Roxburgh writes with one foot firmly in the real world and the other firmly in the world of theological reflection. He helps us wrestle deeply with a challenge left for us by Lesslie Newbigin: can the West be won?[27]

In *The Great Emergence: How Christianity is changing and why*[28], Phyllis Tickle provides a brief survey of the two thousand years of Christianity in order to identify patterns where the church moves through a cycle of relative cohesion, then through a dramatic period of recalibration. She observes that a typical cycle lasts for roughly five hundred years. Tickle notes that while this pattern applies to Christianity it also applies to the other two Abrahamic faiths.[29] She uses the metaphor of a rummage sale[30] to describe the recalibration. Rummage sales function like a hinge. Tickle comments, "We all would do well to remember that, not only are we in the hinge leading into a new five-hundred-year period, but we are also the direct product of the previous one."[31]

Tickle identifies the recalibrations (or rummage sales) as the following events which each have the word 'great' attached[32]: Gregory the Great and the rise of monasticism which saved Christendom; the Great Schism which saw the division of the Eastern and Western branches of the church; and the Great Reformation which saw the division of

---

[27] During a plenary session at the 1973 Bangkok meeting of the World Council of Churches Commission on World Mission and Evangelism, Indonesia's General Simatoupong asked Newbigin a question which had a profound effect on him and coalesced the challenge that he felt was before him for the next twenty-five years, "Can the West be converted?" See Lesslie Newbigin, *A Word in Season: Perspectives on Christian World Missions*, Grand Rapids: Eerdmans, 1994, 66.

[28] Phyllis Tickle, *The Great Emergence: How Christianity is Changing and Why*, Grand Rapids: Baker Books, 2008.

[29] Phyllis Tickle, *The Great Emergence*, 29-30. "... Much the same sort of scheme appertains to Judaism. That is, if one goes back five hundred years from the destruction of the Second Temple and priestly Judaism in the first century CE, one hits the Babylonian Captivity which decimated Solomon's Temple and scattered Judaism away from Judea and into much of the Middle eastern world. Five hundred years before the Captivity... was the end of the Age of the Judges and the establishment of the monarchy... Of late, an Islamic scholar or two has begun to argue that the same kind of cycling can be discerned in that faith's history."

[30] Australians call this a garage sale.

[31] Tickle, *The Great Emergence*, 27.

[32] Tickle, *The Great Emergence*, 13-17.

Protestant churches and nation-states. She concludes that we are now entering the next recalibration, which she terms The Great Emergence.

Religion, Tickle argues, is like a cable that provides social meaning across the centuries. Through this cable we are able to be connected to the past but live in the present as we move towards the future. Developing the metaphor, she says it is as if the cable is holding a dingy in safe water. Occasionally the cable is stretched or broken and requires mending or the dingy is in danger of greater currents and waves. So that there can be safety and predictability again, the cable needs examination and mending. This is what is underway through what she terms The Great Emergence, as Christianity seeks to recalibrate all that has happened since the Enlightenment.

The Great Emergence is a useful metaphor for us. When things that brought meaning and significance to so many for so long appear to be in jeopardy, it is wise to study previous times where similar patterns have occurred. It provides us with perspective and hope while also sobering us to the depth of changes that are underway. The Bible carries examples of these stories for our frame of reference, as does the history of the Body of Christ over the past two thousand years.

In *Joining God, Remaking Church, Changing the World: The New Shape of the Church in our time*[33], Alan Roxburgh uses the metaphor of unravelling. Using his wife Jane's knitting as a metaphor, Roxburgh describes his astonishment when after hours of knitting she unravels her work, in order to commence the pattern again, correctly. She knows that if the work is faulty then continuing won't make a better garment. He argues that sometimes, painful as it is, we have to watch an unravelling. The unravelling of the church going on before us is something similar to his wife Jane's knitting being unravelled.

The denominations that are unravelling are what Roxburgh calls 'Euro-tribal churches'. He uses this term to explicitly describe the origin of these churches and how they function. They are the result of mass migrations from Europe that have formed their self-identity around this. He says, "To a great extent these denominations were formed and

---

[33] Alan Roxburgh, *Joining God, Remaking Church, Changing the World: The New Shape of the Church in our Time*, New York: Morehouse Publishing, 2015.

expanded in the context of strong national and ethnic identities."[34] The unravelling of these churches has progressively grown since the 1960s. This is a pattern very similar to the Australian scene. As a result, Roxburgh notes in North America:

- If you were born between 1925 and 1945, there is a 60 percent chance you are in church today.
- If you were born between 1946 and 1964, there is a 40 percent chance you are in church today.
- If you were born between 1965 and 1983, there is a 20 percent chance you are in church today.
- If you were born after 1984, there is a 10 percent chance you are in church today.[35]

Roxburgh's summary of the challenges facing these churches is similar to the language of the cable articulated by Tickle, "It is not that the ways we have been God's people were wrong. They were developed for another time, and now they are fraying, stretched and torn in the midst of massive social change."[36] Roxburgh then describes some of the technical methods that churches and leaders have employed to negotiate the coming changes: the 1960s and 1970s churches tried relational revolution; in the 1970s and 1980s churches tried Church Growth; in the 1980s and 1990s churches tried the Corporate Approach; and since 2000 the church has experimented with the emerging and missional church. Importantly, he notes,

"There is an increasing recognition across the Euro-tribal churches that tactics, metrics, programs, demographics, health assessments, or strategies for institutional reorganisation are not approximations of the Jesus movement the Spirit is inviting us into across our neighbourhoods. New monasticism, along with counterparts like the Parish Collective and slow church movements, are indicators that after more than fifty years of trying to fix the church, significant numbers of

---

[34] Roxburgh, *Joining God, Remaking Church, Changing the World*, 3.
[35] Roxburgh, *Joining God, Remaking Church, Changing the World*, 6.
[36] Roxburgh, *Joining God, Remaking Church, Changing the World*, 10.

Christians are hearing the Spirit's call to a journey in a different way."[37]

The proposition of Roxburgh's book is that God is initiating a different way. God is missionary in nature and is desiring people to participate in the reign of the kingdom. The incarnation is evidence of this. Our commission (Matt 28:18-20) is not to get church programs and services better so people will come and join our club. We are the ones called to go and live and participate with God in the neighbourhood. Roxburgh challenges us that, "We have to frame our lives around questions about God's actions in our neighbourhoods and how to join with God in these places."[38]

As we have explored the problems facing the church in Australia, we conclude with hope. There is ample data that shows us what is not working and there are useful voices that have helped us understand the social changes that are underfoot. As uncomfortable and threatened as some of us might be with change, our journey is not about comfort but pilgrimage. We have a friend who completed the Camino de Santiago in Spain. It is a long pilgrimage that can take over a month to complete. Asked about the walk our friend (who had prepared well for it) commented that the first week was mainly spent attending to foot pain. Then our friend was able to settle into the pilgrimage and focus on higher matters.

> **Learning**: Western culture is saturated with rapid, discontinuous change, which is causing old models and methods of identity and organisation to unravel. Like many other institutions, church structures and cultures are often not equipped for the challenges and opportunities before us, which is hindering the advance of the gospel and therefore the healing of communities.

We are called to a journey of participation with God in seeding new life in our communities, neighbourhoods and social networks. Many of the models, and indeed the present imagination of the church that has developed in recent centuries, worked well for a time. However, in

---

[37] Roxburgh, *Joining God, Remaking Church, Changing the World*, 23.
[38] Roxburgh, *Joining God, Remaking Church, Changing the World*, 45.

a changing culture these systems now hinder us from the full possibility of sharing in what God is doing today. God is always ahead of us on the journey and promises to shine a light for our path (Psalm 119:105). Our challenge is to look, listen and adapt rather than resist and defend old ways and attack those who see things differently, like religious leaders constantly did with Jesus.

It is important and freeing to remember that Jesus never intended his followers to build churches like we experience today as the only model God will inhabit. The early followers of Jesus practised things very differently and yet God was with them. The church that followed in subsequent centuries evidenced the presence of God until it became more concerned with imitation of its host culture rather than devoting its attention to where God's kingdom activity was found. Throughout Christian history, often after times of lost wandering, God's people have always been drawn back to where and how God was to be found – in Kingdom Communities. Eventually we too will throw off the things that entangle us and weigh us down, in pursuit of the renewing, redemptive and restoring presence of Christ.

We commenced this chapter with the metaphor of Andrew's children and their grandfather trying to understand how each saw the game of cricket. A similar shift is going on for those of us who have inhabited the church for most of our lives. We too need to understand the past and present in order to engage the future. We will now look at life in the early church in order to learn about what early Christian community was like; what things have become and where we might be headed as we re-imagine the possibility of Kingdom Communities in modern Australian cultures.

CHAPTER TWO

Back and Forth

"Many Christians today don't fully realise that racial and cultural integration was an original mission of the first disciples of Jesus."
Jim Wallis

"After this the Lord appointed seventy-two others and sent them on ahead of him, two by two, into every town and place where he himself was about to go. And he said to them, "The harvest is plentiful, but the laborers are few. Therefore pray earnestly to the Lord of the harvest to send out laborers into his harvest."
Luke 10:1-3 (ESV)

Digging holes

Andrew was once touring through the Roman catacombs with his father. Through one particular series of underground tombs the two of them saw where early Christians were able to worship and break bread in relative safety. These incredible underground networks of tombs go for kilometres. The Christians met in these elaborate underground tombs because it was the one place that they could worship and be free from being caught. The Romans would never enter such creepy places because of their superstitious nature, whereas the early Christians didn't fear death and were not superstitious – they were, after all, resurrection people.

The network of graves and tunnels makes one pause to appreciate our early Christian forebears and (for those of us who are free to worship) give thanks for our modern freedom to assemble to worship in a country like Australia. From the fifth century onwards, after the fall of Rome, all of the known catacombs were raided by Goths and Vandals. They took most of the marble coverings from the graves and anything else of value. Over time, without any covering, the ancient skeletons that were placed there were mostly lost.

After the tour, a Korean priest who was talking with the group, became very animated when he found out Andrew and his father were from Melbourne, Australia. He started flapping his arms like he was having a fit. He started repeating, 'Fairy penguins, fairy penguins!' As it turned out he had recently visited Melbourne and taken a tour to nearby Phillip Island, where the fairy penguins parade each night onto the beach after their days of fishing.

So, some small, fairy penguins near Melbourne helped Andrew and his father stand out sufficiently from the rest of the tourists that day and he offered for them to follow for an extended tour. He took them back into the labyrinth of ancient tunnels for several hundred metres until they came to a tomb. This tomb was still half covered with marble. Like all the catacombs, it was dug into the side of the tunnel and was at about chest level. It took a few moments to realise what the two of them were looking at. Right before them, about two feet from their eyes lay the very powdery and ancient remains of an early Christian. The skeleton had not been tampered with for most of two thousand years. This Christian had lived as a member of the early Roman Church. They had closely experienced the legacy of Paul and Peter and no doubt many other biblical heroes they lived within a couple of generations of. She or he had seen all the horrid events of the Colosseum and the martyrdom of saints. It was one of the most moving moments of Andrew's Christian journey and made the two of them pause in silence, wonder and respect.

When we put ourselves into that early Christian's situation we realise that he or she had an extremely different understanding of church compared to our modern experience. The cultural distance of two millennia, persecution, the canonisation of the Bible, the collapse of the Roman Empire, new oceans, different languages, Christendom, colonisation by Europeans of much of the of the world's first peoples and a host of other different variables all separate us from understanding what church was like back then. For a start, there was no Bible yet (the canon wasn't closed until the fourth century), no church building (they were illegal), no seminaries, no denominations, no large congregations, no clergy and no recognition from the state (just opposition). The good news about Jesus' teaching, death and resurrection spread virally and relationally, mainly through a network of households, initially among Jews and then among Gentiles. Luke tells us an edited account of the story in the book of Acts and the subsequent pastoral epistles also colour things in, as do other historic documents and accounts. Various church Fathers and historians help us by adding important stories and testimonies. These all help us understand the times and the culturally challenging demands of following Christ.

Deeper study of the Bible yields so much. Verses, passages and stories are properly understood and not misapplied through surface level reading. It also helps us question and challenge some of the inherited practices that can limit us in our mission and imagination. For example, one thing that some will find surprising, as they study the New Testament books, is the prevalence of female participation in church leadership and ministry. For example, in 2016 Pope Francis took the biggest step yet to properly recognise Mary Magdalene through the degree that put the woman who first proclaimed Jesus' resurrection, as an equal to the male apostles.

Dean and Andrew have found it bemusing and tragic to watch some churches and denominations wrestle with the place and giftedness of females in leadership. Why a gifted female leader who shares our age, experience and education is excluded from certain roles in some churches is painful, certainly for the female concerned as well as for what the church loses. As a nation we have had a female Monarch, Prime Minister, Head of State, Premiers and Governors and there are a growing numbers of CEOs and Board Directors of major companies: yet in some churches a suspicious, medieval worldview remains in place. This was not the case in the early church. Even in many churches that do encourage females into church positions of leadership, very few choose them as the senior leader or executive officer. In modern society where discrimination on the basis of gender is an encroachment on a basic human right, too many churches (hiding behind their religious freedom to discriminate) have become either a disturbing anachronism or target for ridicule and scorn. It is impossible for us to defend any argument that suggests Andrew's daughter should not have the same opportunity as her twin brother, or vice versa.

Recently, Andrew was talking with a colleague from another Christian denomination. She is a senior leader, ordained minister and also a widely published international theologian. She shared with Andrew that she had been invited interstate to an ordination on the condition that she did not go in the capacity as an ordained minister. None of her male colleagues were given this stipulation. Some invitation; come, but we aren't going to recognise your office fully because you are a female. We both know another female denominational executive officer where some churches, which are in her jurisdiction, will not let her preach. Dean's wife, Janette, is an endorsed minister and psychologist. She is a member of the Queensland's Premier's appointed council on domestic violence and chairs the Queensland Churches Together committee on domestic violence. Yet, she cannot preach at some local churches because she is a woman.

How have we created churches with systems that are so limiting, discriminatory and ungracious? The New Testament is filled with examples of female, Christian leadership as well as male leadership. There are a couple of texts that, if separated from the rest of the New Testament and read at surface level can be read against female leadership. However, upon reasoned exegesis they are not as they first present and certainly not for all churches everywhere, forever. Nor are they representative of the general thrust of New Testament ministry. The New Testament has a wide spread of examples of participation at all levels of leadership by females. The early church pushed the cultural barriers of the day far more than some churches do today.

So, what was life like among the early Christians and how did they organise and meet? Many people romanticise about the early church and miss all the really tough stuff of daily life that they wrestled with. This results in too many people giving little value to history and context. Consequently, we miss out on so much. If we examine the Christian movement historically, we will often find that the things we tie ourselves in knots over today weren't significant issues in the early church: ordination, denominationalism, barring females from leading, church property, creeds and doctrinal statements, christenings, the nuclear family, seeker services and clericalism are some that come to mind.

> **Learning:** There is no biblical model of Christian community that only extracts from the local community and context of ministry. Biblically, Kingdom Communities are to be a sign and foretaste of the kingdom of God on earth. They are called to shine light and bring uplift to the community about them.

Going back

Saul of Tarsus hated Christians (Acts 8:1). Although little is known about his birth, we can approximate that he was born five or ten years after Christ. Tarsus was a busy town on a commercial trade route in Asia Minor (generally the same land area as modern Turkey). Saul seems to have been schooled initially in Tarsus, which makes sense, as his letters demonstrate a familiarity with Greek philosophical thinking. However, we also know that he was schooled by a Rabbi, named Gamaliel who was a Jerusalem based scholar.

Paul describes himself as a 'Hebrew born of Hebrews' (Phil 3:5), which was a cultural method of locating himself as someone who did not follow Greek ways. Ultimately, Paul states that he was schooled in Jerusalem (Acts 22:3) and it is quite possible that he lived in his sister's house (Acts 23:16). After Paul's dramatic conversion to Christianity (Acts 9: 1-31) we know that he spent the next ten years ministering in Tarsus and the surrounding vicinity (Acts 9:30; Gal 1:21; Gal 2:1).

Contrary to bias and misunderstanding, Paul was a wonderful architect for the advancement of all the people of God and saw everyone as equal in Christ. As he grew in his understanding of the immensity of what Christ achieved, Paul developed a new ethic for the new covenant people. In his earliest available writing, the Epistle to the Galatians, Paul saw that the gospel transcended any prevailing and limited culture(s) and called us to live into a new reality. He realised that in Christ we became citizens of the kingdom of God. Paul said it this way in Ephesians 2:19-20,

> "Consequently, you are no longer foreigners and strangers, but fellow citizens with God's people and also members of his household, built on

the foundation of the apostles and prophets, with Christ Jesus himself as the chief cornerstone."

Paul envisioned a new covenant people. He saw us living into a healing, compassionate, reconciling, inclusive community formed in Christ, which treated all people, from all backgrounds with dignity and respect. In working through the logical consequence of being Christ's people (who were filled and guided by the Holy Spirit) Paul actually concluded in Galatians 3:28 that, 'There is neither Jew nor Gentile, neither slave nor free, nor is there male and female, for you are all one in Christ Jesus.'

Such a statement had a profound effect on the early Christians who lived within a very patriarchal Roman culture. In the book of Acts in chapter six, we see the story of Stephen being appointed into leadership to ensure provision for Greek widows. This was a profoundly important statement and appointment, both for what happened (see Acts 6:1-8:1) but also for the place of all females in the new community. In a society that did not allow females to hold property titles and which saw welfare for females as an issue only for their families (and if you had no family that was a huge problem) this was a radical move. Females – whether Jew or Gentile – were valued and important members of the community and accordingly deserved welfare if they were struck by personal grief.

The elevation of women as equal to males had another important implication for their welfare. The exposure of baby girls was an occasional practice in Roman culture. As hard as it is to understand in modern, Western society, sometimes Roman families simply did not want more female children and therefore dumped them in the street, to die. Followers of Jesus, moved by the new status of equality of the genders and filled with the compassion of the Holy Spirit, often adopted these infants. These, and other similar acts of compassion, were a key reason for the growth of early Christianity. It is no coincidence that many of the new converts were females who then shared the faith throughout their own households.

It took a while for these new communities who followed Christ to gain the name 'Christian'. Initially they were simply known as disciples or followers of 'The Way'[1]. The title of Christian emerged as a term of denigration similar to how John was called, 'The Baptiser' by the synagogue leaders. Because the word Christian appeared so late in the development of the church, it only appears in the Bible three times; in Acts 11:26; 26:28 and 1 Peter 4:16.

Church or ekklesia?

The word 'church' also appeared late on the scene. As Christianity started to separate from religious activity around the Temple and synagogues and also as it gained traction among Gentiles, the early followers of Jesus started to use the Greek word ekklesia as a name for their gatherings. Ekklesia initially had two popular meanings, which when added together came to be associated with Christian activity. First, in the Septuagint (the Greek version of the Hebrew Bible) ekklesia was used to mean 'the congregation of the Israelites'. It was used for national moments when they gathered for religious purposes or to hear the law read. Second, Greek culture used ekklesia to describe a gathering or assembly of people, whether for religious or secular purposes. It was these two meanings that the early Christians adapted as they formed their own understanding of ekklesia.

Ekklesia appears only twice in the gospels (Matt 16:18 & 18:17) and then more frequently in the rest of the New Testament. There are four major contexts where ekklesia is applied in the New Testament. *Firstly*, it is used to describe a general meeting of Christians. A helpful example is found in 1 Cor 11:18, "In the first place, I hear that when you come together as an ekklesia, there are divisions among you, and to some extent I believe it." Paul was arguing that when the Christians met together they were the people of God. In the following chapter Paul specifically addresses them as a body that he calls the Body of Christ (1 Cor 12:27).

Secondly, ekklesia was used to describe what were generally house assemblies. Because the early Christians had no public buildings and often meetings were illegal, they met quietly in houses (or, as described at the start of this chapter, sometimes in places like catacombs). A similar phenomenon has occurred in China in recent decades with staggering

---
[1] See Acts 9:2; 19:9, 23; 22:4; 24:14, 22.

growth outcomes. As in China, these were often secret meetings and sometimes an enquirer had to be followed and examined before they were trusted enough to be brought into a meeting, because they could have been a spy. Ekklesia is used this way for those who met in Priscilla and Aquila's home (Rom 16:3 & 1 Cor 16:19).

Thirdly, ekklesia is used to describe the entire population of Christians who lived in a city or geographical area. This is often described as 'The church in Jerusalem' (Acts 1:8) or 'The church in Corinth' (1 Cor 1:2), and so on. Remember, there were no denominations back then so the Christians in an area were the church of that area and all identified together. In Acts 1:8 the church had widening geographic understandings that applied to mission: Jerusalem, Judea, Samaria and to the ends of the earth.

Finally, in the New Testament, ekklesia was used as a description for the 'universal' church to which all believers in Christ belonged. This was the meaning that Jesus implied in Matt 16:18 when he said, "And I tell you that you are Peter, and on this rock, I will build my ekklesia, and the gates of Hades will not overcome it." The command to expand this community is also found when Jesus commissioned his disciples to take it to the nations in Matthew 28:18-20,

> "Then Jesus came to them and said, "All authority in heaven and on earth has been given to me. Therefore, go and make disciples of all nations, baptising them in the name of the Father and of the Son and of the Holy Spirit, and teaching them to obey everything I have commanded you. And surely, I am with you always, to the very end of the age."

Importantly, the word 'nations' in Matthew chapter 28 should not be understood as the modern nation-state but as 'tribes and tongues'. That is a reason why the multiplicity of tongues spoken and interpreted by native speakers at Pentecost (Acts chapter two) was a profound statement of the intent of the Spirit towards mission at the birth of the early church. Our understanding of ekklesia becomes important when we start to speak about mission. As we have just seen, there was not the remotest expectation that our modern models of the now-traditional local church were what were to be exported to other nations.

Chapter Two: Back and Forth

The actual journey of the usage of the word ekklesia to the word church in the English lexicon came via Germany, like many other words. Church comes from an old English word cirice, which is derived from Germanic usage of the word kirika, which comes from the Latin ecclesia, which comes from the Greek ekklesia. Andrew's family, being of Scottish origin, still describes the church as the kirk.

There are some important implications for understanding how the local ekklesia understood itself. Early Christians saw themselves as the community of the 'end time'. This is why many people were so willing to give away their material possessions freely, spontaneously and with great generosity (Acts 2:43-47 & 4:32-37). This is why Paul wrote in 1 Cor 10:11, "These things happened to them as examples and were written down as warnings for us, on whom the culmination of the ages has come." The church was called out from Judaism and from the Gentile world to become a new people who were filled and empowered with the Holy Spirit to be a sign and foretaste of the kingdom of God in the world (see Eph 2:11-22).

An expression of this new Kingdom Community was Paul's radical vision for the church to be inclusive, which he wrote about in Gal 3:28. This was a vision that Paul similarly repeated to the Colossian church, in Col 3:11, 'Here there is no Gentile or Jew, circumcised or uncircumcised, barbarian, Scythian, slave or free, but Christ is all, and is in all!'[2] As Manfred Brauch says, "In this new community the traditional barriers of race, social standing, and sex-barriers that divided people from one another and categorised them into inferior and superior classes - are seen to be shattered."[3]

Jesus symbolically appointed twelve apostles as founders of this radical new Kingdom Community. The connection with the twelve tribes of Israel was unavoidable. The new community was formed out of Israel. Luke quoted what Isaiah foretold in Acts 13:47, "I have made

---

[2] The same idea was also expressed by Paul to the Corinthian church in 1 Cor 12:12-13.
[3] Manfred T. Brauch, "Church", in Walter A. Elwell (ed), *Baker Encyclopedia of the Bible*, Grand Rapids: Baker, 1988, 459. Given the vision of Gal 3:28 we need to continually reflect also if current church practice is actually enabling or hindering this becoming a reality.

you a light for the Gentiles, that you may bring salvation to the ends of the earth" (Isa 49:6).

> **Learning:** The meaning and examples in the New Testament of ekklesia are a long way away from most modern expressions of church. While there are elements of gathering and worshipping together implicit in the use of the term, there are equal measures and assumptions about dwelling and being sent every day into the local community.

Today

We now come back to today. Having briefly examined the early Christian understanding of ekklesia, which took decades to emerge, we can begin to make some important observations. We know that the world of first century Christianity was very different to our world. We are reminded that the early church didn't have buildings, seminaries or even the canon of the New Testament. We have noted that there were no denominations and the Kingdom Communities had a singular identity in any given location. We also know that Christians met as the ekklesia usually in homes (and sometimes in odd places like tombs, as previously described). We understand that the vision for this new community that especially Paul encapsulated, was of a Kingdom Community in which all people were equal in Christ. Discrimination on the basis of class, gender or ethnicity was meant to be on its way out in this new community.

Given all this information, we need to ask why the modern church is so preoccupied with certain narrow models of congregation and denomination for its operations, leadership and mission, especially as these models are by and large failing, in terms of growth or the fulfilment of Jesus' social vision. Whereas the early church was generally respected and esteemed by local communities, the modern church is failing in most of the markers we described in chapter one. Our local communities on the whole do not want to come to Sunday worship services and fewer and fewer of our own committed members themselves attend regularly.[4]

---
[4] There are all sorts of reasons for this decline including Sunday morning sport programs, the energy required for young families to actually get to church and then often spend

The back door in most churches is wide open and if you take the time to think of the people who were active in your church just a couple of years ago who have since left, you will see the scale of the problem. If there is a New Testament vision for one people, from every tribe and tongue who are all equal and who all work for justice, we must ask why we stick with this model alone?

There are implications inside the answer to this question for churches, denominations and seminaries. Each of these institutions have emerged as servants and proponents of a model that is under severe scrutiny. The story of Kodak is a timely reminder. Older readers will remember when they used to get photographic negatives printed as photographs. In the old system we would take the negatives to the pharmacy (having no idea whether they were good photographs or not) and come back a week later when the photos were ready for collection. These days with digital photographs available instantly for no cost, we only get the occasional image developed onto photographic paper. It is telling that it was people within Kodak, which was one of the world's largest organisations, who famously developed and then passed on the digital camera, and it was the Kodak leaders who would not change because they decided it would threaten its photographic print business. The model had become too important to change, and history has shown the consequences. We need to seriously consider whether we, like Kodak, want to be attached only to a dated model of church where the key metric is Sunday attendance numbers, or whether we want to support the development of diverse expressions of Kingdom Communities.

If you suspect that the model we are developing requires everything we currently have and know to be thrown out, that is not what we are proposing or developing. As you read on you will notice that we are not about to throw out the baby with the bathwater. We are, however, suggesting the need for significant change in focus and application because of the tough nature of the challenge before us but we still see a crucial and strategic role for local congregations, denominations

---

the whole time trying to keep the kids quiet, people enjoying weekend holiday homes, travel, the distance some people live from the church of their choice, the appeal of Sunday shopping and cafes, the lack of discipleship, etc.

and seminaries as contributors and change advocates of Kingdom Communities. In this hinge moment in mission history, when so much is up for grabs, we believe that local congregations, denominations, seminaries and Christian agencies can make a significant contribution to a preferred future and the advancement of more Kingdom Communities. The example of Kodak reminds us that the defence of past practices that are poorly delivering on the mission, and that persist in the face of discovered improvements, is only to embrace death. Kodak did not need to follow the path they chose. They were in a better position than most to see the future and they could have mapped a timely transition, so their brand continued. They didn't.

Recently Andrew attended the funeral of the minister of his childhood church. This man was a warm, intelligent, humorous, generous, capable minister. His sermons were pastoral and theologically reflective. Each of the churches he led thrived during his ministry. His pastoral care was excellent and there were many families for whom he was a valued, confidential minister and Christlike presence in the midst of life's difficulties and trauma. He performed his ministry with excellence and also maintained a healthy and balanced family life. He lived life well and died well despite a debilitating end. He was an important influence in Andrew's vocational call, so he was determined to attend the funeral to honour his influence, humanity and excellent ministry.

As the service proceeded, each of the churches where he was minister were described. Not all the churches where he was Minister were 'easy' churches but he persevered with grace and determination and significantly unified each of them. Importantly, he left each church well and set it up for his successor. Yet today, each of those churches is a skeleton of their vibrant days and each of them faces closure within a few years. In short, this Minster was brilliant at the model of church that he was formed for, which is now passing away.

This is a well-worn pattern. There is no judgement on Andrew's old minister. In fact, his churches thrived while others were in decline. The eventual decline of the churches that he led is nothing to do with his ministry and occurred well after he had moved on, but it is an important reminder that we cannot future-proof a church and the making of more old-style ministers is not the answer.

The decline of the current model of local church is myriad and complex. There is a vast amount of writing already on this subject. It is genuinely sad for those of us who have benefitted from it, however, over time, while culture, demographics, society, technology, organisations, the social sciences and knowledge have changed, church structure and identity has not. By and large, local churches and the systems they serve have not adapted sufficiently or imaginatively. There has not been sufficient investment in research and development. Like Andrew's father seeking help from his grandchildren about changes in cricket, we also need to face what is not working and encourage imagination and experimentation. Understanding what has framed our comprehension of how church is done is an important part of the puzzle.

Denominations and colonisation

The rise of the modern denomination is an interesting phenomenon.[5] For the first 1500 years of Western Christian history, what is now known as the Roman Catholic Church contained many different streams and orders within its elaborate structure. As time moved on and power consolidated among the church hierarchy and elites, there was less room for divergent views, even when the church was in clear error. The trajectory of what Cox calls the *Age of Belief* became harsher and more bounded. Bodies like the Sacred Congregation for the Doctrine of the Faith and its earlier versions ensured a cohesive (and sometimes unreasonably narrow[6]) theological unity across the church. If an

---

[5] A denomination is not just the head office where decisions are made and executive staff are located. A denomination is the whole system through which leaders, local churches, care agencies, seminaries and staff are mutually united and gain a level of identity and theological familiarity. Alan Roxburgh has done some important work on the deeper European identity which many denominations are founded upon and which is now struggling for meaning. See: Alan Roxburgh, *Joining God, Remaking Church, Changing the World: The New Shape of the Church in Our Time*, New York: Morehouse, 2015, and *Structured for Mission: Renewing the Culture of the Church*, Downers Grove: IVP, 2015, 99-172.

[6] For example, the specific case of Galileo Galilei, who suffered for his scientific discovery and theory, which had dramatic implication on church belief or more generally the 'Spanish Inquisition' which had dubious motives in its policing of orthodoxy.

individual or group was assessed not to be in alignment, they had clear choices: they could repent, face excommunication or worse.

The Protestant Reformation in the sixteenth century changed things dramatically. When Martin Luther and his colleagues protested about certain Church activities[7] and nailed his ninety-five theses to the door of the Wittenberg Castle Church he was branded a heretic. His movement gave rise to the development of Protestantism over the next decades, often in very dangerous circumstances.

Facing excommunication and at severe personal cost, Protestant Christians needed to somehow associate. Needing to identify with other 'protesters' in this new movement, the name 'Lutheran' and 'Protestant' soon stuck. Overtime, as the radicals consolidated core doctrine, they worked through the particular emphasis of their beliefs. Five *solas*[8], or foundational beliefs soon defined the new breakaway group and over time those who identified found each other and developed into what became modern Lutheranism. Over the past five hundred years various streams of Lutheranism have further developed and broken away from their parent bodies for theological, cultural and geographic reasons thus expanding the range of Lutheran denominations. This pattern has continued across other Protestant denominations also, often establishing a pattern of division and competition.

Following this Germanic movement, other European nations also struggled with remaining or departing from the Roman Catholic Church. There were many varying reasons particular to each context that ranged between theology and politics. This era saw the rise of other state churches and breakaway movements that have marked Protestantism including the Church of England (Anglican), the Church of Scotland, Huguenots, versions of Calvinism, Puritanism, Methodism, Baptists, Moravians, Restorationists, Salvationists, Congregationalists and many more. Each sought to improve, alter or respond to a theological or pastoral need in their context.

---

[7] Famously he questioned the sale of indulgences to raise funds for the church and especially the construction of St Peter's Basilica.

[8] *Sola scriptura* (by Scripture alone), *Sola fide* (by faith alone), *Sola gratia* (by grace alone), *Solus Christo* (through Christ alone) and *Soli Deo gloria* (glory to God alone).

Chapter Two: Back and Forth

Slowly over time and aided by colonisation of the 'new world', more denominations and reform movements developed. For example, in the USA, there are over seventy different Baptist denominations and the restoration movement, which is meant to model commitment to church unity, is divided into three main streams.[9] As theological, national, ethical, geographic and pluralistic issues emerged, groups either consolidated or divided, thus creating more denominations. This emerging model of denominationalism has ultimately been exported wherever the Protestant church has migrated in the world. Because of the migratory roots, most denominations are what Alan Roxburgh calls Euro-tribal because, "To a great extent these denominations were formed and expanded in the context of strong national and ethnic identities."[10]

Understanding European colonisation is essential for understanding the context of Australian denominationalism. What is now known as Australia, had been occupied for well over forty thousand years by its first peoples: a series of nations and ethnic groups referred to now as Aboriginal and Torres Strait Islanders. European colonisers initially gave no acknowledgement that these people even existed and early maps simply described the landmass as terra nullius meaning 'nobody's land'. The beginnings of Aboriginal displacement and the contracting of European diseases began in 1770 when Captain James Cook placed an English flag on the beach and named the area Botany Bay[11], claiming the East Coast of Australia for King George III.[12]

Nothing further changed for eighteen years. However, with the loss of the United States as a penal colony, English authorities commissioned Captain Arthur Phillip in 1787 to lead a fleet of eleven ships to Botany Bay to develop a new penal colony. As it turned out, Botany Bay was too

---

9 The three streams of Restorationism in the USA are: Churches of Christ, Disciples of Christ and Christian Churches.

10 Roxburgh, *Joining God, Remaking Church, Changing the World*, 3.

11 Cook initially referred to the area as Sting-Ray Harbor and then Botanist Bay after botanist Joseph Banks' fascination with the new flora and fauna. The name eventually settled as Botany Bay.

12 At least two earlier European expeditions had made landfall on the Australian continent including Willem Janszoon on Cape York Peninsula (1606) and Dirk Hartog on Western Australia at Dirk Hartog Island but both saw no potential in the land nor had any clue about the size of the continent.

shallow and sandy and without drinkable water (in contrast to Cook's description), which led Phillip to send out a search party to find a better harbour.

On 26th January, 1788, near what is now the main ferry terminal at Circular Quay, a new colony was begun at what Philip named Port Jackson (Sydney Harbour). Early reports describe a brutal and very wild landing as the settlement commenced. The initial party was virtually left to perish by English authorities[13] but eventually they grew some food, more supplies came from England, and law and order was established, aided by liberal use of the cat o' nine tails and noose. There was mixed initial success in relationships between local Aborigines and colonists, however European diseases soon tragically claimed many lives. There are early accounts of dead bodies across the northern beaches of the harbour with skin scarred by small pox.[14]

As the new penal colony was being mooted, a chaplain was sought from the Church of England in order to improve 'public morality'. Few wanted to leave the comforts of home until an evangelical cleric named Richard Johnson, with the encouragement of John Newton and William Wilberforce, agreed. Johnson joined the First Fleet and conducted his first public service of worship on Sunday February 3rd, 1788. Besides his religious work, he was regarded as the best farmer in the new colony and had great success with growing the citrus fruit he bought in Rio de Janeiro on the journey. He also had an interest in the Aboriginal people and developed significant relationships. An indication of this is that Johnson and his wife Mary named their first daughter Milbah, an

---

[13] Clive Turnbull, *A concise history of Australia*, Melbourne: Currey O'Neil, 1983, 26. "The early years were unhappy. Out of sight, out of mind, appeared to the colonists to be the attitude of their home Government. They were short of clothes and short of food, eking out their rations with rats, crows and seaweed or, perhaps for the lucky, a fine dog."

[14] W Tench, "A complete account of the settlement at Port Jackson, in New South Wales, including an accurate description of the situation of the colony; of the Natives; and of its natural Productions", London, 1793, in Frank Crowley, *A Documentary History of Australia: Colonial Australia*, Melbourne: Nelson, 1980, 13-14, "An extraordinary calamity was now observed among the natives. Repeated accounts brought by our boats of finding bodies of the Indians in all the coves and inlets of the harbor… It appeared that all parties had died a natural death: pustules, similar to those occasioned by small pox, were thickly spread on the bodies."

Aboriginal name. Johnson struggled to get resources to build a church from the authorities and eventually started one from his own initiative. He was joined by Rev. Samuel Marsden in 1794 as the Church of England (Australia campus) was established. As chaplains, Johnson and Marsden preached, baptised, authorised marriages, prayed for those awaiting execution and then buried them.

Being an excellent farmer, Johnson was given about 400 acres as a glebe. A glebe is a grant of land made to the church for its benefit so as to enable some income for the purposes of mission and ministry. Johnson cultivated this area, which is today known as the suburb of Glebe. The grant of 400 acres created the beginnings of what was to become of significant benefit to the Anglican Diocese of Sydney, which is now the wealthiest Anglican diocese in the world.

As the colony grew so did the size and spread of its brand of Anglicanism, which is still today a strong and distinctive force. What also commenced with these origins was a method of colonisation where models of church with a particular doctrinal emphasis were replicated onto other towns and cities wherever possible. Other than the obvious mission justifications, the key motive for driving this forward was the extension of a Euro-tribal powerbase. Therefore, using the Sydney Anglican denomination as our example because it was the first in Australia, the social imagination and driving force for Christian mission came from a European mentality with regard to how Christianity should be organised. The same forces are still dominant today. The Sydney Anglicans are certainly not the only denomination to colonise and replicate their particular doctrinal emphasis and model of organisation. Many other denominations have subsequently come to Australia and embarked on similar programs, each carrying European or American agendas.

What is important for us to note is the priority and method of mission extension. The denomination extends its particular brand, model and beliefs as far and as wide as possible. Minimum concern is placed on cultural context and attentiveness to what the Spirit is already doing in a place. The model is for the franchise to be extended so as to take new ground. It is very similar to how commercial franchises and corporations expand their business empires. Over the years, Dean and

Andrew have both been involved in strategic planning sessions where denominational leaders have sought to identify areas on the map to plant a new church. Rarely was there any consideration of what other denomination churches might be trying to do in the target community. "Our brand, theology and way" needed to be forwarded.

Denominations spread and divide over time and even sprout new ones for many reasons. Through brief sketches of the origins of two denominations (European Lutheranism and Sydney Anglicanism) we can see the influence of geography, culture and history. Over time, members within the denomination may differ or diverge because of geography, personality, culture or theology and break away and start new churches. Often the new church is formed with a specific emphasis or as a reaction to something in the parent denomination. Practices and rituals are developed and justified because of schism or an aspect of awakening. Often, generations later, whether these patterns are necessary or not, they became impossible to change. They have been wired into the DNA of the denomination.

Today there are many denominations in Australia. They reflect their country of origin and are mostly Euro-tribal. Others are imports from newer movements, especially from the United States, of Asia and the Pacific region. A few generations on, most people in a denomination lose the original cultural meaning of the denomination and see little or no meaning in it. Additionally, as people move from one denomination to another due to increased mobility, denominational stories are diluted. Some older folk remember denominational gatherings as important parts of their Christian formation and identity, but younger people are generally not interested and have lost connection with the original story, which once provided meaningful reasons for association.

The result of this pattern on the modern Australian church scene is that a vacuum has been created. Denominations are usually living in a particular story, which was formed generations ago. This story has diminishing meaning to current church members as they have less connection with the original story. Most church attendees today don't care about denominational affiliation. Less than fifteen percent of people who join a church (from the fifteen percent of Australians who go to church in the first place) do so because of its denominational connection. In other words, denominational loyalty is a relevant factor for just over two Australians in every hundred. Also, as some churches increase in size and outgrow the constraints of the average church, they need less denominational support and resources. The larger a church becomes the less it relies on denominational support and the more it tends to create its own identity and practice.

Baptist churches provide an interesting case in point. Baptist churches originated in Europe when groups of Christians (baptising by full immersion in water) committed to read the Bible together in order to discern how they should respond to various contexts and challenges. Theirs was intended to be an expression of a purer church compared to state churches, which they felt commanded people with what to think and do. Being truly Baptist therefore was about gathering with other believers, reading the Bible together and personally discerning, with a free conscience, how to live out the Christian faith. Sometimes this was done at great personal cost to life and liberty. Freedom of individual conscience is meant to be a Baptist tenant of faith.

> **Learning:** It is so easy and natural for modern churches to colonise, rather than to do the hard work of dwelling, attending and listening to the local community and the quiet, still, voice of God.

If we fast-forward to today, we now have very large Baptist churches with multiple congregations where there is no forum for group discernment and little opportunity to explore freedom of conscience. Due to the size and diversity of big Baptist churches, most policies are made by a Board or an executive. The general trajectory of decision making has moved away from members for pragmatic reasons. It is simply not possible to listen to every voice in a large church. In some modern churches, policies are implemented with little or no opportunity for individual discernment or freedom to express one's conscience. An added complexity is when there are multiple congregations within the one church that meet at different times and sometimes at different locations, whose members live all over the city and some of whom speak different languages. It becomes impossible to follow the pattern of the first Baptists.

However, this book is not concerned with congregational sizes. All churches (large and small) are a critical part of the mix in the mission of the church in Australia and provide community, teaching and guidance to many people. The above illustration is included (and could have been applied to large churches in most denominations) because increasingly in a multi-cultural, mobile, global culture, the denominational practice and story has decreasing meaning and less cause for identity for people, and especially in strong churches. Indeed, the denomination can create a perceived source of tension or drain on resources (for example through needing people on central committees and via affiliation fees), because the original story has been lost or is irrelevant to attendees of their local churches.

Denominations tend to function with a 'typical' or model church and minister in mind because of their beginnings. Each denomination has its own specific requirements that have been formed over the course of their journey and this stipulates some of the qualifications expected of the typical minister for endorsement, accreditation and ordination. We have observed it is always easier for a candidate to make it through the process laid down if they have a pleasant personality, a keen mind, humble aspiration and are from a class and cultural background similar to what prevails within the wider system. The result of this is that most ministers are gifted in pastoral care or teaching. They are solid citizens and faithful proponents of the status quo. Generally 'model ministers' are not prophetic agents of change or evangelists who bring new people into church and create change because those that do generally don't last too long in the system. Yet paradoxically there is increasing pressure on ministers to lead change and produce growth; but are expected to do so within a culture where there is little reward for risk taking. Churches often have boards that don't understand the model of pastoral ministry that their minister was trained for. These are some of the many reasons why stress levels in clergy are unsustainably high. Today, there are more clergy out of church ministry than in it.

Let's be clear why ministers are in constant levels of stress. The denominational selection system favours ministers who will support the denomination and fulfil professional development short courses. The local church wants good leaders who can manage and grow the church, do weddings and funerals, visit the sick, raise leaders and motivate the church to growth. The seminary wants intelligent scholars who can engage with various theological currents and movements. The church board increasingly wants a CEO to turn things around and rebuild the organisation. Potential transferees into the church want a dynamic evangelist. People leaving the church are going to a better option. And the people in the community rate the clergy low for ethics and honesty!

> **Learning:** It is almost impossible today for the modern minister to maintain personal and family health and balance; congregational satisfaction; the applause of the eldership and effective community engagement. Something needs to change.

There is no doubt we are in a period of rapid, discontinuous change when the prevailing models are struggling. Across denominations, pastoral ministers who are called and predisposed to faithfully care for people, have been placed in systems that require (sometimes dramatic) change. Our denominations and local churches have serious sustainability challenges. Seminaries[15] face great challenges too. A generation ago, most responsibility for the preparation of a candidate for ministry was overseen by the seminary. Some even had the final say on whether the individual was ready for ministry and ordination. Naturally a path designed by teachers is going to prepare people for ministry teaching and this is what has occurred. The propensity for ministers who can teach well and offer good pastoral care has established a clear pathway for those with these gifts into church ministry which, in turn, works well in a system where most churches want their minister to be good at teaching and pastoral care. However, there seems to be not much space for true entrepreneurs, activists, prophets, poets, change leaders and strategic change thinkers. This book contends that the task

---

[15] Throughout this book we use the word Seminary (which is short, simple and widely recognised), to include Bible colleges, colleges of ministry, theological colleges, etc.

of seminaries is more important than ever. There is a large and necessary theological and ministry task at hand, which must be in partnership with those at the coalface. God's people need avenues of growth towards intellectual and spiritual maturity that equips them for engagement with modern culture, with a level of professional tertiary rigour that matches with their gifts and skills.

Despite and because of these challenges, denominations, seminaries and churches have to work together to adapt to ministry in the context we face. Given their presence, resources, and perspectives, there is much to gain from a recalibrated networking and cooperation between each of these institutions. What is needed are mature relationships between local churches, seminaries, denominations and agencies that each seek to serve the other as a united force with the end outcome in mind: Kingdom Communities. The time for silos has passed.

Andrew was at a concert recently where the Melbourne Symphony Orchestra was playing one of his favourite pieces, Tchaikovsky's Sixth Symphony, known as the Pathetique. It is a wonderful score, which touches emotions like only Russian composers seem able to do. It has beautiful moments as the violins soar with sweet melodies and then it explores the very depths of human emotion and deep melancholy. Anytime it is played with a decent orchestra Andrew tries to purchase tickets.

There is nothing quite like being transported by such extraordinary music and on this occasion, he was again moved. After the concert he found himself talking with a group of friends. They were comparing notes on the performance of the orchestra; the cello, the oboe and the violas, and so on. He found himself standing back and listened to the conversation, wondering if they were at the same concert? Some commented that, "This bit should have been louder" or "The tempo was too slow" or "The conductor got the second movement wrong". Somehow this group of people managed to attend a concert with a world-class orchestra playing timeless music and all they could focus on was the technical performance of the parts. Each of them was looking for the symphony to be played to their preference. They missed out on what was really happening.

Modern church life can produce similar responses to this. Because we are so conditioned to church being a prescribed model with predictable programs, liturgies, ministry, organisation and feedback loops we fail to imagine that it can be different, and we often miss what God is up to and how we can best respond. We face a predicament; not knowing another way forward and clinging to what we know, yet watching continual decline. Some voices come along with simplistic answers, calling churches to new tactics and techniques and, out of desperation, they are attempted, thus tiring faithful people in the church with another program. Some people will try anything that sounds credible if it will save the church from decline.

The problem is that we face a far more significant challenge. The issue at stake for us is not really technical; after all we have technical ability. The deeper issue is whether we are open to seeing what God is doing in and around us. Too often we don't because we are too invested in implementing and colonising. We are too busy to listen and look. Just because the world is no longer coming to our churches does not mean that the Spirit has retired from calling, redeeming, recreating, reconciling and renewing. It just might be that we are so wrapped up in our own technical church concerns and colonising that we are missing what God is up to all around us as well as within our churches.

There are huge differences in the orientation and purpose of the modern, Western church compared with the earliest churches. How a small, under-resourced, often-illegal ekklesia that had no buildings, seminaries, congregational gatherings, megachurches, or denominations spread to become a tenth of the Roman Empire in three hundred years while the modern church with its freedoms, power, rights and resources is in decline, is a question worth serious thought. We believe a core reason for the difference is because the early church was focused on becoming an interconnected series of Kingdom Communities (or ekklesias) that were attentive to the presence and activity of God about them. They were not focused on programs, seeker-attractiveness and buildings but on God's redemptive, renewing and restorative activity.

Over a two-thousand-year time period, of course many things change, however, the essence of the church has not. The aim of the early church was Christian maturity, which is something that Paul clearly wrote about. To the Ephesian church Paul said that the purpose of the church was,

"To equip his people for works of service, so that the body of Christ may be built up until we all reach unity in the faith and in the knowledge of the Son of God and become mature, attaining to the whole measure of the fullness of Christ." (Ephesians 4:12-13)

To the Colossian church Paul summarised the purpose this way,

"He is the one we proclaim, admonishing and teaching everyone with all wisdom, so that we may present everyone fully mature in Christ." (Colossians 1:28)

Despite the length of years, there really should be no difference in the aims of today's church. It may look different, but these passages must be at the heart of a church's purpose. Christian maturity is still the goal. There is no one single method of doing and being the people of God. Like dancing, there are so many methods that are culturally specific – different steps, movements, dress, music – yet they all stem from the desire for expression. For example, the early church was organised around small house churches (Kingdom Communities) and networks of those house churches across a city. Paul and others would write a letter to the church in the city and it would then be passed around, to be read to everyone via the house churches. These Kingdom Communities often met secretly and emphasised faith, hope and love first, not beliefs or creeds, according to Harvey Cox. They were hard to find and joining them required high levels of commitment. Joseph Hellerman calls them 'strong-groups'[16] because of the level of commitment required to join them. He notes,

"The individual in a strong-group society finds his identity not primarily in his own personal achievements but in the context of the

---

[16] B. Malina, *Christian Origins and Cultural Anthropology*, Atlanta: John Knox, 1986, 19. "[In a strong-group society] the person perceives himself or herself to be a member of a group and responsible to the group for his or her actions, destiny, career, development, and life in general. Correspondingly he/she perceived other persons primarily in terms of the groups to which they belong. The individual person is embedded in the group and is free to do what he or she feels is right and necessary only if in accord with group norms and only if the action in the group's best interest."

group to which he belongs. And crucial life decisions are made in the context of that group as well."¹⁷

Past, Present, Future

In the last section of this chapter we aim to present a simple diagram of some key shifts in the church from its beginnings to the present and the shift we envisage to accommodate the future mission activity of the Spirit and the people of God. **Figure 2.1** below shows in summary form what we are describing.

	Early Church	Present Church	Future Church
Structure:	Distributed network	Hub & spokes	Modified distributed network
Leadership gifts employed:	APEPT (i.e. Apostle, Prophet, Evangelist, Pastor & Teacher.)	PT (i.e. Pastor & Teacher.)	APEPT (i.e. Apostle, Prophet, Evangelist, Pastor & Teacher.)
Expressions of Ekklesia:			
LOCAL	Kingdom Community (met in houses)	Congregation	Kingdom Communities interwoven with congregation and denomination
WIDER	City wide network	Denomination, Seminary and Agencies	Networks of Kingdom Communities, Seminaries, congregations and Agencies
INTERNATIONAL	Inter-city church networks	Councils & Creedal associations	Networks of networks

Figure 2.1 Past, Present & Future leadership

---

17 Joseph H. Hellerman, *When the church was a family: Recapturing Jesus' vision for authentic Christian community*, Nashville: B & H Publishing, 2009, 21. Gendered language is Hellerman's.

Past: Early Church

The early church was structured like a distributed network (see figure 2.2). The term distributed network has been borrowed from computer programming where it describes a situation of data being spread across more than one computer. The term has since been applied to organisational structures to explain a model that has active, interdependent and inter-related nodes but no real central authority. Certainly, there are agreed rules and a common language in a distributed network so as to enable the parts to function but there is no command structure that sits across the top of the nodes. This does not mean that there are no leaders, quite the contrary. Distributed networks depend on self-organising leadership to resource the nodes.

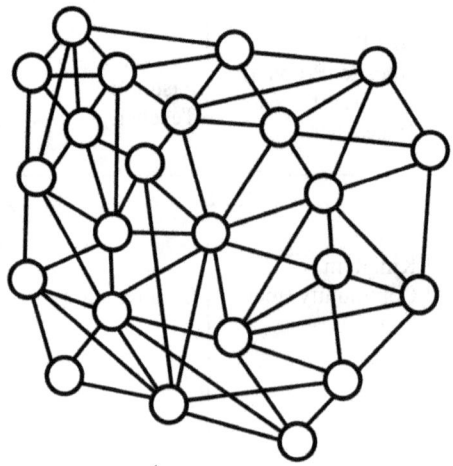

Fig 2.2 Distributed network

In the earliest churches there were certain people with leadership gifts like Apostle, Prophet, Evangelist, Pastor and Teacher. These were gifted people who built up each ekklesia (Kingdom Community). The leadership was not top-down but instead lifted up. Paul is an example of one of these influencers as he travelled widely planting, writing and speaking as an expression of his apostolic gift so as to build up the ekklesia. The vast majority of Christian leaders in local ekklesia supported themselves and were not financially dependent on the church for their income. This is an important point to note because financial independence enables greater freedom to step out in faith wherever one feels led.

As explained already in this chapter, the early church was essentially a series of Kingdom Communities that met in houses and who identified across the city. A typical Ephesian Christian, for example, would have identified themselves as a member of a certain group that met at someone's house which was part of the network in Ephesus. For example, when Paul wrote his letters to the church in Ephesus, Philippi or Colossae the letter was received by the person it was addressed to and then passed around and read at each house when they met and broke bread.

The influence and authority of the city wide church leaders was relational, not legal. A node was free to disagree with advice or counsel if it really felt strongly to do so. Kingdom Communities would resource and support each other as required. Through their network they also expressed practical concern for the other networks and eagerly sought news via letters and travellers across the universal church. We have plenty of evidence of them praying for and passing on resources to those in greater need in other cities.

Present: The church today

Fast-forward to today and things have become very different. The distributed network identified in the early church has been replaced by a hub and spokes structure (see figure 2.3). This functions through command and control. It is often mapped in corporate organisational diagrams with solid reporting lines downwards from a CEO and Board where ultimate authority rests. It usually means those at the bottom of the organisation's chart have the least power and are the least engaged in decision making while being closest to local activity. In most large organisations the greatest resource and knowledge base (people who are in touch with the local context) are rarely consulted or empowered. This is because a hub and spokes model is designed so the outlying parts serve the centre.[18]

---

[18] There is a growing body of literature concerned with organisational shape and structure

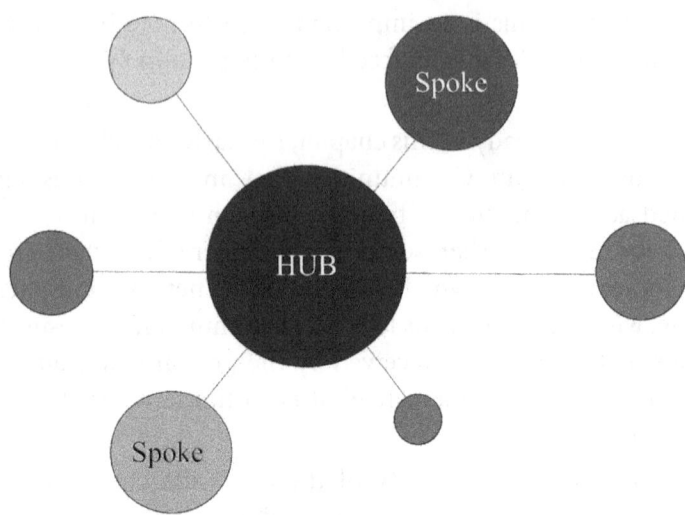

Figure 2.3 Hub and Spokes structure.

Any change of operating model necessitates a shift in practice and effectiveness. For the church, this shift has turned it into a solid, hierarchical institution rather than a community. This change began in the shift from faith to belief in what Cox calls the *Age of Belief*. This has resulted in a concentration of power and allocation of resources to those near the centre and consequently the disempowerment of people engaged in places other than the church. Tragically, it has also resulted in scant attention and concern for people's vocations other than within the church. It has also brought about an understanding that evangelism is about 'bringing people in' rather than sending people out.

The hub and spokes structure has changed the focus of the church as an organisation. The distributed network by its relational and organic nature is always expanding and morphing through new opportunities for encounter and growth (even in the midst of persecution and opposition). A hub and spokes structure creates power for those at the

---

that allows organic growth and empowers all of the people in the organisation. As an introduction to this topic see Frederic Laloux, *Reinventing Organizations: A Guide to Creating Organizations Inspired by the next stage of Human Consciousness*, Brussels: Nelson Parker, 2014 and Ori Brafman & Rod A. Beckstrom, *The Starfish and the Spider: The Unstoppable Power of Leaderless Organizations*, New York: Penguin Putnam, 2011.

centre where resources and strategy are allocated. This explains why many churches develop programs, which are designed for people out of the church but rarely achieve their aim. These groups might grow and keep those in the church busy but at their core, because of the locus of their design, they are not invested in freely sending and distributing people into society and the marketplace.

This has also had a profound effect on the nature of modern church leadership. The professionalisation of paid ministers may well have increased theological knowledge and training standards compared to early church leaders, however, there have been other, less desirable consequences for the church. For example, the nature of ministry has changed from something that everyone participates in and offers their gifts towards, to a small number of individuals doing most of the work, at the centre. In many churches we hear the well known maxim, 'eighty percent of the work around here is done by twenty percent of the people". Even in churches that espouse the priesthood of all believers, there is still often a clergy/laity system that dislocates shared ministry.

The gifts in use in most church systems are also reduced by the hub and spokes model. Gifts that are Apostolic, Prophetic or Evangelistic tend to have been squeezed out. Most leaders in church systems today are Pastors and Teachers. These gift areas naturally bias the church more towards the avoidance of risk. Pastors and Teachers do not generally rock the boat. Perhaps the emphasis on seminary education has also inclined church systems towards Pastors and Teachers and away from Apostles, Prophets and Evangelists – after all most people in seminaries are Pastors and Teachers!

Another consequence of this shift has been the separation of specialised care-oriented ministries from religiously focused ministries (and vice versa). They often function as separate silos in a hub and spokes system. The result has been a dualism between these two areas, which is incomplete and compromises holistic Christian ministry. The story of Churches of Christ in Queensland with the re-imagination of Kingdom Communities in both the religious and care arms is an example we will point to of positive change and for effective mission (this case study is developed in chapters five and six).

Our imagination of church has changed considerably in the modern era from older understandings of ekklesia. The creation of church buildings has altered irrevocably how churches structure themselves, moving church out of the home, away from the table and towards management structures. In addition, the combined effects of belief overtaking faith; the structural separation of religious and care functions; seminaries emphasising Pastor and Teacher; denominations controlling local networks; competition destroying unity and the abolishment of leadership gifts of Apostles, Prophets and Evangelists has reduced the effectiveness of the Christian mission.

Broadly, we see three expressions of ekklesia today.

First, there is the local congregation. This is the group of people who worship regularly at a local level. Usually this is in a church building and participation is generally reserved for certain people with skills appropriate for the size of the audience. The modern congregation has replaced the Kingdom Community as the basic building block of Christian life.

Second, congregations are usually being branches of a denomination. Denominations are essentially groups of Christian churches that associate under the same name, tradition and identity. They often emanate from a similar cultural background. Denominational congregations have superseded the natural relational networks of Kingdom Communities in a geographic area.

Finally, ekklesia can also describe the various Councils and Creedal associations that operate internationally. The World Council of Churches, the Lausanne Movement and various other wider bodies and missionary movements often have small resources in terms of finances or personnel but have wide networks and influence. In an age of globalisation, they are often looked to for strategy, global theological reflection, aid and development, communication and alignment in mission.

Future: The church of the future

Understanding the structure and application from the past opens possibilities for our future. The three aspects discussed (leadership gifts employed, meanings of ekklesia, and structure) each require some comment as we imagine their contribution going forward. We have lost a lot with the adoption of the hub and spokes structure over the distributed network as has been explained, however, we can see some benefits as we imagine forward.

One of the increasingly important requirements for ministry in modern society is the provision of healthy and rigorous governance and compliance. As the scale and breadth of responsibility increases the needs for compliance and good governance increase. When someone is employed, a property is bought, or a grant is applied for, proper governance becomes essential.

We believe that it is possible for good governance in a modified distributed network. Some Kingdom Communities will not require much in the way of governance (for example a Book Club or a Bike Riding group) however, a Men's Shed or a drop-in centre in the community will both require insurance, compliance with relevant standards and appropriate oversight to handle finances and personnel. This is where each level of ekklesia needs to work together mutually.

In the model we develop we see three zones of operation:

- **Kingdom Communities**: The basic building blocks of local engagement and life in the kingdom of God. These can include a neighbourhood group, a men's shed, a school or kindergarten, a chaplaincy support team or a community gardening group. There really is no limit. A Kingdom Community is two or more of God's people who gather regularly to follow certain practices so as to shine the light of Christ through faith, hope and love.

- **Wider Networks**: Clusters of Kingdom Communities from a geographic area or with common concerns for mutual resource and support. This will often be the future for congregations, where Kingdom Communities can be supported as required. A congregation could birth and resource a growing number of effective Kingdom Communities, thus renewing a struggling and ageing congregation. This level of structure can provide appropriate governance and accountability in order to manage buildings, run bank accounts, manage child safety standards, manage personnel, and so on. This can also be a level of interface between denominational care agencies and Kingdom Communities. For example, aged care, social work, refugee support and education all can participate with Kingdom Communities in local engagement or develop new Kingdom Communities themselves within their area of specialisation.

- **Networks of networks:** We think that there is an important future for denominations and their care agencies. In service of Kingdom Communities typically, these will operate across a state or large region and provide good governance, resources and sometimes coordination for all parts of the system for common mission and the flourishing of Kingdom Communities. Education, training, research, insurance, compliance, ethical standards, human resources services, government liaison, communications, legal services, etc. all have important contributions across the system. These areas are all service oriented for the support of Kingdom Communities and function as the backroom. This is not to put their importance down; without a backroom, systems fall down. However, the frontier is where the Kingdom Communities and God's people must be focused.

Leadership gifts for the model that we envisage require the smooth cooperation of Apostles, Prophets, Evangelists, Pastors and Teachers. The church of the future cannot survive with only Teachers and Pastors. However, by the same measure the church of the future needs Teachers and Pastors more than ever! Missionary movements that embark on bold enterprises without care or without reflective and wise teachers usually don't last long and burn up too many good people.

> **Learning:** Kingdom Communities are the basic building blocks of Christian community, formation and mission. Congregations, denominations, seminaries and care agencies need to serve and organise around this biblical foundation.

With these challenges and opportunities before us, we have great hope and optimism for the path ahead. At various junctures in the 2000 year-long spread of Christianity, the church has faced obstacles, reform

Chapter Two: Back and Forth

and persecution, yet it has always adapted. This present moment is yet another opportunity for us to be open to the creative leading of the Spirit. For those who want some evidence for our optimism, we now turn to one of the most significant contributions in the development of Kingdom Communities in the twentieth century, among poor Christians in Brazil.

CHAPTER THREE

Base Ecclesial Communities

"If you are neutral in situations of injustice, you have chosen the side of the oppressor. If an elephant has its foot on the tail of a mouse and you say that you are neutral, the mouse will not appreciate your neutrality."

Archbishop Desmond Tutu

"Then he said to them, "Whoever welcomes this little child in my name welcomes me; and whoever welcomes me welcomes the one who sent me. For it is the one who is least among you all who is the greatest."

Luke 9:48

Fly-in-fly-out!

Known as 'Rocky' to locals, Rockhampton is located about eight hours drive north of Brisbane. For many thousands of years, the area was originally the home of the Darumbal people and was settled by Europeans in the 1850s. No doubt it was easy for Europeans to see the potential of the excellent grazing plains and plentiful supply of water. There are accounts of early battles for the land as the Aboriginal people were dispossessed and regarded as 'non-people'. The continual migration of settlers to the district eventually saw the establishment of several towns and cities.

The town grew and flourished, aided by its position on the Fitzroy River, which has many tributaries and lagoons. It was and still is a great area for agriculture. The town population enjoyed steady growth over the last hundred years and now is home to approximately 85,000 residents. It is a regional hub for business, community and government activity.

To the west of Rocky is a large deposit of black coal. For several decades this coal was a natural resource that supplied a large power station, which provided electricity for much of Queensland. The town, the mine and power station worked well together and were an excellent example of an integrated local community. The local economy thrived, which produced employment, services and opportunities.

In recent years the extensive coal deposits west of Rocky became more than a supplier to the local power station. Australia has many precious commodities (coal, iron ore, gold, diamonds, uranium, oil, and others) and demand from the fastest growing region in the world (Asia) has led to the exploitation of these resources. Rocky's supply of coal is no longer in local demand only. Today, long trains, filled with millions of tonnes of coal, pass right through the centre of Rocky (literally the train goes right down the middle of the road) on their way to the port at Gladstone where they are shipped off across Asia, especially to India and China. The locals in Rocky can now only watch the trains pass through town without any local benefit.

As noted, over the decades coal mining enabled a well-integrated regional town with opportunities for shared prosperity, services, training and a diversification of employment opportunities. Today, however the situation is different because while the mining has scaled up significantly, there has been very little benefit for the town and people of Rocky. The increased mining has coincided with a new practice in mining. In past times, increased production led to a growth in the town. However, now the increased workers are typically fly-in-fly-out (FIFO).

FIFO workers don't live locally. They fly in for condensed work shifts which are squeezed into as few days as possible because they are only there to work. They are not there to live. Then they fly out home. The FIFO workers typically work fourteen days in a row of twelve-hour shifts. They live in small huts provided by the mining company and eat in the company cafeteria. Then they fly home to other cities across Australia and even New Zealand where they have two weeks of rest and recreation with pockets full of generous salaries. The aim of FIFO is to not be a part of the local community at all. Like the mining, everything about FIFO is extractive and created by decisions in headquarters thousands of kilometres away.

The social consequences are significant. There is massive disruption to the workers' families and the FIFO lifestyle has increasing quantities of research that show negative consequences over the medium and long term. The FIFO lifestyle is typically only endured for a year or so and undertaken for purely financial reasons. It is initially seen as a great financial opportunity for young families to get ahead, if mum or dad becomes a FIFO, but soon children and marriages find that they do not cope well with this abnormal practice.

For a town like Rocky, the FIFO phenomenon is cruel. As megatonnes of local resources are scooped up and taken out on trains and ships to foreign shores, there is almost no local benefit. Sports teams get no new players, new families don't move to the town, roads are worn out without local taxes being paid, hospitals are used, the house prices remain stagnant and very few new jobs are created as all the money is siphoned elsewhere. One day, when the mine is fully exploited, all that will be left will be massive holes in the ground where the minerals once were.

This story is not unique to Rockhampton. There are other towns across Australia like Port Headland, Olympic Dam and Wiluna whose experiences we could also have used as a case study.[1] What is new is the FIFO hyper-transportation of the workforce, which causes such massive dislocation to the workers, their families and the local area.

Mining is not new to Australia, indeed the growth and wealth of our second largest city, Melbourne is due to the gold rush of the 1850s and Adelaide benefited greatly from mining as well. Perth, our fifth largest city is still very much based on the resources economy. Across Australia there are cities like Ballarat, Bendigo and Kalgoorlie (and many smaller towns), which have managed to develop with or post mining. FIFO however, extracts from towns, adds little value and eventually leaves them depleted.

Modern church life in Australia is prone to a similar trend. In times past, a local church was an integral part of the hub of a community's life. There were rich layers of connection as people lived, worked and played together. There was little that was extractive about church life. Many tennis, football and cricket clubs, schools, hospitals and nursing homes were initiated out of church life because of deep local connections. It

---

[1] See R. Morris, *Scoping Study: Impact of Fly-in-fly-out/ Drive-in-drive-out work practices on local government*, Sydney: Australian Centre of Excellence for Local Government, 2012.

wasn't hard to listen and respond to local needs because the church lived there too.

Things have changed. Modern forces of mobility, consumerism, entertainment and the high cost of housing have decimated the factors that contributed to healthy local churches. Many local churches now have only one generation remaining if nothing changes. In chapter one we noted this pattern of change and decline. On the other hand, some churches have grown significantly. Driven by entrepreneurial leaders and packaged with specific audiences in mind, there is opportunity for church growth for some. It is these churches, propelled by their eye for success, that have extended their model to other locations often without much attention to serious contextualisation.

Andrew was at a barbeque recently with a young, professional couple. They were very enthusiastic about their church, so he listened in as they spoke of its virtues. The messages were insightful, the music was relevant and professional, people in attendance were all like them and understood their worldview, and on the list went. Andrew was happy for them as so often there are negative stories concerning church life. Clearly the 'vibe' was there for them. He asked them where it was located, and they explained that it was about thirty kilometres from their home. They drove past dozens of churches and suburbs to be at the right church that fitted their requirements. The influences of mobility, consumerism and entertainment are all at play here and their commitment to drive so far for church said as much about their determination to attend this church as it did about the consequence of not living in their own community and among their own neighbours.

Because we are formed by and live among the ever-present forces of mobility, consumerism and entertainment, many of us accept this situation without much thought. It doesn't seem much different to driving across town to a favourite cinema. We reconcile that at least people are in a church. Things have become that desperate! We might reflect on this phenomenon and ask how are local communities being entered and listened to, if this is the preferred method of church life for increasing numbers of people? Have we sufficiently paused and reflected on the damaging effects and possibilities of colonisation from generations past? How will our new franchise models of church not repeat this? What is the cost of implementing this over time?

It is not the intention of this book to argue *for* an old model or *against* modern trends, and nor is it the intention of this book to present any particular church size as ideal. All expressions of church have significant challenges ahead in the changing landscape of Australian society. Models and scale of church are not our primary concern. We are concerned about the activity of the Holy Spirit and the expression of the Kingdom on the earth. Jesus taught us to pray, "Your kingdom come, your will be done, on earth as it is in heaven" (Matt 6:10).

Our culture is unpredictable, shaped by rapid discontinuous chance. Language about successful and failing local church models is often simply a symptom of a struggle to shake off an old and increasingly irrelevant *Age of Belief* imagination. Framed as a mission question, our challenge is, 'How can communities of Christians live, love and embody themselves authentically, humbly, justly and lovingly among their neighbours so that the love and message of Christ may be demonstrated, proclaimed and transformational?' To explore this, we will spend some time among the poor in Brazil.

> **Learning:** Extraction is not a healthy missional and biblical principle. As people trying to follow the Way of Christ we are always called to shine light and bring blessing locally. We are not meant to take away, we add.

Base Ecclesial Communities

Leonardo Boff is a Brazilian Catholic theologian who dedicated his life to theological reflection about Christian ministry in local communities, especially among the poor. Born in 1938, Leonardo and his brother Clodovis (born 1944) were the grandchildren of Italian immigrants. Like most immigrant families, the brothers grew up surrounded by an awareness of dual cultures – Italian and Brazilian. Their father was a teacher and their mother came from a rural family. Both brothers eventually gave their life to ministry and the study of the Christian faith and its call to liberate the poor.

Leonardo is one of the most well known proponents of a school of theology now known as liberation theology. His life as a theological scholar was dedicated to a deep commitment for liberation and advocacy of the poor. He was especially interested in the structural impediments to release the poor from poverty.

Leonardo first studied theology in Brazil and then pursued doctoral work in Munich where his research was concerned with how the Church could be a sign of the divine among the oppressed in a secular world. This pursuit of liberation theology by Leonardo was eventually to come to a head with the Church hierarchy, which was growing increasingly concerned with the rise of Marxist influences at the Munich seminary and elsewhere.

Interestingly, one of Leonardo's doctoral instructors was Joseph Ratzinger who later became Pope Benedict XVI. It was while Ratzinger was teaching in Munich (with students and faculty including Leonardo) that he became aware of and concerned about Marxist tendencies within the Church. A hallmark of Ratzinger's career was that he became a watchdog against any of those tendencies, thus earning the nickname 'God's Rottweiler' - which was enshrined when he became the Prefect of the Sacred Congregation for the Doctrine of the Faith (once known as the Supreme Sacred Congregation of the Roman and Universal Inquisition). Leonardo's brother Clodovis was investigated by this body but was found to be 'not quite Marxist enough' for them to pursue. Greater pressure was placed upon Leonardo who has always held that he was not 'pro-Marxist' but rather 'anti-Capitalist'. The church and Ratzinger disagreed. Ratzinger was appointed as a Cardinal and eventually elected by his fellow Cardinals as Pope. Things did not go so well with the church authorities for Leonardo.

Leonardo experienced ongoing controversy with the Church, which came to a head regarding his position affirming the role of women in leadership. He had earlier hinted in favour of married priests but in

The Maternal Face of God: The Feminine and Its Religious Expressions[2], he argued for the ordination of females as priests. In 1991, Leonardo wrote a series of articles in favour of married priests. It was this later writing which was frowned upon by the Vatican Congregation. When the Church challenged the orthodoxy of his work he resigned as a priest. He continues as a Professor Emeritus of Ethics, Philosophy of Religion and Ecology at Rio de Janeiro State University.

This context and controversy is important because for many in the Protestant church it has meant that they have not read Leonardo's work. There is already a general lack of awareness of Catholic theology in Protestant circles but when tags like 'Marxist' are attached, there is even greater reason for many to keep away. To many people, Leonardo has seemed not only inaccessible but dangerous. He has, therefore, largely flown under the radar and created interest only among academic and Catholic circles in times past. Younger Protestant practitioners whom we talk with today have often never heard of Leonardo Boff.

Boff (and we will change from using his Christian name to his surname at this point because we move away from mention of his brother) writes from real contexts about the empowerment of the powerless for mission and ministry. His life and ministry were with people in communities who were too poor to afford a priest. Consequently, the Church hierarchy often overlooked these people, regarding them as 'the faithful' but nothing more. There was little or no expectation about God in their midst, or their potential for contribution in leadership, ministry and mission. Often, they were unnoticed because there simply were not enough priests to even appreciate them.

The Church was blind to the possibilities within its own people, preferring to maintain its medieval power structures rather than empower the faithful for new avenues of ministry. The influence of Constantine and church hierarchy still continued to dominate. In corporate language, the Church had developed an ecclesiology that was 'top-down' and 'risk averse.'

---

[2] Leonardo Boff, *The Maternal Face of God: The Feminine and Its Religious Expressions*, New York: Harper/Collins Publishers, 1989.

There are very similar circumstances and analogies for us today in the Protestant church in the West. We have the same tendency to keep authority within higher ranks rather than empowering more members of churches for genuine release to minister. Yet as Graham Hill wisely observes, "God doesn't only place the margins at the centre of his life, concern and mission. He begins movements there. And he speaks to society and culture and church from there."[3]

It is uncommon for modern churches to engage in deep, heartfelt listening in local communities. Granted, most churches will respond to a local tragedy, at least in prayer (like a bushfire, school issue or social problem). Some churches use demographic research in order to better understand the local community. This data is usually used to determine where there are families or people who can be easily reached or extracted by being scooped into existing or new programs. That is not what we mean when we speak of listening deeply to the needs of a local community.

Churches also typically attempt to include all their pre-existing historical, theological and doctrinal baggage as they go about their ministry (what Cox calls the *Age of Belief*). While writing this book, Andrew drove past a sign to a church (on the side of the road) each Sunday. The sign simply said, 'Free Reformed Church turn right'. The sign perplexed him. It was attractive and modern and clearly designed to draw people towards that particular church. However, why would a church see it as meaningful to communicate to motorists that there is a worship service for those who hold to a sub-section of a breakaway movement from the sixteenth century on a beautiful sunny morning? Churches can become so consumed with insider church issues that they forget to live and listen to the needs of their neighbourhood.

Denominations are also often prone to multiply the standard 'franchise' model of their particular shape and belief of church. Typically, there is little, real expectation for imaginative new Kingdom Communities to emerge from the bottom up out of the work of God in a local context. This stands in contrast to what must have occurred when Jesus sent his followers in pairs to villages, as described in Luke chapter

---

[3] Graham Hill, "7 Practices for hearing and responding to the margins (especially during elections)", missioalliance.org

ten. Jesus even told them to not take anything but rather to attend to the village first and look for people of peace who invite them in to listen.

Paul also listened and observed deeply when he was in a geographic location and worked with what was already present. In Acts chapter 17 when in Athens, Paul famously noted their altar TO AN UNKNOWN GOD. This was his starting point for announcing the good news and connecting with people of peace in that community. Luke summarised what happened, in verse 34, "Some of the people became followers of Paul and believed. Among them was Dionysius, a member of the Areopagus, also a woman named Damaris, and a number of others" (Acts 17: 16-34).

In 1986, Boff wrote a slim book called *Ecclesiogenesis: The Base Communities Reinvent the Church*,[4] which reflected upon a phenomenon that was sweeping through local Brazilian communities. It was a movement for which Boff had close experience as an activist, guide and advocate. Throughout Brazil, in poor communities where there were few priests, few church buildings, few Bibles and scant theological knowledge, small communities of Christians were gathering for support and witness. It was a growing movement. As Alvaro Barreiro comments, "When the good news is preached to the poor, in a pure, free, and fearless manner, it kindles in them the fire of hope, transforming their lives."[5]

The Christians whom Boff wrote about were poor people who were often oppressed by economic structures. They experienced the daily reality (and often harmful impact) of out of touch, top-down, powerful leadership models employed by business, politics and the church. They longed for something different – something that they could identify with, which would empower them in their daily struggle. They could not identify with the sources of their oppression, but they could identify with the teachings and ministry of a poor carpenter from Nazareth.

Base Ecclesial Communities provided an opening into the experience of a Christian faith community (what we are calling a Kingdom

---

[4] Leonardo Boff, *Ecclesiogenesis: The Base Communities Reinvent the Church*, New York: Orbis, 1986.
[5] Alvaro Barreiro, *Basic Ecclesial Communities: The Evangelization of the Poor*, New York: Orbis, 1984, 1.

Community) for many people when the formal, hierarchical Church appeared inaccessible. As Yves Congar commented,

> "While the entire mystique of the Church affirms love for the poor, and even poverty, and while the Church is really poor almost everywhere, and at times indigent, it appears to be rich and, to tell the truth loudly, or seeking to be such. In this way it has caused itself harm and it has harmed the cause which it exists to serve and which it is really intended to serve."[6]

Boff dates the development of Base Ecclesial Communities from at least the nineteen-fifties. He cites an early story of a 'humble old woman' who was concerned that there were no Catholic Christmas Eve services in her community, whereas the local Protestant churches were able to conduct services, often without clergy. She asked a question, "If there are no priests, must everything grind to a halt?"[7] We in the Western Protestant church should ask the same question about clergy and corporate structures.

The result was the development of lay people to fulfil all the roles necessary, based around solid Christian discipleship. Over time, formational practises became the centre of the community because there were often no priests to offer the sacraments. All that was needed occasionally was someone to coordinate the religious life within it – not a priest. As a result, "Instead of chapels, meeting halls were built and then used for school, religious instruction, sewing lessons, and meetings for solving community problems, even economic ones."[8]

This new movement still contained vision and place for clergy, who would preside over the sacraments, but the emerging model encouraged all from the community to participate as the Spirit gave gifts, from across the community. And Boff was very clear that the clergy were not to take over everything. Base Ecclesial Communities were not the result of a strategic planning meeting among church leaders, who came up with a blueprint. They were an organic, grassroots movement that arose from people in local communities who saw needs and opportunities. It was a

---

[6] Yves Congar, *Power and Poverty in the Church*, Baltimore: Helicon Press, 1964, 10.
[7] Boff, *Ecclesiogenesis*, 3.
[8] Boff, *Ecclesiogenesis*, 3.

very real product of active listening from the bottom up. The Spirit was breathing new imagination that didn't fit with the church hierarchies' traditional template.[9]

The central idea of Base Ecclesial Communities was built on an understanding of the church as a living community rather than a material structure or institution. Boff writes,

"The communities are built on a more vital, lively, intimate participation in a more or less homogeneous entity, as their members seek to live out the essence of the Christian message: the universal parenthood of God, communion with all human beings, the following of Jesus Christ who died and rose again, the celebration of the resurrection and the Eucharist, and the up-building of the kingdom of God, already underway in history as the liberation of the whole human being and all human beings."[10]

Thus, a movement was born that came to be termed Base Ecclesial Communities. Boff wrote *Ecclesiogenesis* to tell stories of renewal and growth of local Christian communities with a theological underpinning about what was going on. The resistance he found himself facing was with the Catholic Church authorities, regardless of whether these communities brought meaning and liberation to the local people. It didn't fit the prevailing models.

Ecclesiogenesis is a wonderful resource, especially for those who seek to live intentionally in their local community as a sign and foretaste of the kingdom of God. It helps those who have a local commitment for mission and ministry that is not oppositional but is neither an agent of the institutional church. People who carry this sense of mission are

---

9 Boff, *Ecclesiogenesis*, 7. Boff adds, "There can be a genuine renewal of the institutional framework of the church, springing from the impulses of the grassroots communities, without the church losing its identity of being distorted in its historical essence. The church sprung from the people is the same as the church sprung from the apostles… After all, the problem of church does not reside in the counterpoint of institution and community. These poles abide forever. The real problem resides in the manner in which both are lived, the one as well as the other: whether one pole seeks to absorb the other, cripple it, liquidate it, or each respects the other and opens itself to the other in constant willingness to be put to the question."
10 Boff, *Ecclesiogenesis*, 4.

often misunderstood by those in the leadership positions of churches, whether Catholic, Protestant, clergy or laity.

Ecclesiogenesis can assist activists and practitioners. These are people who often want to get on with the task at hand. They don't want to attend to all the structural programs and committees associated with institutional church life. They are often misunderstood or given an easy label of rebel or maverick or assumed to be against the local church. This is because they are often people who are not motivated by helping build the structure and programs of the current Church. Their vision is local and outward. Sometimes their writings and behaviour threaten the power structures in the institutions of which they are a part. As Harvey Cox reminds us in his description of the *Age of Faith*, this was not what apostolically wired activists faced in the earliest centuries of the church as it thrived.

Ecclesiogenesis argues that Base Ecclesial Communities are a vital sign of renewal within the church. They help people move away from the structure and hierarchy of the Church as a goal, thus signifying a new action of the Spirit. Boff commences the book with a clear diagnosis that many people who are in positions of church leadership know too well,

> "The church has acquired an organisational form with a heavily hierarchical framework and juridical understanding of relationships among Christians, thus producing mechanical, reified inequalities and inequities. As Yves Congar has written, "Think of the church as a huge organisation, controlled by a hierarchy, with subordinates whose only task it is to keep the rules and follow the practices.""[11]

Boff identified three streams of energy that contributed to the rise of Base Ecclesial Communities[12]: a scarcity of priests (Brazil had many thousands of local communities unable to access an insufficient supply of priests); the consequent rise of the laity; and an imagination for a different form of church expression. He warned the Church, 'Do not seek to box this phenomenon within theological-pastoral categories distilled from other contexts and other ecclesial experiences.'[13] We echo that emphasis for Kingdom Communities.

---

[11] Boff, *Ecclesiogenesis*, 1.
[12] Boff, *Ecclesiogenesis*, 2.
[13] Boff, *Ecclesiogenesis*, 2.

Chapter Three: Base Ecclesial Communities

He reflected that church history is filled with the creation of 'never-before-experienced novelty'. The evolution of the church, as inspired by the Spirit, is fluid. He says the story of the church is not predictable or 'rectangular' but 'pluriform'. This is the same observation offered by Cox for what he calls the emerging *Age of the Spirit*.

Boff's Base Ecclesial Communities are specifically Christian in their practice and mission. They are not simply groups identifying local need and finding a solution. To do that would be similar to what any local service club like Rotary or Lions Club provide so well. Base Ecclesial Communities are an expression of the Kingdom with a particular purpose of renewal through concern and empowerment of local people and communities, especially the poor. They are a positive response for the church, which should be already concerned with local needs and community building rather than hierarchy and structure. Boff adds, "Jesus was not much concerned with the institution, apart from demanding that it live in the Spirit in which all expressions of human togetherness ought to be lived."[14]

There is a natural tendency for powerful and educated people to dominate hierarchies and structures, which operate vertically. Powerless and alienated people have generally less say (or access for a say) in decision making in hierarchical structures. Hierarchical forms of church governance reflect this. Local community groups are naturally far more inclusive because they operate informally and horizontally within their own networks. Therefore, Base Ecclesial Communities have a natural tendency to make participation accessible to more people.

This is an important concept to note with the modern trend for larger and more professional churches. While large structures enable increasing levels of technical and professional presentation, they also sever participation of increasing numbers of people. Andrew remembers talking with a colleague who had a lack of musicians in his mega-church. Andrew actually laughed and said that his church had many thousands of people on any given Sunday so there must be musicians. His colleague responded that this was the problem; there were not enough musicians good enough to play in front of thousands of people!

---
14 Boff, *Ecclesiogenesis*, 7.

Boff also notes that if Base Ecclesial Communities are to be able to keep the community spirit alive among members then generally they need to stay small. They cannot replace the local parish function, or they will be taken up with administration and structure. Members need to function at a level where they maintain personal relationships with each other.

The vision that Boff articulates is one where Base Ecclesial Communities and the local church are subsets of a greater whole. There is still a clear role for the local church or parish as well as the Base Ecclesial Community. In fact, today, many small local and regional churches still effectively function as Base Ecclesial Communities. Boff's description and analysis of Base Ecclesial Communities opens the possibility for unified and broad contribution from local churches and denominations in the development and sustainability of active Kingdom Communities in local areas as well as healthy local congregations. There is no polarity in the existence and function of both expressions.

In the late 1990s and into the first decade of the new millennium, across Australia and New Zealand, many small intentional faith communities started up. They argued that they were the future of the church and more missional than existing churches. They often called themselves 'emerging churches' or 'fresh expressions' and argued that they were built upon an incarnational model of church, rather than traditional churches which were primarily attractional. Their particular target of scorn was often, sadly, the megachurch. This was unfortunate on at least two levels. An unnecessary polarity was developed between some exciting new mission experiments and really good churches that often also had wonderful mission initiatives. Sides were developed and that is never helpful and not the spirit of unity that Jesus wanted among his followers.[15]

Also, by cutting themselves off from leaders and churches with experience, stability, wisdom, maturity and resources, these experiments often only lasted a few years. Good initiatives simply petered out when the pioneering leadership became tired or drawn to another initiative. Today across Australia there are perhaps a couple of these communities

---

15 See Matt 22:37-40; John 13; Rom 2:10-11; 1 Cor 12 -13; Phil 2; Eph 4:1-6; 1 Thess 1:9.

still in existence. A few more survived by jettisoning much of their emerging church regalia and becoming what look very much like, modern and growing local churches. An experiment of greater mission focused possibility ended in a sad whimper.

A central vision of this book is the integration of mutual and enmeshed relationships between local nodes and the wider Body of Christ. We see no reason for division between the two models nor should there be any pressure to select one model as the correct path. In chapters five and six, using the case study of Churches of Christ in Queensland, the multiplication of Kingdom Communities at denominational level is described in more detail.[16] The creation of Kingdom Communities enabled meaningful links between churches and care agencies and the general public. There are wonderful, generative possibilities that were experienced through mutual collaboration and unity, which we will describe. Boff was very clear about this as he developed his theology of Base Ecclesial Communities and we seek to integrate the best of Boff's reflections to our mission context today.

A key challenge is how to do this without one smothering the other. By using the term Kingdom Communities, we are aiming to point to a new mode for mission that can have a mutual and unifying relationship with the local congregation and denomination. One does not yield power over the other and one is not more important that the other. Like any healthy partnership, both are mutual and interdependent parts of a greater whole and important members of Christ's Body. A Kingdom Community is a place where people can access something of the kingdom of God.

Across Australia in thousands of towns and suburbs there are church buildings that are only used for a couple of hours on Sundays. They might have the occasional meeting or activity throughout the week, however a casual drive past many church buildings reveals that the doors are

---

[16] Where Boff uses the term 'Base Ecclesial Communities', Churches of Christ in Queensland used 'Kingdom Action Places.' Others have alternative names for the same idea. For example, Churches of Christ in Victoria & Tasmania describe 'Communities of Hope and Compassion' and New Hope Baptist Church in Melbourne employs 'Communities of Hope'. We have settled on 'Kingdom Communities' as a meaningful and simple description.

closed, and the car park is often empty. There is only one reason why these facilities aren't opened up and given to Kingdom Communities: insufficient Kingdom vision. Groups with an interest in stamps, coffee, poverty, pre-schoolers, food-banks, exercise and teaching English as a second language can all engage with people who will never come to the usual church programs. We must remember that church members as well as denominations do not truly own their buildings, they are trustees of them for a greater cause; service in the kingdom of God.

Boff devotes a whole chapter[17] to the area of ecclesiology. He revisits the meaning of the word predominantly used in the New Testament which has now been adapted as 'church' (ekklesia). Today the broader understanding of the New Testament word and the associated discipline (ecclesiology), have been colonised by modern, corporate, material understandings of the word church often minimalising relationality. There is nothing in the Bible that suggests that church needs to be like a modern congregation. The New Testament meaning and use of ekklesia allows for far more imaginative, diverse and organic concepts of how we can build Kingdom Communities that reflect and enable access to the kingdom of God.

Boff identifies four meanings of the church, which are all referred to in an interchangeable fashion in society. The categories identified are Base Ecclesial Communities; parishes; the hierarchical institution, which is predominantly managed by clergy; and the universal church. For Boff, the crucial point to qualify as a church in any of these categories, is the centrality of Christ. He says, "In order to formally be church, the consciousness of this reality must be there, the profession of explicit faith in Jesus Christ who died and was raised again."[18]

When asked about the development and validity of Base Ecclesial Communities, Boff responded, "Are we now going to tell these people that they are not church, that they have certain "ecclesial elements", but that these do not actually constitute the essence of church?"[19] For him, Base Ecclesial Communities were real churches – as valid as any other

---

[17] Boff, *Ecclesiogenesis*, 10-22.
[18] Boff, *Ecclesiogenesis*, 11.
[19] Boff, *Ecclesiogenesis*, 13.

expression. His arguments are important in his context in the Catholic Church in Brazil but help us greatly too.[20]

So?

While Boff was writing within his own Catholic, Brazilian context, there are also principles that apply in our context. We have sought to identify areas of overlap so far. We now seek to name and briefly discuss some of the core principles from which we can learn.

Firstly, churches should give ministry back to ordinary people. Ministry does not belong in the domain of clergy, paid specialist staff or within the walls of the church. The vast majority of Jesus' ministry was outside the walls of the Temple and the synagogue. The vast majority of Jesus' problems came from the synagogue and Temple leadership. Ministry training exercises for Jesus' disciples were in streets and villages where real people and real needs existed. Paul was clear to the Ephesians (Eph 4:12-13) and to the Colossians (Col 1:28-29) that the goal of ministry was guiding people towards maturity in Christ. Initially, the church during the *Age of Faith* practised this but by the advent of the *Age of Belief* it had built walls and structures that took ministry away from ordinary people. This disabled too many people from participation in ministry.

When Andrew was a local church minister he was automatically made a member of the pastoral care team. This group of faithful people visited those who were frail and aged and also attended to practical needs like 'meals-on-wheels'. The team were modern saints and gave their time and gifts to this ministry. At one meeting the team were moving through their list of who was ill, and someone said something like, 'Doris isn't very well, I think she needs a visit from the minister.' This was code for, 'Doris needs a real visit, this is serious'. Andrew challenged it. He explained that the members of the committee were older, wiser, better gifted and already had long-term relationships with people like Doris. They were all the ministers. Andrew's task, according to Ephesians, was to equip people on the team for works of service and ministry. Our

---

[20] It is not possible to work through all of Boff's defences in regards to Base Ecclesial Communities. The interested reader is encouraged to read chapter two of *Ecclesiogenesis* for further detail.

trouble is that most people in our churches have 'learned' how it works: so, Doris expects a visit from the minister (even if she doesn't know him or her well) because that's the way things work.[21]

Secondly, the work of the Spirit cannot be tied down within church hierarchy and structure. God does not live inside church programs and buildings alone. Intellectually and theologically we know this, but practically we often function as though God lives on the church property only and programs run on the premises are extra special. We need to realign our practice with our theology. The Holy Spirit is not restricted by church programs and buildings but rather has gone ahead of us into our neighbourhoods, schools, relationships, workplaces and networks as well as among strangers and refugees. Our task is to discern patterns of God's activity and partner in the work of healing and reconciliation through faith, hope and love.

Thirdly, disciples are best formed through regular formational practices combined with deep engagement in their local community, not through an isolated program in a church. In recent years, the priority of discipleship has been rediscovered in many churches, which on the face of it is an important discovery. How can a church grow people towards maturity if they will simply depart elsewhere at the first point of discomfort?

The call to discipleship is latent in any gathering of Christians. Discipleship (the active pursuit of doing all that you can in pursuit of Christ and his teaching), as well as Christlikeness, focuses us towards God the Father, Son & Holy Spirit (vertical), inner transformation (internal) and also in response to human need and relationships (horizontal). Learning Bible verses and points of theological truth are important but need to be applied. They are not the full requirement of authentic discipleship in Christ.

The idea of the Spirit's active presence calling us to mission focused action is developed by Alan Hirsch in *The Forgotten Ways: Reactivating the missional church.*[22] Hirsch argues that the Spirit is in our midst and

---

[21] Out of courtesy for Doris and the pastoral care committee, Andrew visited her but also commenced a change in pastoral care training and theology at the church.
[22] Alan Hirsch, *The Forgotten Ways: Reactivating the Missional Church*, Grand Rapids: Brazos, 2006.

is constantly promoting a deep impulse towards mission that he calls, 'Apostolic Genius'. Hirsch says that Apostolic Genius is present in every community of Christians but often suppressed by structures and lack of imagination. He comments, "It [Apostolic Genius] is there, only the more institutional forms have simply forgotten or suppressed it, because its primal and uncontrollable nature represents danger to the institution itself – it is so different and uncontrollable."[23]

The idea of Apostolic Genius as a force, creating movement and expansion has some similarity with Boff's idea of ecclesio-genesis. Boff too, describes a life-force driven by the Spirit. The force that he describes is a creative Spirit that, in effect, births or creates (genesis) new possibilities for mission shaped communities (ekklesia). This is where the book title, *Ecclesiogenesis*, is derived.

Fourthly, Boff reminds us that the typical local church is not God's singular model for Christian community and never has been. In the previous chapter we noted the different forms and models that can represent the concept of ekklesia. In particular we noted that there were three primary models that a reference to ekklesia can refer to: the local households where Christians met (Kingdom Communities); the Christians across the city, for example in Jerusalem, Colossae, Philippi or Rome (networks of Kingdom Communities); and the universal church (networks of networks).

While we are at pains to stress there is nothing essentially wrong or bad about the current expression and imagination of local church, we must remember that it does not appear in the Bible and is not the only model or approach for Christian community. Just because something is not in the Bible does not make it wrong, or we wouldn't drive cars, use data projectors, have a band in church or have small groups. By the same measure, just because something is not in the Bible does not make it right. While there is an abundance of theological justification (often called ecclesiology) for modern church practice, the evidence over the past half century keeps reminding us that lots is not working, within and outside the church. Researchers like Alan Jamieson, statistics cited in chapter one, and an abundance of personal anecdotes remind us that it

---

[23] Hirsch, *The Forgotten Ways*, 77.

is not working for many people. Consultants like Rowland Croucher at John Mark Ministries[24] and Keith Farmer[25] have been raising the alarm for years about the toll that this model places on leaders. In Australia, there are more ex-leaders of churches than leaders of churches.

Helpfully, Boff reminds us there are other creative avenues that can work mutually with current expressions of local church. Each can have an important and meaningful contribution as they seek to build Kingdom Communities that promote the reign of God's kingdom. Throughout this book many examples are told to help show the breadth and scale of possibility for Kingdom Communities. They are not a threat to the current expression of the church but an addition. We explore the statewide case study of Churches of Christ in Queensland in the chapters five and six to demonstrate how dynamic, unifying and effective the possibilities are.

Fifthly, Boff reminds us that the current congregational model is limited in its ability at mission. It originates from the model of a pastoral, 'holding' container within European villages in an era when the world was considered as already evangelised. It was designed in a 'hub and spoke' era so that all the parts are reliant upon it. It has an inbuilt tendency towards being centred around: top-down leadership (including clergy, Elders and small group leaders), programs, pastoral and teaching focused clergy, pastoral care, budgets, buildings, and people who 'come' (rather than people who are sent). This is why churches value and report on weekly attendances, rather than how many are sent throughout the week. The modern congregation and denomination tend to reproduce through colonisation, if it reproduces at all. It typically prioritises 'holding' activities over sending. This model doesn't generally incorporate apostolic, prophetic and evangelistic gifts.

The local church is built upon a hub and spokes model. **Figure 2.3** shows the model in visual form. Like a bicycle wheel, a hub and spokes model of church has a centre that has direct relationships with its nodes at the extremity of the organisation. Ministry to children, youth, young adults, women and men, among others, all report in to the centre

---

[24] jmm.org.au
[25] http://www.mentoringnetwork.org.au/2012/01/

which manages the resources that enable them. The type of governance employed at the centre of a hub and spokes model is very predictable. Typically, there is a Board (or equivalent), that oversees an Executive Officer (Minister), who oversees the hub and the spokes. The size of the church may change some layers of management but ultimately the model is the same: there is a centre and there are parts that are expected to serve the centre and conform to the central preference for doing things.[26]

Most people, when given responsibility in a church essentially are given a task that reports in to the centre through a leadership structure. The centre determines the priority of the program and the leader's task is to care for the people in their area and build the area of responsibility so that it might contribute to the whole system. When these leaders see missed opportunities or needs that are outside their responsibility they need to receive permission from the line of report to change their plans. This can often be bureaucratic or discouraging.

Often the centre is unable to adjust to the challenge that the leader identifies because change is hard in a hub and spokes model; it really only works well when everyone rolls together in the same direction. In *Ecclesiogenesis*, without using this specific language, Boff describes how local parishes struggled to adapt to Base Ecclesial Communities as they emerged. The centre didn't seem to know how to allow for a new Base Ecclesial Community that wouldn't report to the centre. This will be a challenge for modern churches also as more Kingdom Communities emerge.

> **Learning:** Kingdom Communities, like Base Ecclesial Communities, are bottom up, grassroots communities formed around listening, empowerment, servanthood, formation, relationality, faith, hope and love. These are the things that shine light and transform neighbourhoods and communities.

---

[26] Alan Roxburgh, *Structured for Mission: Renewing the Culture of the Church*, Downers Grove: IVP, 2015, 111-123. See for further information on description and challenges of a hub and spokes model in church life.

In the previous chapter we introduced an alternative structure, called a distributed network, which is closer to what the early church employed. **Figure 2.2** presents this alternative model of organisational life in visual form. In a distributed network there is no central management. Each Kingdom Community is free to self-organise and identify with other Kingdom Communities, which through positive support or interaction can benefit it. Each Kingdom Community is flexible and is able to respond to needs quickly and with minimum stress. In *Structured for mission*, Roxburgh describes in greater detail the history and development of the distributed network for organisations. In particular he traces the development of electronics companies who have adapted to this model. He also explores possible implications of distributed networks for Christian denominations and movements.[27]

The absence of central management control does not necessarily mean an absence of authority or structure. Even the most radically anarchaic groups have natural authority and structure if you examine them. In the case of the early church, the omission of salaries, buildings, formal qualifications and constitutions did not mean an absence of authority or structure. We can see the flows of authority and structure in the various New Testament documents that we have availaible. What is apparent is that the set up was more relational (similar to family structures) and mission focused than what we have inherited in our modern church model. The connection was through a common commitment to the Way of Jesus.

A Snake and a Garden

Australia is well known for its wide variety of deadly snakes. Many of them make their homes in urban places near waterways and parks. As a result, most Australian children grow up knowing what to do if they see a snake. It is drummed into children by parents and schools. The first response is to not panic. Most snakebites occur because people panic, which causes the snake to panic. Whereas, if you freeze and the snake can find another way out, it will take that opportunity and slither away.

---

[27] Roxburgh, *Structured for Mission*, 125-136.

This is easier said than taught. How does it go in practice? Actually, it works. When Australians occasionally see a venomous snake, they freeze, watch the snake slither away and remember the moment for the rest of their lives. Very few people are hurt by snakes in Australia. If people are bitten it is usually the consequence of misadventure: an accident (stepping on one) or trying to kill it or kick it off the pathway. We had to put this to the test recently when visiting one of the churches in Brisbane's southern suburbs. After a meeting, Dean, Andrew and the local minister were summarising their time together. The three were standing near a children's play area when an Eastern Brown Snake casually slithered out of the garden to within two metres of them. Being one of the deadliest snakes in the world their childhood training of standing still kicked in (so to speak). The three of them continued the conversation but stood still as the snake looked around and found its escape via an alternative route.

The same principle applies in moments of transition. Don't panic. Stop, observe and calmly and prayerfully reflect on what is going on before taking any action. This principle also applies to the wider church in this current cultural moment, which is filled with challenges. There is little to be gained and a lot to be lost through panic and knee-jerk reaction. Certainly, significant changes must inevitably come, however the method and attitude invested in any new experiments will determine much about the success of any new ventures. This is one of the mature and significant points that Boff reiterates. Base Ecclesial Communities were a wonderful new addition and contribution to the mission of the church that added possibility, not a competitive alternative.

The emergence of Kingdom Communities is not intended to represent a challenge to the local church either. Indeed, the experience in Churches of Christ Queensland was that the greater the investment in Kingdom Communities, the greater the growth of the traditional churches as well. History suggests that experiments like these will fall over without local churches and denominational support and resourcing, especially in their initial and transition phases. Wise leaders from churches and denominations will understand this and be sensitive about how to step back a little to let these communities grow, mature and multiply.

Andrew's grandfather was a very good gardener. A trip to his house always involved tours of the extensive vegetable and fruit garden in the backyard where the grandchildren would pick all the tomatoes, carrots, potatoes, raspberries, passion-fruit and plums they wanted. In summer, they would then take a bucket of raspberries and strawberries inside to their grandmother who would allow them to sprinkle on some sugar, which was a great treat. There was one part of the yard that had a special fascination. It was the glasshouse. Inside this small, glass, A-framed hut he cultivated the next season's seeds and seedlings. Sense of time was lost as he taught us how to cultivate new plants. There was joy in the act of creating.

This metaphor of a glasshouse is useful as we unpack what is required in the next steps of the transition before us. Glasshouses are safe places. They are designed to control the environment, while young seeds and seedlings take root and grow. They protect the new seedlings from being destroyed by a storm. Glasshouses have an inbuilt watering system that simulates gentle, misty rain, which is run by a clockwork timer. Even the soil is a careful blend of potting mix designed to balance the right nutrients so that the plants will grow successfully.

The intention is that one day the seedlings will be taken from the glasshouse and planted in the garden. They will hopefully be given water and it will be helpful if the ground is somewhat prepared, but this is their real world, where they will be expected to grow and develop into mature and fruitful plants. Mature plants yield food and seeds for the next generation of plants, which would again be cultivated in the glasshouse for the forthcoming year.

If Kingdom Communities are going to grow, develop and help extend the presence of God's kingdom in local communities, then the church will need wise and caring 'gardeners' who can create safe places for these new-style leaders and communities in which to be cultivated. The skill and abilities needed from these gardeners require people who can nurture leaders and teams in the practices required to live as salt and light in local communities and networks. They will understand that the purpose of Kingdom Communities is not to add numbers to existing church attendance on Sundays, although this may occur. They will understand that the multiplication of Kingdom Communities is not so as to boost denominational annual statistics, although that too may happen.

The function of these gardeners is apostolic. Their concern is towards the development of agents of community blessing and kingdom presence so that Kingdom shalom is expressed. Because these gardeners are apostolic, their influence is not primarily hierarchal but relational. Their authority flows from their own personal and spiritual authority and experiences and they bring exhortation and challenge as needed.

Kingdom Communities must be genuine in their motivation. There is nothing worse than finding that an impure motive lies beneath the surface of what appears to be good and wholesome neighbourly interest. They cannot be a sneaky way of drawing people back to church. They cannot be subject to inappropriate wider structural control. Their essential value lies in the relational sensitivity and concern expressed for what God is doing locally. It is in the development of Kingdom Communities that people are formed for the journey towards Christian maturity as the group prays, breaks bread, dwells in the Bible and shares life in the neighbourhood together.

These groups can easily multiply as members who are well formed in these practices move to other locations and start similar groups. It is quite normal to expect connectedness with the sending Kingdom Community. Each new Kingdom Community carries its own, unique DNA formed by the makeup of members, culture and geography. Some will be small (two or three Christians[28]) and some will be large (for example, the school cited in the Introduction). Some will have a particular charism towards justice, care for the environment, the disabled or disadvantaged – the sky is the limit. This is how a network of Kingdom Communities begins; with the needs of that particular community. This, too, was how the early church grew and spread. This is the natural beginning of a distributed network, which can't be limited.

Local churches can make a wonderful contribution. Obviously, many members of local churches already live in a local environment. There

---

[28] Jesus said in Matt 18:20, "For where two or three gather in my name, there am I with them."

is nothing to stop existing church members from attending to their own local neighbourhood; this was Jesus' commandment after all (see for example the exercise described towards the end of chapter seven). As mentioned, some churches may have gifted individuals, who can contribute as 'gardeners'. However, churches have many other potential ways to give themselves to their community as God has always intended. The challenge will lie in the 'de-structuring' of many groups from existing church programs. The *raison d'être* must always be towards the Kingdom of God and the local context as well as for the members of the group; it cannot be compromised by funding, hierarchy, branding, and so on, which are all extensions of top-down power. Choirs, children's groups, parent support groups, play groups, book groups, soup kitchens, hospitality for refugees, seniors drop-ins, financial counselling, among others. all become Kingdom Communities – places where people can access the kingdom of God.

In 1958, Frank Beale and Harold Finger pioneered new mission work in Papua New Guinea. Frank was joined by his wife, Win, who was medically trained. The sending of missionaries to "convert the lost souls" overseas, was part of every denomination's expansion strategies back in those days. Much can be debated about the efficacy of these efforts for both the lost souls and the missionaries and their families. However, a reading of Beale's records of their time in PNG, and the principles he articulated, sound positively familiar to us.

Beale believed that mission stations or missionary outposts should only be established at the invitation of the local people; he believed that missionaries needed to "develop a sense of belonging" to a community before anything else, and that they also needed to learn the beliefs and practices of the groups they were reaching. He argued that it was the role of Holy Spirit to change people from within; the missionary as much as the people being 'reached'. He also advocated the gospel being presented as "God's love revealed in Jesus" and not as a law-based system of "do's and don'ts". One of Beale's strongest beliefs and practices was that the missionaries came as friends, often to the extent that if the missionaries walked into a village, but there was no villager prepared to introduce them, or there was hostility towards their presence, they would simply move on (echoing Luke 10: 1-12). All the while, these pioneers had a vision of a Papua New Guinean church that would be in existence some fifty years later, self-supporting and reaching out. The work progressed relatively quickly from the pioneering stages. In 1961, a site was chosen for a hospital complex at Bunapas, and by 1964 work had been established in six villages, four of which had schools, and there were three locations that had medical work, each a new Kingdom Community. Additionally, the fledgling churches (more Kingdom Communities) in the regions were growing.

Beale and the others sought to replace themselves in order to establish a truly indigenous form of church in Papua New Guinea. Sometimes this was not easy, as Beale himself reflected, "At times missionaries experienced heartaches as they watched the indigenous church make decisions". Yet they knew that, just as they had been led by the Holy Spirit and allowed to make and learn from their own mistakes, so too could the indigenous Papua New Guinean church. Frank Beale's summation of his and Win's time in Papua New Guinea pays testament to that belief, "I spent fifteen years being scared and out of my depth. Then when the growth took place it was like body surfing. Working with the Holy Spirit means that you are being carried along with your head only just above water and if you don't ride with it you get dumped and left behind. It was the greatest fifteen years of my life."[29]

> **Learning:** Kingdom ministry should incline towards the creative, organic and relational rather than mechanistic, top-down or hub and spokes. Fruitful leaders are more like gardeners who know what to grow, in what location and in what season.

The bias of this book is towards local geographic areas or as they say in viticulture, the terroir. That has always been how and where the Holy Spirit has primarily directed the growth of the Kingdom. However, in a networked and mobile society we would not want to be too rigid to name the potential for 'networked' Kingdom Communities. These communities could function in a very similar fashion to locally based

---

[29] Geoff Risson and Craig Brown, *The Church from the Paddock*, 108-109.

Kingdom Communities with one difference: they would be networked through common interest or need rather than locality. The networks may flow through a workplace, a profession, international students at a university or in other creative ways.

In Brisbane, Steve Drinkall has drawn together a network of professional young people who experienced a disconnection between their Christian faith and vocation. The group is called the 'The Society of the Brown Cardigans' (a bit of a laugh at the perception of their vocation). Most had continued to try to faithfully go to church but never experienced any encouragement for how they spent most of their days in their vocation. Typically, the people that Steve has drawn together are professionals; engineers, accountants and lawyers. Churches tend to only draw upon the contribution of such people for boards or financial contributions. Yet for the people in Steve's group, their profession is their vocation and each of them really feels that God wants them in that field. Each has expressed that they felt God was calling them to ministry, but not to lead a typical local church. The Brown Cardigans Society has enabled members to realise that their ministry is to be God's person serving in their chosen profession. Steve has drawn them together for mutual encouragement where they could meet other people with a similar conviction.

In Warrandyte, on the outskirts of Melbourne, Derek Bradshaw is the proprietor of Now And Not Yet. Not only is it a great café with good food and excellent coffee (it has to be in Melbourne) but Now And Not Yet is also a social enterprise based around social and community objectives, where the profits are directed to local projects like Create Space Art Studio, Blur support group and Tamil Feasts to support asylum seekers. Some of the staff and a growing number of customers are a vital part of the enterprise. The mission of the café is clearly displayed on the website. There is no limitation on a Kingdom Communities' engagement in social enterprise, compassion and justice – indeed being Christian, these will naturally be reflected.

There are other possibilities where Kingdom Communities can develop with a tendency towards being networked rather than local. Migrants sometimes settle across a city yet keep close relationships with each other in their new land. Artists also often tend to gravitate towards other creative people who understand the necessity of their lifestyle and means of expression. We believe that the possibilities are endless.

So, what do these local (and networked) Kingdom Communities look like, how do they function and what do they do? To discover more we will now uncover some case studies from a small missional order that has practised as a network of Kingdom Communities for twenty years in Australia, New Zealand/Aotearoa and Thailand.

CHAPTER FOUR

Into the neighbourhood

"The call of God is a call to the neighbourhood."
Simon Carey Holt[1]

"Whenever you enter a town and they receive you, eat what is set before you. Heal the sick in it and say to them, The kingdom of God has come near to you."
Luke 10:8-9 (ESV)

The dockside slum of Klong Toey, Bangkok, is a world away from the tourist strip of nearby Sukhumvit. On Sukhumvit everything is cheap and Western tourists pour through the seedy side streets, the retail shops and the bars in search of their thrills. Bangkok, Thailand, is one of the world's great mega-cities. It is home to approximately 15 million Thais and the expatriates who are posted there in one of South East Asia's vast economic hubs. In Bangkok you will find all life's extremes: beauty, ugliness, wealth, poverty, greed and generosity.

The dockside slum of Klong Toey has generated such a tough reputation over the years that it is almost impossible to get a taxi to take you there from the airport. In an area that is under a couple of square kilometres, over 100,000 people make their homes along with the floods, drugs, humidity, smog, crime, heat and very loud televisions. Many inhabitants of Klong Toey are migrants from poorer provinces in rural Thailand trying to make a better life. You will also find refugees from nearby Myanmar, some living in shipping containers. They are a small but significant part of the biggest urbanisation movement in history across the globe.

In the midst of the heat, density, bright lights, cheap thrills and horrendous traffic there is a small group of Christians who also make the slum their home, by choice. Together they are called Urban

---

[1] Simon Carey Holt, *God Next Door: Spirituality and Mission in the Neighbourhood*, Melbourne: Acorn, 2007, 88.

Neighbours of Hope (UNOH), Bangkok.[2] Together about eight adults plus their children have moved to the slum from the wealth and comfort of Australia and the United Kingdom. Each individual is well educated and has left a profession to pursue this calling in order to participate as a sign and foretaste of the kingdom of God. As a result, in all sorts of ways, this small Kingdom Community is a witness to the truth of Jesus' beatitudes, in surprising ways. The group has grown too. They have been joined by neighbours who are attracted to the life and example that is so visible – not much is hidden in a slum.

Although far too humble and focused on their neighbourhood to make any claims themselves, it has been our experience that UNOH (and the many groups like them, including the examples we share throughout this book) are the emerging future of Christian mission in the twenty-first century. UNOH, and groups like them, follow simple, Christian practices in their neighbourhood every day. They live with their neighbours, they love, listen, break bread together and discern what the Spirit is calling them to do. This might lead them to bathe a dying man, care for a disabled neighbour, start a kindergarten for children, throw a party, enable better pathways to education, hold a prayer meeting or put on a neighbourhood meal. The results are varied, fascinating and inspiring but certainly not always glorious. That such tremendous fruit of Kingdom proclamation and demonstration can come from a tiny node of people who are willing to take Jesus' commission seriously amongst a hundred thousand poor Thai Buddhists proves the power of the principle that this book is exploring: when a small, committed group of Christians lives faithfully in a neighbourhood, in partnership with the Holy Spirit, the kingdom of God really does come on earth. It happens something like this.

Over time by following basic practices such as regularly breaking bread, listening to neighbours and living in the neighbourhood, team members have been able to share together and weave local stories and

---

[2] UNOH was founded by Ash & Anji Barker in Springvale, Melbourne in 1993 and subsequently established Kingdom Communities in some of the neediest neighbourhoods in Melbourne, Sydney, Auckland and Bangkok. The Barkers have now moved to Birmingham where they have created another Kingdom Community in a very poor part of town.

Chapter Four: Into the neighbourhood

experiences. In the midst of regular conversation, the team is able to discern something of what the Holy Spirit seems to be up to. For example, one member told stories of the excellent handicraft skills that some of the neighbours had. Another shared that she had been offered suitcases full of Westerners clothes from expats who had too much to take home – except who in the slum would need a suit? All of the team was aware that there were women in the slum who were doing the mind-numbing task of sowing undergarments for the department stores at very low wages.

Stories like these were floating around the UNOH Bangkok team when the idea for Second Chance developed. The vision of Second Chance was to be a place where donated clothes and local people could be given a second chance. After some basic research and the acquisition of seed funding from supporters, a two-level building on the main road by the slum was rented. Goods were received and some of the local women working for department stores on poor wages were invited to come and use their creative skills. They were also paid a fair wage, which was considerably higher than what the department store offered.

Today, Second Chance has become an extraordinary operation and sign of the kingdom. The downstairs area has been converted into a shop-front where local Klong Toey people can shop for affordable and quality items made by local women from the goods that have been donated. The creativity is beautiful. Jeans are turned into handbags. Suits are cut down into teddy bears. Shorts, shirts, dresses and shoes are all available too. Upstairs the women gather each day to sow, design and share life. Several women are now employed. A handicraft business has been started where other local women can design and make jewellery. UNOH, through its local and international supporters, has created a distribution network. There is a similar story about a cooking school[3], an employment education café and a grocery home-delivery service that all started from the small team called UNOH Bangkok. Some projects endure while some are for a season.

When you talk with the people whose lives have been dramatically altered by steady, ethical employment (which has literally given them

---
[3] See cookingwithpoo.com

a second chance), what is telling is that the material blessing is not the greatest benefit. What they comment on first is that they are now a part of a community that is like a family. Some have also become Christians and the UNOH team is working hard to contextualise how to develop a Thai slum faith community that extends their current model of local, neighbourhood presence. The kingdom of God is making inroads through attentive, creative and loving neighbours in the slum and lives are being changed.

> **Learning:** Kingdom Communities have always been the most fertile and effective expression of the transforming and renewing work of God. Enormous power and possibility come about when a small group of people work together for the transformation of their community. As Margaret Mead famously said, "Never doubt that a small group of thoughtful, committed citizens can change the world; indeed, it's the only thing that ever has."

Luke chapter ten is a famous training passage about Jesus' sending of the seventy to villages where he had planned to go. He asked them not to take anything and to not get distracted on their way. There are many fascinating parts of this passage that require contextual work and understanding as we have both dwelt in this rich passage for years. A colleague from a pastoral team that Andrew led ended up memorising it because the team dwelt in it every week!

Many ideas are found in this passage. One is the idea that Jesus sent his followers ahead of him to dwell dependently on local hospitality in a village or neighbourhood. They had no strategic plan, no prepared answers, no resources and no agenda. In fact, they didn't even understand why they were really there, other than that Jesus had sent them. Their instructions were to locate a person of peace, settle in and join that household.

As they joined in the economic life of the household they also contributed. There were no free riders! The people who Jesus sent would have soon found themselves working in the garden, drawing water from the well, tending to livestock, cooking or working on building repairs. They would have soon blended in to the local environment. In doing this, they would have heard lots of the local news and gossip. Stories of who was ill and who was struggling would have entered into the day-to-day conversations as they went about their business. These situations would have been the entry points for ministry because we know that when they returned they told incredible stories of joy about what had occurred.

So much of modern ministry is predetermined by plans and goals. We think that we are the ones in control and determine to set goals and plans for God. We are so often focused on doing, that we forget about being God's people. To appreciate what God is up to requires an ability to listen and adapt.

A *technical* solution is something that requires expertise or procedures to which we already have access. Ronald Heifetz and Marty Linsky are authors in this area and explore these challenges.[4] There are many issues that we face in daily life and ministry that require this sort of know-how. Much in church leadership is technical: how to curate a worship experience, the design of a sermon, leading a meeting, developing a strategic plan or solutions to the needs of the children's ministry.

There are some things, however, that we do not have the ability to respond to through our usual resources. These are called *adaptive* challenges because, "They require experiments, new discoveries, new behaviour, and adjustments from numerous places in the organisation or community."[5] This was the challenge that Jesus placed before his followers by sending them to villages and neighbourhoods without any resources. They had to learn new skills of attending, listening and discerning in the moment– and they eventually experienced marvellous results. They had to draw upon God's Spirit.

---

[4] See Ronald Heifetz & Marty Linsky, *Leadership on the line: Staying alive through the dangers of leading*, Boston, Harvard Business School Press, 2002, Ronald Heifetz, *Leadership without Easy Answers*, London: Belknap Press, 1994, and Ronald Heifetz, Alexander Grashow & Marty Linsky, *The Practice of Adaptive Leadership: Tools and Tactics for Changing your Organization and the World*, Boston: Harvard Business School Press, 2009.
[5] Heiftez & Linsky, *Leadership on the Line*, 13.

When churches approach mission they usually start with the resources and imagination that they already have. These are technical skills. This is a reason why so often a church will start another church with a worship service - they already have this know-how. The danger of this approach is that this is also a potential method of colonising.

Colonisation is a process of control and domination by which one body yields power over another's land, method or culture. The word comes from the Latin word for inhabit (colere). It has caused untold damage over centuries of Christian activity and Christian mission, often accompanying European colonisation. There are many horrid stories across the centuries of damage caused by senseless expansion of damaging models and practices. We are only beginning to come to terms with the damage this had on indigenous people and cultures. Appropriate and sensitive contextualisation was not applied. As Sparks, Soerens and Friesen remind us in *The new parish: How neighbourhood churches are transforming mission*, "History shows that faithful presence can too easily be forfeited by our missionary agenda."[6]

In February 2008, former Prime Minister Kevin Rudd apologised to what is termed the 'Stolen Generations' for their suffering from sometimes well-meaning but damaging practices of the past. Recently, while on a walking tour with a local indigenous guide in the Flinders Ranges in South Australia, Andrew noticed the following quote on a plaque which shows the damaging practices that occurred via colonisation, "If the missionaries heard us kids speaking our language they would refuse to sell my mother groceries at the store – she would have to wait until the next week or travel to the next town to buy flour and sugar."[7]

As we seek to advance the reign of God in suburbs and communities we do not want to again be agents who create more damage. Our mission is to see healing, uplift, restoration, reconciliation and redemption after

---

[6] Paul Sparks, Tim Soerens and Dwight J. Friessen, *The New Parish: How Neighbourhood Churches are Transforming Mission, Discipleship and Community*, Downers Grove: IVP Books, 2014, 43.
[7] Attributed to Bill Couthard and inscribed on a plaque in a sacred meeting place of the Adnyamathanha people at Wilpena, Flinders Ranges, South Australia.

all. This why the model and practices applied by the UNOH team in Bangkok are so mature.

An Extraordinary Community Centre

In South Auckland, New Zealand the local UNOH team have many generative Kingdom stories to tell of their own. Theirs are stories that have emerged from the application of similar practices to the UNOH Bangkok team. Living in a well known and tough part of Auckland that has a reputation for high levels of crime, unemployment, drug use, family breakdown and violence the UNOH team faced a dilemma: were they going to see the community through the same lens as the 'experts' who live elsewhere or as neighbours? Experts tend to view from the outside whereas neighbours have a common interest in the dreams, aspirations and possibilities for their local community. UNOH team leader Dave Tims said it this way in a TEDx Manukau talk, "People told me that nothing good comes out of our neighbourhood but it all depends on your lens."[8]

Tims suggests that authorities and experts have a conflict of interest because the worse things get, the more funding that is handed out to them. Therefore, if they tell bad stories they get more money and ultimately things need to stay troubled. There is no motive to improve; actually, there is a motive to make things seem worse. He calls this a 'deficit lens'. If you change the lens and ask questions like, 'What if this is a good place?' 'Where are the bright spots?' and 'Where are the voices of the people to be heard?' then you generate very different results.

In 2011, Randwick Park was a boggy field. Surrounded by the estate houses of the area, it was a bit of a 'no-man's land', frequented rarely except by bored young people looking for mischief. Visually, it looked pretty unappealing, filled with mud, rubble and graffiti. Yet, today it is a genuinely beautiful community asset and place of gathering, socialising and pride. The journey of how this came about is inspiring.

The UNOH Auckland team is a Kingdom Community made up of committed Christians who follow Jesus' teaching to love their neighbour.

---

[8] Dave Tims, TEDx Manukau, "Don't just live here, be local: Community led development from the inside," November 2015. https://www.youtube.com/watch?v=W9JKWx7flGk

Logically, they extend this command to loving the neighbourhood also. They live locally, listen to and care for their neighbours. They don't seek to colonise, but rather they advance the welfare of the community through joining it. Theirs is a quest for the common good and human flourishing. They understand that transforming a community is not primarily about building parks, churches or buildings. Too many local authorities have stories to tell where just weeks after completion, facilities are destroyed, vandalised or simply not accessed.

The UNOH team understood that transformation is about people. Tims observed, "People have a deep, deep desire to belong: to be known, to be someone. Therefore, as neighbours we had to create a place where I could look into someone's eyes and they could look into my eyes, which is sacred, vulnerable treasure."[9]

Being local residents, the team soon realised that there was no place for gathering in the neighbourhood. There was a boggy local field, described above, which the local authorities had given up on but no place where the community could gather safely with pride. The community was a consequence of generations of application of experts' deficit lenses. It was disempowered and disillusioned.

The UNOH team knew that for anything positive to happen, the community needed people within who were an interested, listening presence. It needed ordinary people who could listen, speak truth and create a sense of belief and possibility. The community also needed something visual that would demonstrate clearly that their community was a positive and safe place. The team went to the local authorities and sought permission to manage the field. No one else was having any success with it so after deliberation the management responsibility was freely given.

They immediately started a community-wide consultation and asked the local residents what they would like to see done with the space. Everyone was listened to and respected and after a series of meetings a blueprint was drawn up. Zones within the reserve were broken down into stages and projects, while volunteers were sought to make paths,

---

[9] Dave Tims, TEDx Manukau, November 2015.

regenerate old streams and mow the lawns. Permission for the mowing of lawns was not easy to obtain as the council still wanted their own staff to do this. However, the UNOH team ultimately won the contract on the basis that local people had far more vested concern for the condition of the reserve than a person on a tractor once a month. Tims says, "When ordinary people have input into others the encouragement, sharing and kindness to each other and to mother earth starts to see a process of real transformation."[10]

Today events are held with concerts and dancing and the Randwick Park area is a remarkable symbol of transformation. The area is cared for and locals take pride in it because they 'own' it. Everyone is a park security officer. There is pride, confidence, belief and an amazing sense of community throughout the neighbourhood. The lawn mowing business has now generated four local jobs from within the community.

The experience has also empowered the community to respond to other areas of need. For example, the community had been waiting on the authorities for five years to provide a bus shelter for old people and children. Nothing was ever done. So, the community, initiated again by UNOH in a smaller but similar process, built one itself. It was what they wanted, made by local people and generated a great sense of local pride – and now it keeps old people and children sheltered while waiting for the bus.

Learning: Extraordinary fruit develops when faithful, attentive people listen for local needs and draw out the heart's desires and dreams embedded within their neighbours and networks.

Defending the community

Mount Druitt is approximately fifty kilometres west of the centre of Sydney. Formerly part of the land occupied by the Darug people, its growth and creation was a result of 1960s and 1970s social policy. This resulted in the construction of large numbers of public housing estates.

---
10 Dave Tims, TEDx Manakau, November 2015.

Today, the area has a lot of negative social stigma from those who live outside it. For those who live in Mount Druitt, it is their home and community, regardless of the high crime, domestic violence, drug usage and an occasional riot (a decade ago).

Jon and Lisa Owen moved to Mount Druitt for about a decade as the team leaders of UNOH Sydney. In that time, they recruited a diverse team of people who each came to live and serve in the local area. Over time some of the team have moved on to other initiatives and jobs, taking with them the formative experience of their time in Mount Druitt. Others have moved out of formal membership with UNOH but stayed in the area as partners and friends in the ministry. Jon and Lisa did not reside as missionaries, they joined the community as neighbours.

At the rear of their home they constructed an annex that enabled afterschool activities for local children. This made their house a centre of local community life. Lisa had (and still has) close friendships with many neighbours and Jon is a passionate advocate, especially for local young men. You can't walk too far down the street with Lisa or Jon, without being stopped by someone for a catch-up. For over a decade, along with their team, they threw themselves into the local community, Jon as a chaplain at the local school and Lisa at a local prison. They both helped run the local community centre, which initiated contact with a lot of local Aboriginal youth. Fairfax reporter Tim Elliot commented in the Sydney Morning Herald, "It's a fair bet that if Jesus Christ were around today, he'd be doing what the Owens are doing in Mount Druitt. They feed the poor and house the homeless. They lead the lost and counsel the conflicted."[11]

Despite all the daily activity, they also experience local emergencies, which happen somewhat regularly. Situations like youth being caught up with the police, schoolgirls becoming pregnant and young people being kicked out of home. Jon has regularly made the observation that simply getting to school can be a major achievement for many of the local kids. Because of his local public presence and advocacy, Jon was rated as one of Sydney's top 100 most influential people. He was unlike any of the other 99 on that particular list!

---

[11] Tim Elliot, *Sydney Morning Herald*, "House of Hope", 20th January 2012.

The UNOH Sydney team loved their neighbourhood. Mount Druitt was their home and they were there by choice. Jon and Lisa have recently left the area after more than a decade but their legacy, and that of the team, continues on; in the community garden, the local school, the community centre, and in the faces of the many local people who are their friends.[12] They were fierce advocates for their neighbours. This is a key reason why we have specifically included this case study: because the work of the Kingdom that was led by Jon, Lisa and their team will continue long after any organisation is present. This is a key idea within UNOH. That the positive effects and practices continue after the visible scaffolding of the team is removed.

In 2015, a documentary called 'Struggle Street' was aired by SBS. The aim of the series was to introduce viewers to some of the people and personalities who live in one of Australia's toughest and poorest suburbs: Mount Druitt. What it actually presented were clichéd characterisations and general belittlement for comfortable, professional people to view from their armchairs and 'tut tut'. The show was dubbed 'poverty porn'. Jon and the mayor led a national campaign that aimed to pull the series from being telecast because of its unfair and damaging stigmatisation. It just reinforced the negative stereotypes of the area. It is no surprise that Jon was at the forefront of the campaign; he was defending the people and the neighbourhood that he loved.

Four Commitments

These stories from Bangkok, Auckland and Sydney have introduced us to three of the UNOH teams. There have been others we could have shared if it wasn't for our commitment to keep to a reasonable word count.[13] Each has been made up of different individuals and located

---

[12] The legacy also continues in the lives of the neighbours who still live in Mt Druitt as well as the team who were formed in that Kingdom Community who have moved on to serve the kingdom in other creative ways. For example, Jon and Lisa left UNOH to serve on the team at The Wayside Chapel in Kings Cross, where Jon is now Pastor and CEO – another example of a Kingdom Community.

[13] A particular case-study we would cite would be the UNOH Broadmeadows team in Melbourne where Brad and Colleen Coath are immersed in a local primary school as well

in vastly different contexts. The only similarity is the poverty of each neighbourhood and the UNOH commitment to bringing hope to those in poverty. These three case studies have been included to show the amazing things that can happen when a small group of committed Christians, on a tiny budget, live locally as a Kingdom Community.

There are four basic commitments that we learn from UNOH for the formation of a Kingdom Community regardless of context. None of us have to move communities to build one although some might choose to do so. The commitments described here are not intended as a prescription or a formula. They are identified here so as to sharpen the focus and nature of any Kingdom Community you may be drawn to establish or in which to participate. For Dean and Andrew, it simply doesn't seem possible to establish a Kingdom Community without each of these being carefully considered and contextualised.

1. Living Local

This is as simple and as complex as the challenge sounds. Being a neighbour means attending to the local area. The neighbourhood needs to take priority over many other possible choices. We live in a networked and mobile society where so much activity is designed to take us away from being present locally. Therefore, the decision to live locally has an impact on a number of areas of our lives: the schools we send our children to, how we do church, the sporting clubs we join, the relationships we cultivate, the shops and cafes we frequent, the time we spend in our street talking with neighbours, and so on. Every decision we make to depart from our local area is a choice not to be engaged locally. This is not meant to make our local area a prison, but we should remind ourselves that living locally is a conscious and sometimes inconvenient choice. This can result in some wonderful and creative initiatives as we seek to attend to our neighbourhood, but we do have the constant cultural obstacles of independence and mobility to overcome. Just think about how we live.

---

as with refugees at the nearby asylum seeker centre. We have elected to use older UNOH case-studies that have survived the test of time.

Chapter Four: Into the neighbourhood

The design of a typical, modern suburb is all about retreat from the city. Everything in the design of modern housing is away from good neighbourhood relationships. For example, it is easy to get in your car inside your garage, raise the door with a sensor, and drive out of the driveway without seeing a neighbour. There is no opportunity for even a simple greeting – even cars have well shaded glass to hide you. On your way back home, you reverse the routine and once out of the car, spend most of your time in the family room, which is positioned at the rear of the typical house, away from the street. The demise of snail mail now means that you don't even have to check the letterbox. You can go for weeks without seeing a neighbour in a modern suburb.

In the documentary presented by Tim Ross, *The streets of your town*[14], the evolution of Australian housing since the 1960s is explored. It is well worth watching. Ross observes that there are no windows onto the cul de sac on which the newest houses are located. Its owners only enter and exit the property via the automatic garage door. They even comment that the front door is only used to receive packages and guests! These are real design obstacles in modern life for those of us who take Jesus' command to love our neighbours seriously (Matt 22:34-40).

Simon Carey Holt observes,

"I believe the neighbourhood remains a fundamentally important context of urban life and deserves to be taken more seriously by those who live in one. I believe that in ignoring the health and wellbeing of our local neighbourhood, we're ignoring the glue that binds the wider city together and makes it a genuinely human environment."[15]

Sarah and Andrew are a young couple with two pre-school aged children. Their neighbourhood is a typical suburban street as we have just described. They realised the hurdles that were against any sense of community in their street, so they came up with a fun project to change things. One long weekend they dumped a pile of wooden sleepers and soil on their front nature strip right next to the road. They began to dig holes and fit in the uprights and soon had the framework established for a garden bed.

---
14 See http://www.abc.net.au/tv/programs/streets-of-your-town/
15 Holt, *God Next Door*, 14.

Local children came to investigate this strange new occurrence. Aided by the presence of their own children, the other kids were invited to join in the creative, building process. Soon there was a street-wide construction process of children building a garden bed and filling it with the soil on their nature strip. Once the soil was added, they handed out seeds and seedlings of various herbs and each of the children discovered the joy of planting. They all then helped water the garden and saw the nature strip was transformed.

The street-side herb garden started growing well and now in that street just before dinner time most nights the children and their parents come to collect whatever herbs are needed for the evening meal. As they pick their fresh herbs the parents catch-up on their day, right outside Andrew and Sarah's home and the sense of neighbourhood and points of connection grow. There are rich lessons for us in this simple story as to how we can creatively attend in our local context.

As discussed earlier, not all Kingdom Communities are local and some networks flow across vocational or interest groups. The principle of living local that we are exploring here still stands. Whether our concern is explicitly local or networked through things like amateur radio, sport, painting, a book club or within a profession, we need to really live in that place: prayerfully, attentively and creatively.

2. Liking Local

Simon Carey Holt, reminds us that, "The neighbourhood is what is right in front of [us] day by day yet a reality that stretches far beyond my own little world. It's where we live … all of us."[16] It is easy to talk poorly about a neighbourhood. It is easy to call a place a 'dump' or to use language that suggests you would love to get out at the first opportunity for a better area given half a chance. However, Dave Tim's language and approach to Randwick Park offers an alternative approach. Tims argues that we need to check what lens we are using. Is it a deficit lens or one of possibility? A commitment to a local area has to start with a belief that every neighbourhood is unique and special.

---

[16] Holt, *God Next Door*, 152.

Every environment has unique possibility for God's creativity and possibility. UNOH have demonstrated that in the toughest of neighbourhoods. Biblically and theologically, we know that God is already at work ahead of us, so we should ask if our language opens or closes us to God's activity. Sadly, not all Christian communities are open to this, preferring rather to stick to their spiritual enclaves and comfort zones where they are unchallenged. We are reminded of Richard Rohr commenting that, "All of life is grist for the mill."[17]

He continues the same line of thought in *Falling Upward: A spirituality for the Two Halves of Life* by wishing,

"Why didn't someone tell me that earlier - that this life is the raw material that I need to take seriously? Every day, what's right in front of me is the agenda. And even more, the natural world all around us has all the lessons that we need for life, love, death, and salvation. Really! Just look and listen, and note how Jesus himself seems to have looked and listened to lilies, birds, hens, sheep, "red sky in the morning," green and dry wood, moth and worm, etc. You can see how merely believing doctrines and practising rituals is very often a clever diversionary tactic to avoid my actual life - to avoid the agenda that is right in front of me every day, which is always messy, always muddy, always mundane, always ordinary - and all around me."[18]

The language that each of us use about place and community is important. One of the core responsibilities given to humans by God as stewards, is the authority to name (Gen 2: 19-20). We must take seriously the names that we give to a community and place – both formally and informally. Sparks, Soerens and Friessen comment,

"Just as God called humans to care for the land, they are also called to steward what they make with that creation. This is referred to as the built environment. The built environment is a powerful demonstration of our reciprocal relationship with the created world. The ways that humans

---

[17] Richard Rohr, *Everything Belongs: The Gift of Contemplative Prayer*, New York: Crossroad, 2003.
[18] Richard Rohr, *Falling Upward: A Spirituality for the Two Halves of Life*, Hoboken: Wiley and Sons, 2011, 66.

design structures end up forming their lives and remaking them."[19]

One of the easiest and most fun ways to meet your neighbours is with a friendly dog. Dogs can be the most inquisitive animals that just bowl up to a stranger's dog (followed by the stranger) and introduce themselves. If you have a dog, you will probably find yourself on an early morning walk with the possibility of falling into conversations with neighbours on a regular basis. That has been Andrew and Dean's experience.

Andrew's dog is named Bella and she is a Labrador crossed with a Golden Retriever. Every morning she enthusiastically demands her walk, which is a great way of rising early. As Bella and Andrew walked along local streets they developed a circuit, which had maximum time when she could be off the leash at a local park. They found themselves being at the same park at the same time each morning where Bella would bound up to any other dogs to sniff and play. One of the dogs was named Amber and another was named Scout. While the dogs would sniff, run and play their owners chatted light-heartedly about the weather (a Melbourne thing), the football (another Melbourne thing) and other light topics. Eventually it seemed natural to introduce themselves by name. After all, they knew each other's dog's names.

Andrew met Trish and Dawn who were the owners of Amber and Scout respectively. Every morning the dogs would bound up to each other excitedly for a play and the owners would stand in the middle of the park chatting come rain, hail or shine. One day a new dog came past. Chloe was owned by Vince, who lived just across from the park, and pretty soon they joined the early morning small group on a regular basis. The group kept on growing like this and over the course of about a year other dogs joined. They actually got to a record of fourteen dogs one morning.

It was quite a group and at Christmas they even held a dog 'Kris-Kringle' where everyone bought a wrapped five-dollar present for the dogs! Some mornings, owners would bring their children for the experience and the group travelled closely with one couple through the

---

[19] Sparks, Soerens & Friesen, *The New Parish*, 104.

husband's cancer treatment. Andrew formed the clear feeling that they were their closest support network judging from the intimate details that they shared and the prayers that they invited from him – the resident Christian!

One morning was particularly memorable when a very tired Trish turned up to inform the group that she had become engaged the previous evening to Steve. The dog group was the first opportunity she had to share her exciting news. Everyone celebrated with her and as the group dispersed she came over to Andrew and asked if he did weddings for non-church goers. Interestingly, she said words to the effect that as a couple they loved the neighbourhood. They had bought a house there and had already become involved in a hockey club where Steve was a coach. Their dream was to live there for the rest of their lives and watch their children grow up through the local schools. They asked Andrew, as a neighbour and friend, to do the wedding, which they held at a local park as an expression of their sense of belonging locally.

Groups like this dog group and commitments like Trish and Steve's are wonderful examples of how to live and like locally. In a similar pattern, Dean's walking with his two dogs at a local Brisbane Park and the ensuing meetings of a regular group of neighbours follows a similar story of listening, engagement and belonging.

3. Listening Local

Despite being in some version of full-time Christian ministry for most of his adult life, Andrew still braces himself for a reaction before people find out. When he shares what he does, it is easy to see all sorts of assumptions being made. As a result, he has developed a strategy where he tries to avoid sharing what he does for as long as he can. Make no mistake, Andrew is quite centred and settled about his vocation but knows that an increasing number of Australians aren't used to talking with a minister and is well aware that two thirds of Australians rate ministers low for ethics and honesty. The best strategy he has found is to let people get to know him for who he is, for as long as possible before anything to do with Christian ministry enters the conversation. Once his occupation is in the open people usually place certain expectations, constraints and value judgements around anything discussed.

The art of listening is a lost skill in modern society. Everyone is making so much noise and fewer people are listening. If you visit a contemporary church, there is rarely any silence. Every moment is filled with noise and one is left to wonder how we can ever hear the still, small voice of God? Yet people talk all year about the minute of silence at an ANZAC service and how powerful it is. No wonder psychologists and therapists are in such demand.

A commitment to live local is a commitment to listen locally. There are all sorts of ways to listen but most of them start with quietness. As the old proverb says, 'The quieter you become, the more you can hear.' One way of learning what things are of concern in a neighbourhood is through the practice of active listening. This practice involves a commitment for a set time each day of not speaking, but simply listening. It produces very valuable and insightful fruit.

Here's a way to practise intentional, local listening exercises. Andrew did this for six months when he started as a minister in a new church. Each weekday morning, he would go to a local café and order his favourite coffee. Then he would sit at the counter or at a table and read the paper while paying attention to what was going on around him. He was present at the same time most mornings for about thirty minutes with no agenda. Some days he would just read the newspaper, magazine or a book. Some days he would talk with the owner. He just listened to what was going on around him and was fully present. He listened to the background music, the coffees being ordered, the news and the bits and pieces of conversation that floated around the café. It wasn't really 'eaves-dropping' as much as taking a daily sample of conversations.

On some days, especially Mondays, the discussion was about the football results. Other days all sorts of topics were covered like weddings, funerals, school balls, chapel services, relationships, cars, employment, health and illness, fitness, fashion, concerts, television, finances, real estate, weather (it was in Melbourne) and many other topics. Andrew just sipped his coffee and let it all just occur around him. His objective was to listen to what was going on and hear what preoccupied local people.

After about three or four months Andrew realised that some general themes were emerging. The suburb that this was conducted in was upper middle-class, so people dressed smartly and professionally. Yet, as he listened to the heartbeat of the neighbourhood he realised that this was just a disguise that hid people's deeper issues. There were three major themes that emerged through the listening. Firstly, there was anxiety about relationships. People were concerned about marriages, partners, children, friends, and so on. Secondly, there was anxiety about finances and job security. It came up in conversations about retrenchments, mortgages and house prices. Finally, there was an existential aspect in some conversations about the meaning of life. People would comment about a funeral, a wedding, a christening, or church school chapel service and wonder what it all meant.

The only way that Andrew could recalibrate and understand some of the deeper things that were going on in his new church neighbourhood was through listening. No one was going to tell him this information. Not only did these listening exercises cause him to slow down and understand what was on people's hearts at the café but it also caused him more generally to see the value in quietness and listening. It impacted the rest of his ministry in that context. Through listening we are better positioned to glimpse what God is up to. As Sparks, Sorens and Friesen say,

> "Once that you believe the Spirit is at play in the neighbourhood, that wisdom is calling out in the streets, that God was at work before you got there, your task is listening – listening to join in with all the redemptive hopes of the people in your neighbourhood."[20]

4. Loving Local

Jesus' greatest commandments to the Pharisees, his disciples and consequently those who represent him in the world today was to love God, self and neighbour (Matt 22:37-40). Of all the passages in the New and Old Testaments, these must be the most well known and urgent for the Western church. This is why we have used some examples from

---

20 Sparks, Soerens & Friesen, *The New Parish*, 143.

Indonesia and Thailand, where the centrality of this command is still practised. Biblically, it is really impossible to be a follower of Jesus and not attempt to live out this teaching.

Yet as we have examined, the orientation of the local church away from attending to the local combined with modern house design makes this a real challenge. Take for example the story of Colleen and Jim. They were a typical couple with lives filled with all sorts of activities, but they were asked by their minister to lead a small group. Wanting to understand a little more about what was required before committing to this role they asked him to describe a healthy small group. He described their job as the frontline of the church's pastoral care. He continued, "Good leadership will see that the group meets regularly, cares for one another if needs arise, participates in whatever study-series the church is following, prays for each other and incorporates new members who join the church, whom the minister for small groups will allocate."

The two of them discussed and prayed through this request and agreed that they had the necessary gifts to do the job and also that they should probably help out a little more than they were doing in the church. They concluded that leading in this way was a sign of contributing to the church and they felt they did need to help out more. They signed on and were sent a list of names of people who had registered to join a small group. The names on the list were all recent arrivals to the church who weren't yet in a small group and were from all over the city. Initially they didn't know anyone, but their gift of hospitality soon broke the ice and over the first term they started to appreciate the diversity of group members.

As happens with people in any setting, some group members shared thoughts and feelings quickly and openly while others took some time to open up. Eventually the group started to feel safe to other members and the group gained a sense of momentum. One day they received an email from the church small groups minister asking them to incorporate a couple that were new to the church and had requested to join a small group. They agreed and the next time the group met the new people turned up. They seemed pleasant and a good fit, but the change did cause the group dynamics to freeze up for a while as the group recalibrated. A new person in any group makes a new group.

Chapter Four: Into the neighbourhood

Over the rest of the year this happened twice more as other people joined the church and consequently the group. It was bulging, yet struggling to find connection. Something else kept occurring that Colleen and Jim felt hindered momentum. Every four to six weeks the church would launch into a new series on a topic. One series was on boundaries, one was on missions, one was on financial stewardship and one was on evangelism. The group had committed to align with the church teaching program, but they felt they were getting whiplash as they jerked around different topics. There was no time for deeper communication and honest discussion about struggles and opinions on the topics being covered, let alone getting to personal needs within the group.

In the middle of winter something else happened. Literally, almost all the group members were sick at the same time. Most were just colds and flu but two were more serious. One group member had a kidney infection that required hospitalisation and one suffered a badly broken leg. Colleen's natural method of care was to make meals but she herself had the annoying cold and the challenge of doing the cooking and getting the meals delivered all over town was too hard, between managing her own job and family. She realised that care was best done locally but wondered how this could be done when group members lived so far apart. The church small groups minister organised a training night to teach how to do better pastoral care for all leaders. He suggested that a quick email was often enough to let people know that you were there for them and that leaders need to be realistic about what they could achieve. Something started to become unsettled deep inside Colleen and Jim. How could this group move from being a small group into a community if they lived so far apart and they couldn't even make meals for each other when they were sick?

One day, the couple's fourth grade son, Noah, came home from the local school and announced that his best friend's mum, Meg, was ill and had to go to hospital. Colleen knew Meg quite well, as she lived up the street and they used to walk the children to school when they were younger. She determined to call immediately to check in on her. However, the small group was coming, the meal wasn't cooked, the house looked like a bomb and the kids needed to be supervised doing school reading. Jim got home late from work and pitched in, but the result was that there was no time to call Meg.

The next morning Colleen called Meg and was horrified to find out that she had an aggressive cancer that required extensive and invasive treatment. During the phone call Meg also let her know that another young mother from around the corner had the same thing. It was one of those moments for Colleen when the value of good health becomes acute and her cold no longer counted. She swung into action. She knew that Meg's wider family lived interstate and that she would be struggling for practical support. This was where Colleen came alive – by helping those in need.

Meals, school pick-ups and cleaning the house were the practical ways that Colleen always responded in moments like this. She organised a meal roster with some other local friends for both the mothers who were undergoing treatment and helped out in other practical ways as needed. Two of the small group members also lived in the same area and they were also recruited onto the roster. Colleen's gifts were perfect for this sort of thing.

Throughout this experience a shift occurred within Colleen and Jim. Whenever the small group gathered for its regular meeting, Colleen and Jim's hearts seemed somehow to be less and less in it. They persisted out of faithfulness but the latest series on church membership seemed so disconnected when they were asking questions like, 'Why do some people suffer?' and 'How can we help more with local needs?'

Requests from the church for help at working bees, going on the family camp, for Jim to join the eldership and for giving towards the property extension just no longer were priorities. They had no philosophical problem with any of it but somehow, they felt a pull into the neighbourhood at the cost of church activities, especially with two local families in such need. The couple needed to decide. Did they care for each other, support those who were pitching in locally among the families in their moments of need and cease to be a link in the church small group program or did they stay? There didn't seem to be any space in between these two options.

Chapter Four: Into the neighbourhood

They met with the small groups minister, who while sympathetic to their dilemma, was focused on the purpose of the church small group program – that was his job. It was the building block of the church and needed to support the overall body. Colleen and Jim went away confused. They didn't want to leave the church, but they needed to step back in some way. So, they resigned as small group leaders. The church didn't seem to have any position for a couple who wanted to focus on caring for the neighbourhood.

Meg went downhill very suddenly. What was understood to be a medium-term diagnosis tragically turned to short-term. Meals, prayer and help were all they could offer as Meg's family approached their farewells. In her last week, Colleen was with Meg when she asked if she would, 'Do the service, say a few words and farewell me?' Meg explained that she had no religious connections but didn't want a celebrant who didn't know her to do it.

So, on a Saturday morning at a local funeral parlour Meg's family and friends along with many people from the local neighbourhood and primary school gathered to farewell her. The two other families from the small group who had faithfully stuck out the journey were also there. The service had tears, poems, a Bible passage from John's Gospel, jokes as some funny stories were told about Meg and a moving reflection from Meg's husband and children. It was tragic, beautiful and local all rolled into one – but mostly tragic.

Most of the small group members had dispersed into other groups but Colleen and Jim and the other two local families kept meeting. They developed a pattern that gave them a sense of rhythm, helped by a retired seminary lecturer they had met at church, who knew a thing or two about missional orders. Late on Sunday afternoons they gathered in Colleen and Jim's backyard for a barbeque meal where, including the children, they caught up on the week, broke bread and drank the wine that was before them on the table. Then a group member would open a Bible passage from the common lectionary, which was easy to access on the web. It was a simple, ordered set of Bible readings. And then the group asked, what had God been saying that week and how should they partner with it? Then they prayed for each other and their neighbourhood.

Colleen and Jim have never formally left their local church because they never had reason to leave. They have friends there, it has a good youth program and they relate well with the minister. One thing they learnt about getting too involved in the church was that most of the activities drew them away from their local neighbourhood. It wasn't intentional but that was the outcome. Most, if not all, of the church activities were centred around the church. The choice forced on Jim and Colleen was to spend all their time at church or to attend their neighbours. It was never communicated like that but there are only so many hours in a week. If you asked their minister about them he would probably say that they were a great couple with a lovely family, but they didn't quite make church their priority.

It doesn't have to be this way. As we have previously discussed, the modern local church, with all of the challenges facing it still has many wonderful possibilities through which to contribute in local presence and mission. Indeed, the retired seminary lecturer from their church functioned as a gardener for Colleen and Jim. Yet, if we are to take Jesus' commandment about loving our neighbour and His commission of making of disciples seriously, then priorities need to change. We need to invest far more prayer, support and training in the 'Colleens and Jims' than in maintenance of internal church structures.

> **Learning**: Kingdom Communities are present in the tough situations of life in ways that congregations cannot be present. The light of Christ is shone best through prayerful, Christlike, relational friendship and presence. These are moments and contexts in which God calls his people to be present.

Our resources and energy need to be more focused on how many leaders and Kingdom Communities we can see established, resourced and sustained rather than how many people come to services and programs in our churches. This is our very real challenge if we wish

Chapter Four: Into the neighbourhood

to take the call to discipleship, harvest and love of neighbour seriously with the weight that the New Testament places upon them.

The exciting news is that it is possible. We have explored some biblical and theological frameworks for Kingdom Communities. We have also uncovered several case studies from Brazil, Thailand, Indonesia and across Australia where this is already happening. In the next chapters we look at a whole denominational system in Queensland, where this transformation has begun to take root among its churches, care agencies and in many other creative forums.

CHAPTER FIVE

Kingdom Communities in Queensland

"The world we have created is a product of our thinking; it cannot be changed without changing our thinking."

Albert Einstein

"The Spirit of the Lord is upon me, because he has anointed me to proclaim good news to the poor. He has sent me to proclaim liberty to the captives and recovering of sight to the blind, to set at liberty those who are oppressed, to proclaim the year of the Lord's favour."

Luke 4:18-19 (ESV)

We turn now to explore the case study of the transformation of Churches of Christ in Queensland, based on the theology and principles outlined in previous chapters. From 2010 to 2017, Churches of Christ in Queensland (a mainline Protestant denomination) changed from near collapse to a transformed movement and added 190 new Kingdom Communities to what was already in existence across Queensland. We believe that this is an important case study for four reasons:

First, it demonstrates that the theory explored in previous chapters really works in practice. It opens missional possibilities, unifies people, focuses an organisation on its deeper purpose and invites more people to participate meaningfully.

Second, it occurred in Australia where the context is of diminishing interest and participation in the Christian church. The Australian 2016 Census data continues to show a consistent fifty-year decline in the number of people identifying as Christian. This decline in the percentage of Australians identifying as Christian, is correlated with declines in most denominational memberships and consequent local church closures.

Third, despite the prevailing demographic data we believe that this case study illustrates that growth is still possible on a wide scale. Whilst the majority of Australians may not be interested in Church as it has been traditionally understood, many are still drawn to places of genuine compassion and spirituality – what we have called Kingdom Communities.

Finally, it offers a blueprint, based on real life experiences, for thinking about local as well as large scale church culture change aimed at enabling more of the light of Christ to be shone in local communities.

The Background

In 2009, after a long period of difficulty and conflict, Churches of Christ in Queensland was in a parlous state. The Conference of Churches of Christ in Queensland, which was established in 1883, was described as coming within a whisker of folding.[1] There were seventy affiliated local churches (half had under fifty members); generally, dwindling congregation numbers; a property and finance agency; and various care services that had separated from the Church into their own sub-departments. There was a general view that 'Kenmore' (the State Conference Office located in the suburb of Kenmore) was irrelevant, full of silos and there was significant and widespread distrust.

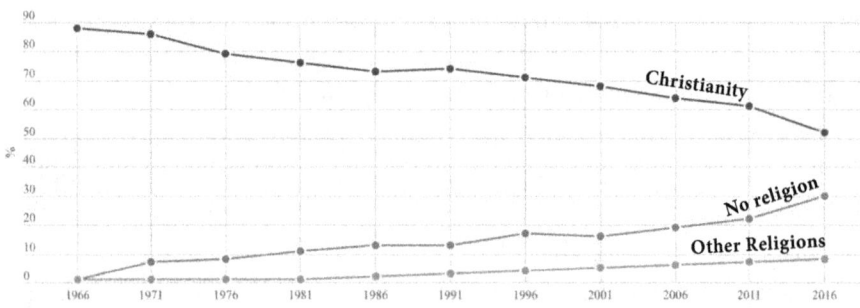

*Figure 5.1 Share of religious affiliation in Australia from 1966 to 2016.
Source: ABS Census 2011 and 2016*

One of the many benefits of association is that despite the grave situation there were still a few capable leaders who continued to believe in the possibilities of the denomination. Central to this conviction was a deep awareness of community need and commitment to the

---

[1] Geoff Risson & Craig Brown, *The Church from the Paddock: A History of Churches of Christ in Queensland 1883 – 2013*, Second Edition, Kenmore: Churches of Christ in Queensland, 2016, 163.

original mission of the Churches of Christ in Queensland movement. The first step towards rebuilding the whole system was to bring about organisational alignment through a new constitution. It was voted in at the November 2009 AGM and signalled commitment to a fresh start. This new constitution brought in new governance and structural changes, some new people at the top and a widespread resolve to pull together for the sake of the kingdom of God.

These changes sought to bring about three improvements:

1. Unity. The decision was made to integrate all departments and areas of work and mission into one organisation, with one mission.
2. Better utilisation of resources.
3. Development of a collective sense of zeal for the mission of the denomination.

The new constitution created a Council, which was elected by delegates from affiliated churches who served as the stakeholders and guardians of the mission. The Council then appointed one skill-based Board of Directors who served as the legal, governing body for the whole of Churches of Christ in Queensland. The Board, in turn, appointed a new Chief Executive Officer (CEO) who had responsibility for all functions within the Conference, including Care Services, Property and Finance, and Church Mission and Ministry. The aim of the newly created constitution was: one Council, one Board and one Executive with one mission; to be one body forwarding the gospel.

The new Board and Council invited Dean to take up the newly constituted role of CEO. Dean and his wife Janette, a psychologist, relocated from Melbourne to take up this challenge, commencing in February, 2010. The first six months were largely about listening and healing through travelling, meeting and listening to local leaders in churches, care services and communities across the large State of Queensland. There were many important encounters, but Dean recalls three formative experiences from which important insights emerged on his first trips to Cunnamulla, Charters Towers and Maryborough.

What was understood by the word 'church'?

Cunnamulla is Aboriginal for 'long stretch of water'. It is situated along the Warrego River, about nine hours' drive west of Brisbane. Cunnamulla is a community of approximately 1200 people living in beautiful, red earth, outback country. As the new CEO of Churches of Christ in Queensland, Dean, together with his wife Janette and David Swain (Director of Care Services), drove out to Cunnamulla to meet staff and volunteers at the child and family care centre. A meeting had also been arranged with the Mayor and CEO of the Shire of Paroo, as Cunnamulla is the largest of four towns that make up the Shire.

Dean was pleasantly surprised by the warmth of the meeting with the Mayor and CEO, having wondered beforehand whether the local leaders would really want to meet with Church leaders from Brisbane. In fact, the opposite was the case. The best crockery with country scones, jam and cream were laid out in the Council boardroom, and, during the conversations, the CEO and Mayor both said how much they appreciated what the church was doing in their community. They both spoke at length of children and families being uplifted. It turned out both the Mayor and the CEO had their children attending the child care centre; so, they were speaking from first-hand experience.

Their language was significant and important. Back at headquarters in Kenmore there were two directories: one that listed Churches of Christ in Queensland's seventy churches, and a separate one that listed the care services, which included several not-for-profit entities. As indicated earlier, the two areas operated independently following years of conflict. A church was defined by being in the Church directory. A care service was listed in the Care directory.

Churches of Christ in Queensland did not believe that it had a church in Cunnamulla because nothing was listed in the Church directory. Yet, much needed child and family services were being provided to the community by Churches of Christ in Queensland Care. Churches of Christ in Queensland language reflected how the world occurred to them, which was that they had a care service at Cunnamulla, only. However, the local leaders' language (which reflected how the world occurred to them) was to greatly appreciate what the Church was doing in their community. They were using the word 'church' to describe their understanding of a single entity that encompassed caring services as well as local worshipping communities. This insight was reinforced to Dean in other communities visited. Virtually all local community leaders saw Churches of Christ as a Christian denomination that was providing a range of caring services in addition to local, worshipping congregations. They implicitly saw Churches of Christ in Queensland as a big 'C' Church, whereas Churches of Christ in Queensland saw itself in terms of little 'c' churches, with care services as separate operations.

Over a number of decades, Churches of Christ (like many other denominations) created a huge division in governance structures, operational strategies, resource allocation, brands and language; separating and centralising their caring services, housing services, education services, and so on, away from their local congregations and Christian missional imagination. Yet Dean experienced that local community leaders, as well as the many people accessing the services, saw no such division. For good or bad, the wider community perceived it all as the 'Church'.

What constituted being a church?

Not long after the visit to Cunnamulla, Dean met with the Church of Christ members at Charters Towers, west of Townsville. Once a strong church birthed out of the gold rush era, Charters Towers Church of Christ had declined to nine elderly folk who met each Sunday in one of their homes over lunch. The church building had become run down and too difficult to maintain, and it was sold to another denomination. Dean joined them in their home for a traditional roast dinner on a sweltering hot Sunday. They prayed together, broke bread and shared a cup of juice as part of the meal and warm fellowship. After lunch people went on their way, to reconnect again the next Sunday.

A few days later he travelled down to meet with staff, volunteers and residents at the Churches of Christ Seniors Care facility at Maryborough, where he joined them in their weekly worship service. There were about eighty residents and family members present. They were accompanied by a lady on the organ, sang some great old hymns with gusto, prayed together, shared in communion, and a retired minister preached a rousing 'come to Jesus' sermon. That was followed by lunch and warm fellowship.

Dean was puzzled that Charters Towers was listed as one of the Churches of Christ in Queensland's seventy churches in the Church directory, whereas Maryborough was listed as a care facility in the Care directory. Both comprised a group of people meeting in their homes (the aged care facility is their home). Both shared in prayer and Communion on a Sunday. Both groups pastorally cared for one another. There was no doubt that Jesus was present at both gatherings. A question was brewing within him. What criteria was being employed to define the group in Charters Towers as a church while the group in Maryborough was a care service?[2]

Dean realised that Churches of Christ in Queensland had simply assumed what all other denominations did about what a 'real' church is and is not. A real local church seemed to require a group meeting every Sunday morning, ideally in a designated church building, for worship, songs, Communion, a sermon, and an offering. If a group was doing this, then all things being equal, they were counted as a legitimate member of the Churches of Christ in Queensland 'club'. Furthermore, if the attendances on Sunday morning were growing, they were counted by fellow church leaders as a model of success. This would be typical in most denominations.

Yet, the confusion of what did and did not constitute a legitimate church went even deeper. The aged care home at Maryborough met together every week in a chapel, hymns were sung, a sermon was preached, and traditional Communion was served with love and care to those in the community. By the ideal understanding of what was church (above), the Maryborough group certainly looked like a traditional church; and with regular attendances of more than fifty people, it was a bigger congregation than half of the seventy listed churches. Despite this, it still wasn't seen as a church.

---

[2] In 2010, Churches of Christ in Queensland's website and brochures described the denomination as being comprised of 70 local churches, various care services and other ministries.

Meanwhile, Charters Towers had no minister, no sermon, no music, no hymns and no programs. Yet, presumably, because it had dwindled from an original Sunday morning congregation, worshiping in a stand-alone church building, it was still counted as a legitimate ongoing expression of an affiliated church. If questioned, they would justify, "For where two or three gather in my name, there am I with them." (Matt 18:20).

However, to show how inconsistent things had become, other groups with similar numbers of people who met regularly for prayer, Bible study and Communion in Churches of Christ's affordable housing complexes, or other aged care homes, retirement villages, on the back deck of a minister's home, in cafes, men's sheds, or every Wednesday morning in the park, and so on, were not counted as real churches. Such groups were commended; however, the implicit cultural assumption was that they needed to be progressing further toward the more traditional shape of real church. Dean reflected that because they were, in essence, indistinguishable from the Charters Towers Group, that other criteria were being culturally applied in the definition of what was and was not a church.

Of course, we are of the view that both examples of Maryborough and Charters Towers were legitimate expressions of ekklesia. That is, they were groups of faithful Christians gathering together to love God and to love one another in the presence of Jesus, and in a context that made sense for them in their community.

> **Learning:** Ekklesia does not refer to a building or a denomination in the Bible. Ekklesia refers to the Body of Christ (two or more people who have placed their faith in Jesus Christ and gather regularly to pray, worship, open the Bible, build community and break bread).[3] Each 'ekklesia' is a member of the universal church. History and experience show that this can occur in many contexts, forms, settings.

Two Stories of identity

From Cunnamulla, Charters Towers, Maryborough and many other meetings with leaders in local communities, two groups of stories

---
3 John 3:16; 1 Corinthians 12:13.

emerged about who the denomination called Churches of Christ in Queensland were. The interesting fact is that both stories were true.

The first story, or metanarrative, was the one already described from the 2010 website. Churches of Christ in Queensland consisted of seventy local churches, various care services and other ministries. It was a story of self-focused survival, closed ranks, fear, judgement, resistance to change and often was tainted by competitiveness. The subtext of this story, which was repeated behind closed doors from church Elders across the state, went something like this, "We are a small denomination that is slowly dying. Half our congregations have fewer than fifty ageing regulars, they can't afford a paid minister, and many can't afford to maintain ageing church buildings. Younger people are not coming to church. There has not been a new church planted by our denomination for years. If we don't start planting churches soon we will be dead in a few decades."

The second story was that Churches of Christ in Queensland consisted of more than two hundred places that had at least some people among them who were endeavouring to live out the way of Jesus. In local communities, Churches of Christ was seen as the church, 'with sleeves rolled up' and greatly valued around Queensland for the love and care that was brought to children, youth, the homeless and the elderly. The State Government held 'this' Churches of Christ in Queensland in the highest regard, particularly for its work with at-risk children, youth and families.

Having spent six months listening to and pondering some of the mindsets across the denomination, Dean started to pull together the threads. Churches of Christ in Queensland had large resources and the capacity to grow, if everyone worked together. The tough legal work had been completed through the new constitution. As CEO, his challenge was cultural and theological. To achieve this challenge, he had to find a common, generative story for everyone that explained what God was up to. There was a growing, life-giving, other-focused story full of possibility that gave meaning and value to a traditional story that was meaningful to those who lived inside it. Somehow, Dean needed to guide the two stories towards a unified whole.

Confronting the predictable future

Running in parallel with all of this travelling, listening and reflection, were the many discussions with the Executive Team, Board and Council about the perceived predictable future decline of too many churches. There were some strong exceptions, however many were depressed and on a path towards extinction. Despite public statements of positivity, the traditional story was still dominant. Dean observed that many people wanted change, but they lacked the words to explain a better future that included unity, more resources and a strong mission focus. There was a lack of alignment about what a future could actually look like that achieved these aspirations.

Many discussions were had concerning the default future versus a hoped-for future. Realists pointed to the statistics and commented that if everything continued as it had been headed over recent years, there was no future. They were tired of undelivered goals like, "Twenty more churches by 2020". Despite hope for a better future, deep down inside, the majority view of the future was continued isolation, decline and closure of many churches; the stronger Care area heading its own way and probably separating away from the Conference altogether, into a stand-alone not-for-profit; and, a couple of the larger churches separating from the Conference because they saw no value in continued association. Churches of Christ in Queensland was still at-risk of folding.

The situation was confronted by the Senior Leadership Team, Board and Council and collectively everyone agreed that they could not achieve the deeper intention of the constitutional reform without a new, unified mindset and a common narrative. Decline, fragmentation or silos were not the preferred future for Churches of Christ in Queensland. Collectively the leadership determined that a new future was needed from the most generative parts of the existing stories. They all asked critical identity questions like, who are we as Churches of Christ? What do we stand for? What are we trying to forward? Why do we believe that it's critical for us to forward it? What does it mean to be a church of Christ in a local Queensland community today? How does that inform what we do and how we do it?

Identity going forward

At the November 2010 AGM Conference, late into Dean's first year, he presented to the delegates feedback from the months of conversations around Queensland and among the leadership community. It was summarised through the two stories about who Churches of Christ in Queensland were and what they wanted to become. As both stories were true and supported by plenty of anecdotes and evidence, it was widely agreed that a way was needed that sought to combine the best of each. In essence the whole AGM was led through an experience of positive dissonance as they held the two stories and the predictable futures that flowed from them. The result was that the meeting determined that they needed to unfreeze the prevailing cultural mindset of depression and decline by contrasting it with an equally true story of influence and possibility.

An old parable spoke to the choice,

A grandfather was teaching his grandchild about life. "A fight is going on inside me," he said to the child. "It is a terrible fight and it is between two wolves. One is evil—he is anger, envy, sorrow, regret, greed, arrogance, self-pity, guilt, resentment, inferiority, lies, false pride, superiority, and ego." He continued, "The other is good—he is joy, peace, love, hope, serenity, humility, kindness, benevolence, empathy, generosity, truth, compassion, and faith." The same fight is going on inside you—and inside every other person, too." The grandchild thought about it for a minute and then asked the grandfather, "Which wolf will win?" The old grandfather paused and then replied slowly, "The one you feed."

Churches of Christ in Queensland was at a major juncture. There was a clear choice that would affect future capacity and culture as well as their ability to maximise the fulfilment of their mission. There was a choice. The first was to continue with a dying and depressing story filled with self-focus, excuses, inferiority and resentment. The second was a story of life, creativity, boldness and growth. The overwhelming majority of assembled delegates acclaimed the second story and supported a number of steps aimed at creating a new predictable future.

> **Learning:** The stories we tell matter. How the world occurs to people shapes how they feel and behave. The lens through which we automatically see and make sense of situations is shaped by the stories we hold about the past (why things are the way they are) and the future (where all this is going). Our individual and tribal stories shape our reactions, thinking and behaviour into the future.

Kingdom Communities

A key action from the AGM's positive affirmation for Dean and his team was to promote with as many groups as possible (from both the church and care areas) the second and preferred story. They needed to generate a story about identity and purpose that engaged as many people as possible as they moved forward. The team constantly found themselves saying, "We are not just seventy churches. We have over 200 places where at least some people are endeavouring to live out the way of Jesus."

Gerry Weatherall, the Head of the Mission Department, came up with the image of each place being like a Wi-Fi router. The idea was that if you can connect to the router then you can access all that the internet has to offer. So, the challenge in the story became, 'What if every group that Churches of Christ in Queensland was involved with, became a place where people could access the kingdom of God?' In other words, a Kingdom Community.

Acknowledging that many of the two hundred places did not immediately see themselves as a Kingdom Community, the leadership nonetheless imagined a future where every church and care centre/program would become one. They saw a future where anyone encountering a church or care centre/program would be able to access and experience something of the kingdom of God. The shared vision invited further questions like, 'What should be going on in such a place? How should people be behaving? What would people see and experience when they came in contact with a Kingdom Community?'

In our preceding chapters, we have canvassed a range of local examples from across Australia, Indonesia, Thailand and New Zealand that demonstrate how Kingdom Communities, as a concept, are spreading like a (healthy) virus. They have not come about from a grand strategic meeting. They are often local, and their leadership is low key and highly relational. In this Churches of Christ in Queensland case study, the beginnings were different. Kingdom Communities came about through an intentional Action Learning journey that sought to find answers by asking fresh questions rather than starting with predetermined solutions.

Understanding a Kingdom Community

A Kingdom Community was defined as a place where the kingdom of God could be accessed. It was understood as a place of light in the community and inspired by Jesus' words that, "You are the light of the world. A town built on a hill cannot be hidden. Neither do people light a lamp and put it under a bowl. Instead they put it on its stand, and it gives light to everyone in the house." (Matt 5:14-15)

The kingdom of God, often referred to as the kingdom of heaven in Matthew's gospel for the meaning that idea brought to Jewish hearers, is referred to many times by Jesus and other Bible writers. The kingdom of God is the sovereign rule or dominion (kingly power) of God. It was not specifically referred to by this name in the Old Testament, however the idea appears in the prophetic literature. God is frequently referred to as the King and ruler over his people, thus implying that he has a kingdom. Rabbinic teaching understood Israel as the custodian of this kingdom because it was the custodian of the Law.

In the New Testament we learn that the kingdom was initiated through Christ's earthly ministry and, as George Eldon Ladd says, "It will ultimately be consummated when the 'kingdom of the world has become the kingdom of our Lord and of his Christ.'"[4] The kingdom was Jesus' central message (Matt 4:23). The Sermon on the Mount is about the righteousness required to enter the kingdom (Matt 5:20) and many of Jesus' parables refer or illustrate it. The Lord's Supper, initiated by Jesus, looks forward to the coming of the kingdom on earth in its

---

[4] Walter A. Elwell, et al., (eds), *Baker Encyclopedia of the Bible, Volume 2*, Grand Rapids: Baker Books, 1988, George Eldon Ladd, "Kingdom of God (Heaven)", 1269.

fullness (Matt 26:29 & Mark 14:25). Jesus taught that the kingdom was present; it came in an unexpected manner and that it was taken from Israel and given to a new people (Matt 21:43 & Mark 12:9).

The concept of a Kingdom Community was to be a presence in the community where a group of people were intentionally trying to practise or live the Way of Christ and thus demonstrate and announce the Lordship of Christ over the world. It meant that they were seeking to love God and put him first in their lives; to love one another; to care for the poor, sick, vulnerable and oppressed; to tell, train and encourage others in the Way of Christ, inviting them to join in; and to live a rich and fulfilling life through following the Way of Christ.[5]

A Kingdom Community was envisaged to be a place where the kingdom of God is evident. It is where the fruit of the Spirit is evident because there is love, joy, peace, forbearance, kindness, goodness, faithfulness, gentleness and self-control (Gal 5:22-23). As the team kept thinking through what a Kingdom Community should be, they noted it should be a place or environment where people could:

- Find their way to God through an encounter with Christ.
- Feel safe.
- Have access to a decent roof over their head, and enough good food and clean water to be healthy.
- Belong: they could feel connected and be a valued part of a community.
- Care for one another and feel loved and cared for themselves.
- Feel valued and able to contribute.
- Feel able to acknowledge and be free from past sins and mistakes, and to find peace with God, others and themselves.
- Be their true and best selves.
- Find with renewed sense of purpose and hope that their life has meaning.
- Take responsibility for themselves and contribute to the greater good.

---
[5] See, Matt 22:37-40; 25:35-36; 28:18-20; and John 10:10.

- Be honest and talk straight with one another – there are no mind games or manipulation.
- Experience wholeness, uplift and healing.

They realised that if the churches and care centres/programs were to really become Kingdom Communities, where people could access the kingdom, then they had to train and help people to understand what it really meant, and they also needed to develop a culture where the values, thinking and behaviours were of the Kingdom Way, rather than those often found in communities and not necessarily the culture and behaviours associated with traditional church or care centres/programs. Paul described the contrast clearly in his letter to the Galatians, here translated by Eugene Peterson in *The Message*[6],

"It is obvious what kind of life develops out of trying to get your own way all the time: repetitive, loveless, cheap sex; a stinking accumulation of mental and emotional garbage; frenzied and joyless grabs for happiness; trinket gods; magic-show religion; paranoid loneliness; cutthroat competition; all-consuming-yet-never-satisfied wants; a brutal temper; an impotence to love or be loved; divided homes and divided lives; small-minded and lopsided pursuits; the vicious habit of depersonalizing everyone into a rival; uncontrolled and uncontrollable addictions; ugly parodies of community. I could go on. This isn't the first time I have warned you, you know. If you use your freedom this way, you will not inherit God's kingdom.

But what happens when we live God's way? He brings gifts into our lives, much the same way that fruit appears in an orchard—things like affection for others, exuberance about life, serenity. We develop a willingness to stick with things, a sense of compassion in the heart, and a conviction that a basic holiness permeates things and people. We find ourselves involved in loyal commitments, not needing to force our way in life, able to marshal and direct our energies wisely. Legalism is helpless in bringing this about; it only gets in the way. Among those who belong to Christ, everything connected with getting our own way and mindlessly responding to what everyone else calls necessities is killed off for good—crucified. Since this is

---

[6] Galatians 5:19-26, Eugene Peterson, *The Message*.

the kind of life we have chosen, the life of the Spirit, let us make sure that we do not just hold it as an idea in our heads or a sentiment in our hearts, but work out its implications in every detail of our lives".

> **Learning:** Creating a new language of Kingdom Communities helped people to see with fresh eyes. It helped bypass the interminable arguments that leaders seemed to want to have about the merits of established churches versus emerging churches, and ministry versus mission – which arise from their predetermined views about words such as church and mission.

Accountability

Measurement and reporting had always been an integral part of the history and culture of Churches of Christ in Queensland. Each year directories and annual reports were published which listed the number of churches, members, Sunday attendees, baptisms, the number of aged care centres, child care centres, housing units, clients cared for along with many other indices. By introducing the idea of Kingdom Communities, the Senior Leadership Team had to come up with some measurable definition that was more than just a place that had a Churches of Christ label attached. Although ruthless, one of the senior ministers commented, "It has to be more than just giving people peanut butter sandwiches."

After various discussions, the team came up with the following definition of a Kingdom Community for the purposes of measurement. A Kingdom Community is a group or active network that:

Fig 5.3 Shining the Light of Christ Annual Report

- Has twelve or more people who connect with an identifiable rhythm and regularity,
- Contains at least three people who would self-identify as members of the Churches of Christ in Queensland mission movement,
- Is designed to give people in the community access to the kingdom of God, or in other words, 'there is a danger they will meet Jesus,'
- Has some definable and nameable leadership and governance, and
- Has traceable links to Churches of Christ in Queensland.

There was nothing unchallengeable about the definition. It was a definition created for Churches of Christ in Queensland at a particular time so that they could be accountable about how many Kingdom Communities there were; how many new ones had been started; how many people were involved, and so on. They also continued to record the historical statistics that had always been kept over the past century. The statistics provide a compelling account of the transformation that was underway through Kingdom Communities (see figure 5.2).

From the Annual Reports	2009 - 10	2016 - 17	% Growth
Total number of Kingdom Communities*	207	398	92%
Number of people regularly connecting with KCs	30,000+	40,000+	33%
Number of affiliated churches	70	69	- 1%
Average weekly attendances at affiliated churches	6,220	7,808	26%
Registered Clients receiving care	14,282	20,598	44%
Number of foster and kinship carers	667	1,000	50%
Number of Family day care and in-home carers	276	286	4%
Number of housing places	583	1,268	117%

Number of independent living units	556	1,074	93%
Number of approved operational aged care beds	1,355	1,812	34%
Number of registered volunteers	740	1,627	120%
Number of staff across all areas	2,907	3,333	15%
Total revenue ($000)	$138,970	$259,041	86%

Figure 5.2 Churches of Christ in Queensland Statistics Comparison: Financial years 2009/10 to 2016/17
* Kingdom Access Places were not defined in 2009-10. The number 207 is compiled of 64 affiliated churches, 6 indigenous fellowships, and 137 individual care services which totalled over 30,000 people connecting with all of these services.

The Tipping Point

A tipping point is a moment in time when a group, or a significant number of group members, rapidly change behaviour by widely adopting a new view of themselves and/or the world. Malcolm Gladwell, in his book *The Tipping Point: How little things can make a big difference*, defines a tipping point as, the moment of critical mass, the threshold, the boiling point. "It is the magic moment when ideas, trends and social behaviour cross a threshold, tip and spread like wildfire."[7] When a tipping point occurs, most of the group or population innately shift to the new view and act accordingly.

In 2010, the predominant worldview both at State level and among many of the smaller churches, was that Churches of Christ in Queensland was slowly dying – the first story. Many of the care services saw themselves as 'Care' first and not part of the Church and there was little, if any, identification with who Churches of Christ were as a movement or denomination.

Following the constitutional and organisational structural changes, the transformational aim was to get as many stakeholders as possible (both churches and care leaders) to shift their perspective about Churches of Christ in Queensland to the second story. This shift required

---
[7] Gladwell, M., *The Tipping Point: How Little Things Can Make A Big Difference*, London: Abacus, 2002, back cover.

the entire organisation to see, believe and start acting as though it was a movement with over two hundred presences throughout Queensland. The aim was to get enough people sharing this second view so as to create a tipping point.

As an organisational psychologist, Dean understood that, if there was a shift in the way the world occurred to people through the second story, then emotions and behaviours would also generally shift. People constantly gather their own evidence, often without being aware that they are doing so, to support the story they hold. Therefore, shifting the story involved changing the things that people automatically cued into for personal opinion and navigation. To use a metaphor, it was about changing the lens through which they saw Churches of Christ in Queensland. Steve Zaffron and Dave Logan, in their book *The Three Laws of Performance*[8], list this phenomenon of how people perform correlating to how situations occur to them. It is called their first law of performance.

There are many examples of events confronting people with jolting awareness about their subliminal attitudes (including prejudices and biases) towards others. A current example is with refugees. To believe the media headlines would be to assume that many refugees are terrorists or looking to 'bludge' off Australian welfare. When you actually meet and get to know these people you discover they are not very different from us, with their own dreams for freedom, opportunity and safety. Jesus' parable of the Good Samaritan (found in Luke 10:25-37) is a powerful story that confronts preconceived views about the way the world can be seen.

Stephen Covey, the author of *Seven habits of highly effective people*, describes a shift in the way a situation occurred for him while travelling on the New York subway on a Sunday morning.

> *" People were sitting quietly - some reading newspapers, some lost in thought, some resting with their eyes closed. It was a calm, peaceful scene. Then suddenly, a man and his children entered the subway car. The children were so loud and rambunctious that instantly the whole climate changed.*
>
> *The man sat down next to me and closed his eyes, apparently oblivious*

---

[8] Steve Zaffron, & Dave Logan, *The Three Laws of Performance: Rewriting the Future of your Organization and your Life*, San Francisco: Jossey-Bass, 2009.

to the situation. The children were yelling back and forth, throwing things, even grabbing people's papers. It was very disturbing. And yet, the man sitting next to me did nothing.

It was difficult not to feel irritated. I could not believe that he could be so insensitive to let his children run wild like that and do nothing about it, taking no responsibility at all. It was easy to see that everyone else on the subway felt irritated, too. So finally, with what I felt was unusual patience and restraint, I turned to him and said, "Sir, your children are really disturbing a lot of people. I wonder if you couldn't control them a little more?"

The man lifted his gaze as if to come to a consciousness of the situation for the first time and said softly, 'Oh, you're right. I guess I should do something about it. We just came from the hospital where their mother died about an hour ago. I don't know what to think, and I guess they don't know how to handle it either.'

Can you imagine what I felt at that moment? My paradigm shifted. Suddenly I saw things differently, I felt differently, I behaved differently. My irritation vanished. I didn't have to worry about controlling my attitude or my behaviour; my heart was filled with the man's pain. Feelings of sympathy and compassion flowed freely. "Your wife just died? Oh, I'm so sorry. Can you tell me about it? What can I do to help?" Everything changed in an instant.[9]

Communications

A very deliberate strategy was undertaken to promote the new story about who Churches of Christ in Queensland was and what they stood for. This was not about spinning a concocted position, as both stories were still true. It was about deliberately promoting the life-giving story rather than allowing the dying story to dictate feelings and behaviour. Communications were to become essential in building toward the new tipping point.

A monthly magazine called Networking was published with stories and photos that reflected the story that Churches of Christ in

---

[9] Stephen R. Covey, *The Seven Habits of Highly Effective People: Restoring the Character Ethic*, New York: Rosetta LLC, 1989, 30-31.

Queensland had over two hundred Kingdom Communities where at least some people were fiercely committed to forwarding the gospel and had a heart to become part of a transforming movement that again focused on the essentials of Jesus. The magazine was backed up by a new website and development of a social media strategy that promoted regular examples across the Movement of who they were, what they stood for and how striving to authentically live out this commitment was making a difference across the State. Whenever Dean was asked to preach in a church the same message was told of who they were, what they stood for, and the possibilities of renewal.

It was a big undertaking to get a hard copy of the Networking Magazine out every month, as well as to build a social media presence from scratch to 14,000 followers, but it proved to be very important in helping everyone associated with Churches of Christ in Queensland to hear the new story that the Movement was up and about and there were already two hundred Kingdom Communities making a difference in local areas across the State. Instead of isolated silos, there was again a shared sense of everyone being a part of one movement focused on forwarding the gospel through a holistic strategy – bringing love and uplift where it was most needed – physically, mentally, emotionally and spiritually.

Finding a Common Mission

As people were encouraged to live into the new story of being one movement, it became clear that it would be of great assistance if everyone shared a common mission or purpose that provided a compass point for everything we did. So, the question became: What is it that everyone would put their hand up for to say "Yes! I'm committed to that"? Previously there were separate plans, separate mission statements, different names and branding, separate marketing taglines and separate strategy documents. They reflected the separate silos of activities that Churches of Christ had fallen into and from which they had now chosen to move away. Many local churches had even dropped 'Church of Christ' from their name in favour of calling themselves an unrelated name, which probably reflected the fact that they no longer saw advantage in being associated with the Churches of Christ brand. They did not want to be associated with the old story of identity.

On the listening tours around the State in Dean's first months, he heard and read of each area's desire and targets for growth. For example, the aged care services spoke of having more aged care beds with higher occupancy; the childcare services spoke of having more child care places with higher occupancy; the housing services spoke of having more social and affordable housing units and more clients; and the local churches spoke of having higher Sunday attendances and new church plants. Everyone desired numerical growth in their domain. In fact, people were already praying for God to increase their domains and provide much needed growth in numbers. Behind the prayer there was a back story of increasing financial difficulty caused by falling numbers and a clear lack of unity.

On Dean's first trip to St George (an outback town just over five hundred kilometres west of Brisbane), he visited Churches of Christ in Queensland's aged care service called Warrawee. The Movement provided the only residential aged care service in that community. After greeting, meeting and touring the facilities, Dean asked the staff if they could direct him to the Churches of Christ child care service in St George. He was met with blank looks. The fact that Churches of Christ also provided the only childcare service in St George seemed to be unknown to the staff members at Warrawee. This was a problem of branding because the childcare centre was called Tom Thumb. When Tom Thumb was mentioned, the staff immediately knew where it was, although they did not know that it was owned and operated by the same organisation that owned and operated Warrawee.

The point of this story is that the two services operated totally independently of each other in the same small community (population 2,647 at 2011 census). Warrawee was part of the aged care stream that reported up to an area manager and general manager for aged care. Tom Thumb was part of the child care stream that reported up to a different area manager and general manager for child youth and family services. St George was a small community, yet it was later discovered that in some cases, Churches of Christ in Queensland were caring for children in the childcare centre and their grandparents in the aged care centre. Churches of Christ were intimately connected with families without realising it. Similarly, in many communities, the Movement's local church had little, if any knowledge of, or involvement with, the care services in the same community and vice versa. Sadly, this silo approach had become entrenched in communities all over Queensland. Good care and ministry was being completed but the focus of leaders was on delivering and growing their own services without any notion of collaboration with others, let alone asking what the community most needed.

In mid-2011, seventy or so of the State's leaders came together for a retreat over several days to discuss the possibilities of the new story, and the overall desire to again have unity of purpose and collective effort. What arose out of these discussions was God-given and formative for the years to come.

The presence of God was manifest amongst the group who gathered for the retreat and on the second day there was a collective realisation and repentance of the fact that everyone was trying to grow their own work in isolation. The gathered leadership realised that they were the ones who needed to be lifting up their eyes and asking the community and God for what was most needed across the movement. Despite the genuine belief that clients and congregation members were being put first, it dawned on everyone that they were in fact putting their frameworks, goals and paradigms first.

The God-given realisation on the morning of the second day of the leadership retreat was a unanimous coalescing of hearts and minds. No matter what each leader was involved with, everyone wanted to bring more of the light of Christ into communities and to do all they could to enable the light of Christ to be shining more brightly, particularly for individuals and families doing it tough.

Bringing the light of Christ into communities became a rallying phrase and mission statement across the whole of the Movement. This meant that whether people were worshipping God on Sunday morning, teaching English to refugees, caring for an at-risk child, caring for a homeless person, caring for a frail, aged person, caring for a troubled teenager, providing coffee and pastoral care to the family of someone critically ill in hospital, providing a sense of belonging and fellowship via a men's shed, or a lady's quilting group ... whatever was being done under the umbrella of Churches of Christ in Queensland, everyone agreed that they were they were together bringing the light of Christ into communities. Together they were fulfilling the Great Commandment and Great Commission.

Matthew 22:34-40 (The Greatest Commandment),

"Hearing that Jesus had silenced the Sadducees, the Pharisees got together. One of them, an expert in the law, tested him with this question: "Teacher, which is the greatest commandment in the Law?"

Jesus replied: "'Love the Lord your God with all your heart and with all your soul and with all your mind.' This is the first and greatest commandment. And the second is like it: 'Love your neighbor as yourself.' All the Law and the Prophets hang on these two commandments."

Matthew 28:19-20 (The Great Commission),

'Therefore go and make disciples of all nations, baptizing them in the name of the Father and of the Son and of the Holy Spirit, and teaching them to obey everything I have commanded you. And surely I am with you always, to the very end of the age.'

By putting up front the collective desire to bring more of the light of Christ into communities, they were also putting at the fore their collective desire to stay true to God's three core pillars; love of God, love of neighbours, and the making of disciples.

Learning: The power of the new mission statement 'Bringing the light of Christ into communities' shifted the dominant question of individual leaders from concern only for their area, towards the wider community and also how as a part of a big team they could enable more of the light of Christ to be shone into communities. It shifted the focus from themselves to others.

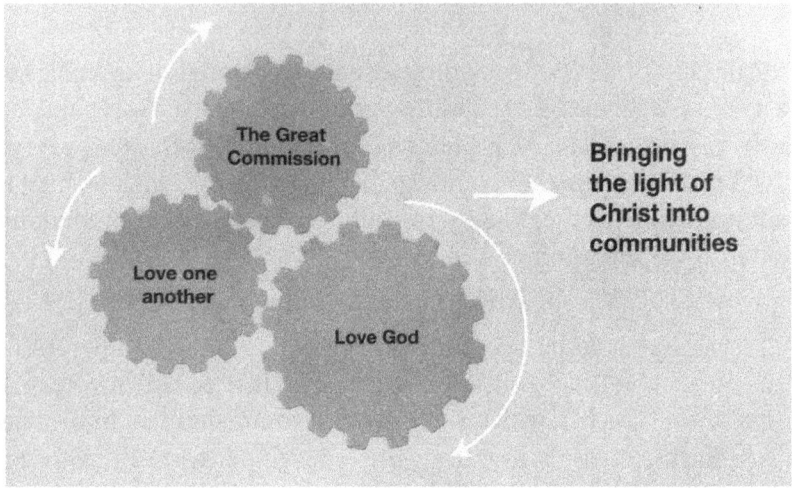

Three Pillars Fig 5.4

To address the challenge of shining more of the light of Christ into communities, the team purposefully placed the community at the centre of the model and worked with local leaders to understand what was needed. The question would no longer be how could Churches of Christ in Queensland grow their services but how could they help where there was need in the community? This opened up new and expansive questions that needed thought and reflection. These questions included the following: If they were aiming to bring more of the light of Christ, what were the greatest areas of darkness and need in each community? What were the demographics? What assets and services were already in the community? If their care services and local churches were to work together, how could they achieve better outcomes for each community? What was the best shape of involvement in the community that would be most helpful from a holistic (physical, mental, emotional and spiritual) viewpoint?

> **Learning:** Creating a mission statement that focused on uplifting others rather than growing the services Churches of Christ wanted to deliver, shifted everything; how they looked at things, the questions they asked, and strategic planning.

As those questions emerged and were unpacked, the team continued their visiting and listening to local community leaders about what was most needed to bring uplift and light to their community. Dean recalls several community leaders telling him that their community did not need another church building. They pointed out to him that there were already plenty of church buildings with underused capacity for those who wanted a Sunday worship experience. The team recognised that any argument for planting new churches needed to have a much deeper understanding of what we were trying to do and why.

In one rural community, they met with the mayor and a group of other local leaders. Dean shared about the new mission as a body that wanted to work with local leaders so as to bring uplift and therefore enable more light to shine in their community. He asked them what the greatest areas of darkness were in their community. They looked at each and then quietly answered, "Drugs! Drugs are smashing our community." Dean was taken aback as it appeared to be an idyllic community. The conversation turned to the hidden darkness of drugs and the impact on individuals, families, crime, healthcare providers and so forth. After some discussion, they directly asked him, "Could Churches of Christ help?" At the time Dean had to answer truthfully. He said that he did not know, but that Churches of Christ was committed to stay in conversation with them and bring whatever resources and networks they could, so that together they might see if a difference could be made.

In another Queensland regional community, Dean met with the head of police for the region. He was also a member of the local Church of Christ. They spoke about bringing the light of Christ into communities and Dean asked him about the greatest areas of darkness. He persisted by asking what were the issues that took up most police time in the region. The regional chief answered, "Domestic violence and drugs." A passionate conversation then pursued where the regional head of police spoke first-hand about the breakdown of culture, families and community. He felt things had deteriorated over his thirty plus years in the force and strongly supported the push to focus on bringing the light of Christ into communities. He believed the Christian faith was the best vehicle to bring any chance of rebuilding community; however, his experience was that too many church people were focused on Sunday morning services and doctrinal issues. They seemed to have little time and energy for really taking Christ's light into the darkest places. He commented that it seemed to be the case for all the denominations.

In both these encounters, the question is writ large both for Churches of Christ in Queensland then and for us today. If we stand up and say that our collective mission is to bring the light of Christ into communities, then how can we respond to the real challenges community leaders are facing? They are challenges that don't fit into our neat and organised doctrinal boxes and church practise. During both encounters, Dean recalls thinking, as CEO of the Movement, that Churches of Christ in Queensland provides aged care, child and youth care, social housing and local churches. They don't do drug prevention or domestic violence intervention. They don't have a specialist unit that could be asked to work with those community leaders. Do they therefore say that they can't help? After all, they can't be expected to be all things to all people.

Yet, the new, clear mission statement of 'Bringing the light of Christ into communities' was more than just a feel-good aspiration. They were faced with a major challenge. They needed to be fair dinkum about putting the physical, mental, emotional and spiritual needs of the community at the centre of their response through working with those who felt similarly called to try and make a difference. They realised that their response would take them into unknown and uncomfortable places, where big questions of funding, resources, capacity and strategy all loomed large. It was a God-sized challenge.

In the Gospels of Matthew and Mark, the account of Jesus healing the sick and teaching a large crowd of over five thousand is told (Matt 14:13-21 & Mark 6:30-44). As evening approached, the disciples indicated he should send them away, so they could buy themselves some food. It seemed a sensible and pastoral observation. They had very limited resources and no obligation to the crowd. After all, Jesus was tired before he had even started the day and, out of the goodness of his heart, he had spent hours teaching and healing their sick. In terms of fairness, it should have been the other way around. The crowd should have provided food for Jesus and the disciples.

Yet, Jesus said to his disciples, "They do not need to go away. You give them something to eat". This defied logic as the crowd only had a few loaves of bread and a couple of fish between them. Jesus asked them to bring what they had, and then he did the rest. The gospels recall that the number of those who ate was about five thousand men, besides women and children, with twelve basketfuls of broken pieces left over.

It was a miracle. It was a miracle that has since been repeated throughout history when faithful and committed disciples brought whatever they had to Jesus, and trusted and believed in God's ability to feed and care for his people. Jesus commanded us to love God with all our heart, mind and soul and love our neighbours as we love ourselves. He commissioned his followers to show and teach people the way of life he had lived and taught. There were no qualifiers to the commission. There was no preamble or safety clause that exempted discomfort or allowed release if circumstances didn't fit with strategy and resources.

In an address he gave in 1912, William Booth, the founder of the Salvation Army, said,

"*While women weep, as they do now, I'll fight*
While little children go hungry, as they do now, I'll fight
While men go to prison, in and out, in and out, as they do now, I'll fight
While there is a drunkard left,
While there is a poor lost girl upon the streets,
While there remains one dark soul without the light of God,
I'll fight - I'll fight to the very end!"

Booth articulated a heartfelt commitment. Everything else would somehow be sorted through the lens of commitment and higher priorities, especially when he didn't know how. John Wesley similarly put the call out in the 1700s, "Do all the good you can, by all the means you can, in all the ways you can, in all the places you can, at all the times you can, to all the people you can, as long as ever you can."

Martin Luther King Jr articulated, over and over, a vision of communities where black and white people were all viewed as equal children of God. In the language we've used above, King promoted a dream that was at odds with the prevailing story. His legacy flowed from his dream and commitment to seeing the kingdom realised, where all are created equal and had a place at the table of humanity. He was prepared to march, go to prison, be beaten, and ultimately give his life to that purpose. Everything was seen through the lens of that commitment, with arising problems tackled and sorted through as best they could.

Great movements are fuelled by passionate commitment to a God-given call. As Tom Wright says, "It is not so much that God's Church has a mission; but rather God's mission has a church."[10] Churches of Christ were discovering that it was the mission that needed to come first. Structure, strategy, financial plans, policies and processes needed to serve the mission.

The challenge that we need to continually address is that over time the identity and functioning of all organisations and institutions becomes what they do. They become defined by what they do and how they do it, rather than why they exist. Churches of Christ was no different but was attempting to change. The good news and key turning point was a growing awareness of the gospel call and community need, together with a collective commitment as a Council, Board, Executive Team and key local leaders, to do whatever it took to live into the new story with an overriding commitment to bringing the light of Christ into communities.

We now turn to explore the cultural, structural and strategic changes that were pursued to promote Kingdom Communities across Queensland which transformed the denomination, along with two of the theoretical frameworks that underpinned these strategies.

---

[10] Tom Wright, *Simply Christian*, New York: Harper One, 2006.

CHAPTER SIX

From Silos To Kingdom Communities

"Don't have people working in silos; have them working across the team."
Patrick Lencioni

"For the body does not consist of one member but of many. If the foot should say, "Because I am not a hand, I do not belong to the body," that would not make it any less a part of the body. And if the ear should say, "Because I am not an eye, I do not belong to the body," that would not make it any less a part of the body. If the whole body were an eye, where would be the sense of hearing? If the whole body were an ear, where would be the sense of smell? But as it is, God arranged the members in the body, each one of them, as he chose. If all were a single member, where would the body be? As it is, there are many parts, yet one body."
1 Cor 12:14-20 (ESV)

The word silo comes from the ancient Greek word *siros* which was a pit for holding grain. Today we know silos as large structures that are usually above the ground but nevertheless have the same purpose; they hold grain and keep it separated from foreign material and hazards to the purity of the stock. A couple of these brief case studies introduce us to the silos that Dean encountered in Queensland.

On one of his early travels Dean went to a town where Churches of Christ were providing aged care and child care services. The services happened to be located on land next door to each other. Dean noticed that the grass nature strip out front was mowed to a certain point and then not mowed beyond that. On enquiring about that situation, he was advised that aged care only paid for the grass to be mowed at the front of their place. Child Care was responsible for mowing the grass out the front of their place. As Churches of Christ Care owned both properties and ran both services, something was clearly amiss.

In 2011, many communities throughout Queensland were impacted by very significant floods. Many lives were lost and hundreds of thousands of homes and community facilities were devastated. There were many extraordinary examples of people rallying to help out neighbours and strangers. Churches of Christ in Queensland had industrial laundries and kitchens in most of their aged care facilities. In an attempt to mobilise the significant resources across Churches of Christ facilities in response to the emergency, Dean indicated that they should offer to take in muddy clothes, sheets and general laundry for local communities whose homes were impacted by the floods. This suggestion was met with resistance by several of the local service managers who asked; who was going to pay for it?

After being told to help each community where possible and to account for the additional cost separately, managers got on board and even began to take initiatives of their own such as making sandwiches for displaced children at a local school. The protectionist mindsets began to open up, but both of these examples reflected an underlying silo mentality within Churches of Christ in Queensland, largely driven by the system of budget setting and financial accountability processes that the organisation had set up.

The silo mentality was even enshrined in language at the time. One senior leader spelled out his view at an early Executive meeting, stating, "We (Churches of Christ in Queensland) do aged care, child care, housing and churches." He was articulating four separate sets of services (that often didn't communicate) which were clearly brought into alignment with the new mission statement, "We bring the light of Christ into communities."

Prior to taking the role as CEO of Churches of Christ in Queensland, Dean practised as an organisational psychologist. It was a rewarding and varied career and in addition to the substantial experiences he had at ministry and governance levels with Churches of Christ in Victoria and Tasmania, it prepared him well for the challenge of leadership in such a complex and transforming system of churches and care services.

In his professional practice Dean had a formative experience in 1995 when he was invited to participate in a week long gathering of

Action Learning practitioners with Professor Reg Revans. Revans was not only a brilliant academic and Olympian but also was a pioneer of Action Learning, so it was a privilege to be with him and participate in the gathering of practitioners from around the world. The gathering was convened in London by Lord Butterfield, who was a very strong advocate for the work of Professor Revans and its potential to enable effective, large scale change.[1]

Dean was greatly influenced by that week, listening and discussing first-hand the principles that Revans used to revolutionise the coal industry in service of Britain's World War II and post war demands. Revans subsequently moved to Belgium where he headed a national project aimed at raising Belgium's productivity. Working with five universities and twenty-three of the country's largest businesses, Revans' collaborative approaches succeeded in raising Belgium's industrial productivity growth rate above that of the USA, Germany and Japan. Revans was subsequently awarded with the nation's top honour by the King of Belgium, and he was later nominated for the Nobel prize.

A central piece of Revans' work was that managers learn best and produce better outcomes by engaging and learning from and with each other. He discovered that bringing together six to eight managers with shared experience in an area (for example, managers in a mine, ward managers in a hospital or experienced hands in a factory), who had some passion for solving problems and making things better in their area of work, led to real improvements on the ground. Levels of engagement, ownership, influence and practical gains were all significantly higher than the more traditional hierarchical or motivational approaches to change at the time.

Revans called these groups of team leaders 'Action Learning' groups. He found these Action Learning groups were best used for problems where there was no known or correct answer. It was in contrast to what

---

[1] See https://www.actionlearningassociates.co.uk/action-learning/reg-revans/ and Reg Revans, *ABC of Action Learning*, Surrey: Gower Publishing, 2011. Also, David L. Dotlich, & James L. Noel, *Action Learning: How the World's Top Companies are Re-creating their Leaders and Themselves*, San Francisco: Jossey-Bass, 1998, and William J. Rothwell, *The Action Learning Guidebook: A real-time strategy for Problem Solving*, Training Design, and Employee Development, San Francisco: Jossey-Bass Pfeiffer, 1999.

he called 'Programmed Knowledge,' which was all the things that had a clear and correct answer (for example, the solution to a crossword puzzle, or the quickest route of travel from Adelaide to Perth). Revans spoke about areas of endeavour that required fresh questions and thinking. He asked questions like, what was the one question, that wasn't currently known, that if an answer could be found, would significantly catapult the organisation forward?

Revans' method of operation was to set up small groups in the workplace under investigation to pursue such questions. He empowered groups of six to eight practitioners with shared experiences and emotional involvement to significantly move things forward, by meeting regularly to discuss, experiment, share learnings and agree on ways of advancing and achieving breakthroughs. Revans is the author of a widely used saying, "There can be no learning without action, and no action without learning."

Today many leading companies like Google, Space X, General Electric, Anderson Consulting, Whirlpool and the US Department of Defence employ models based on principles of Revans' work. Some principles that underpin Action Learning include:

- Attacking problems (or opportunities) not puzzles. A problem has no existing solution whereas a puzzle has a right answer that isn't presently known (for example, a crossword).
- Posing questions from conditions of ignorance, risk and confusion, when nobody (including the experts) knows what to do next.
- Learning by doing, which means experimentation and risk must take place.
- Searching for reflection from experience. The major resources that any manager has are his or her experience and knowledge of the work situation. Learning by managers consists mainly in new perceptions of what they are doing and in their changed interpretations of their past experiences. It is not any fresh program of factual data, of which they were previously ignorant but which they now have at their command that enables them to surge forward.

Put simply, Action Learning is a process where people try out new ways of doing things relevant to a specific issue or project. They follow a process of observation and reflection about what happens, learn from it, and make modifications. It is a continuous and intentional process of learning from actions taken.

Action Learning on the Sunshine Coast

In the previous chapter, we explored the first eighteen months of Churches of Christ in Queensland's journey towards unity of mission and one common story. Once there was genuine ownership and commitment of the new mission (Bringing the light of Christ into communities) there needed to be a way to harness the enthusiasm and give legs to the energy around how the new mission would be implemented. Describing an attractive vision was important, but the words would become hollow unless there was a practical, on the ground strategy that engaged people to move ahead. The easier part of being a leader was to talk up a vision. The harder part was the implementation of strategies that encouraged and enabled people to actually move toward their preferred future. Talk was easy. The challenge before the leadership team was how were they going to bring more of the light of Christ into communities?

The experience on the Sunshine Coast was an important step forward. Having been explained by Dean, the leadership personnel concerned decided to use Revans' model of Action Learning as a way of moving forward into the unknown. They initiated a small learning group to explore a possible way forward by inviting local leaders from the wider community, including local ministers, local care managers, and other passionate local leaders. These people were invited to come together to grapple with the question of how can Churches of Christ in Queensland enable more of the light of Christ to shine in that community (in this case the Sunshine Coast)?

This question was a good Action Learning question. It was not a puzzle that had a predetermined correct answer. There were any number of possible answers. Therefore, it was a challenge that needed to be wrestled with. The answer and implementation for that community, at that point in time, was interwoven with the commitment and passion of the people who answered the question and came up with a possible strategy.

The site of the Sunshine Coast was deliberately chosen as 'low hanging fruit.' There were three strong local churches and several well-regarded care services in the area. The then Senior Minister at Nambour Church of Christ was an early adopter of the idea and he had already built good relations with the neighbouring Church of Christ Sanctuary Park Seniors Village and developed active ministries engaging with the wider community. He championed the Action Learning group idea locally and encouraged the other local leaders to participate. So, eight local leaders started meeting for the first time to look at what Churches of Christ in Queensland might be able to do to enable more of the light of Christ to be shining on the Sunshine Coast, beyond the services that were already offered.

The Action Learning group was named a Strategic Action Leadership Team (SALT), which emphasised Jesus' metaphor for why and how his followers should engage in missional presence: to be the salt of the earth and the light of the world (Matt 5:13-16).

The first thing the SALT discovered was that they had no common idea of what the major areas of darkness and need were on the Sunshine Coast. This was despite the fact that each of them provided particular services in the local area. Therefore, research was undertaken to determine what were local areas of need or darkness. Interestingly, men's health emerged as a major issue, despite the sun and sea and apparent idyllic retirement destination of the Sunshine Coast. They learned that there was a hidden story of significant depression, mental and physical health needs and a high suicide rate amongst men. It was largely hidden because men would not talk about it or seek help but was well known to wives and healthcare professionals on the Sunshine Coast.

The idea for a men's shed emerged from the SALT discussions. It was the first men's shed for the region and was carefully and creatively designed as a way of creating a Kingdom Community with a focus on men's mental health. Once the SALT agreed to the strategy there was high energy to roll out the men's shed. Through brainstorming, cooperation and networking, spare land was identified next door to the Churches of

Christ Care retirement village at Nambour. Through local contacts, a huge shed was donated by one of the big companies who had written it off after recent floods. Men from the churches and retirement village excitedly became involved, and a big hardware chain donated equipment through its community fund to support the fitting out being done by the team of volunteers. Incredibly, up to one hundred men (and supportive partners) became involved in the birth of a new Kingdom Community.

Opening of Men's shed Fig 6.1

In the middle of this activity, a former church minister, Mark, emerged as a natural leader for the group. He felt that God was calling him to this work. He loved working alongside the guys. Mark was given a title of Mission Action Partner (MAP), as the role evolved into something more than being a chaplain, although it certainly involved chaplaincy. The role had an apostolic and entrepreneurial side to it, as part of Mark's calling was to establish other men's sheds and Kingdom Communities. He intentionally sought out others who could partner in order to enable more of the light of Christ to uplift and transform the lives of individuals, families and communities in other places.

Supported by the SALT, Mark had a huge impact and led the introduction of healthcare sessions through inviting local GPs and health professionals to come and talk at the shed about topics like prostate and bowel cancer and mental health matters. As relationships started to form, it became known that some blokes were doing it "real tough". They were battling hard realties like depression, loss of the family farm following severe financial stress, or quietly battling cancer.

Bowl Fig 6.2

Mark suggested that prayers be offered in support of these guys and a regular prayer group naturally formed. Tim, the Senior Minister from the Nambour Church of Christ, was also actively involved and before long numbers started to swell at his church on Sunday mornings. The shed was not designed as a strategy to increase Sunday morning attendances, however, it seemed to naturally occur. A number of the men said that they went to Church years ago but had drifted away. They could relate to Mark, who was also a member of Nambour Church of Christ, and also to Tim, who happened to also be Chair of the SALT that established the men's shed. Some men felt they wanted to bring their family back to reconnect again, as it was a place that was community minded, relaxed, relevant and caring.

The other interesting thing that happened was that the guys started making toy trains and doll houses to give to Churches of Christ child care centres along with many other projects. They also became involved in helping some of the farmers that were doing it tough, thus building further relationships and shining more light in the community. They decided to do a display stand at the annual Nambour Show to profile the men's shed. An exercise book was available for anyone to put their

Chapter Six: From Silos To Kingdom Communities

contact details down if they were interested in joining. Over 200 put their details down.

This experience provided more community connection and growth in one year than Churches of Christ had witnessed anywhere in Queensland for two decades. It was catalysed by local leaders coming together because they were passionate about seeing what might be done to bring uplift and shine the light of Christ into one area of darkness in their community.

This work continued to grow with other men's sheds commencing through the collaboration of local church and care service leaders across Queensland. In a few years Nambour, Mackay, Townsville, Bribie Island, and Toowoomba had men's sheds running in collaboration with local churches and care services. The momentum generated by the shed gatherings and an expanding desire to shine the light of Christ to those doing it tough, also expanded to teams who provided food relief, practical help and pastoral care to farmers and rural communities affected by bushfires, drought and floods. Today, thousands of lives have been impacted in Queensland communities that would not have been reached through more traditional models of church alone.

Action Learning in Townsville

In North Queensland, a SALT was formed by local leaders from Churches of Christ in Queensland's child, youth and family care services in the area, indigenous leaders and several people who were keen to birth a new faith community in Townsville.[2] Facilitated by Churches of Christ in Queensland's new Executive Team, the Action Learning question was, 'How can we best bring more of the light of Christ into the Townsville community?'

What followed was quite extraordinary. Having followed a process of wrestling and research, the Townsville SALT envisioned an integrated campus that would bring together all of Churches of Christ in Queensland's services and active people onto one site. They dreamed of

---

[2] There had previously been a Church of Christ local church in Townsville but it had folded following a number of years of difficulties. The 2010 Conference Council were very keen to see a new Church of Christ church rebirthed in Townsville.

a campus that was big enough to invite other like-minded organisations to also come together onto one site. Churches of Christ care services had staff providing separate child, youth and family services out of rental premises across Townsville. There were also separate and unconnected efforts being made by Churches of Christ people with indigenous folk from the area. The SALT wanted to create a space where worship services could be held on the campus.

The new Churches of Christ worship centre on the Townsville campus Figure 6.3

Because there was already better and integrated communication across the many areas (formerly silos) of Churches of Christ in Queensland, the property manager was made aware of a site that initially seemed way beyond what might be possible to purchase. It was originally a campus of James Cook University and had been sold to developers who subsequently went into receivership. The site had been unoccupied for several years. Churches of Christ were able to acquire the substantial campus, whose zoning was locked for community use, from the receivers for a greatly reduced figure.

The site was made fit for purpose, and all of Churches of Christ in Queensland's existing services were relocated onto the site. Church services were commenced in an old gymnasium space under the leadership of Barry, a Churches of Christ minister who had recently returned to Townsville from ministry in the USA. Despite having suffered a stroke, he offered to help out and eventually became the first minister and chaplain for the site, helping to shape a holistic Christian culture of the new campus.

Having established the new integrated campus, Churches of Christ in Queensland was soon after invited to take over a retirement village across the road which was experiencing financial difficulties. A deal was struck, and the group of elderly folk living in 120 units were successfully integrated into the wider community family with a sense of belonging and connectedness that they didn't previously experience.

The Indigenous community at the same Townsville campus Figure 6.4

Arising out of the SALT's discussions, a large men's shed was built on the campus in one of the vacant buildings, and today is enthusiastically used by men from the church, retirement village, and many others in the community. Subsequent to the men's shed they also opened a women's shed! Also, suitably screened men are working in conjunction with the primary school across the road to provide mentoring for kids who do not have a dad.

These, and many other initiatives, all grew out of a SALT comprised of a group of local leaders who had a growing desire to enable more of the light of Christ to be shone in Townsville. In the space of a few years, Churches of Christ in Queensland had gone from having no local church and separate care services, provided out of different rented premises, to a thriving integrated Kingdom Community, providing a whole range of spiritual, mental, emotional and physical love and support to the wider community. Along the way other common mission organisations have also moved onto the campus, renting office space and contributing to the life of the community. Today, the Churches of Christ's Vincent Campus in Townsville is well known and regarded by the community and government and is seen as a major community presence in the area.

Churches of Christ's Vincent Campus in Townsville Figure 6.5

Shining more light

Having commenced the initial SALT on the Sunshine Coast in 2011, by 2017 there were thirty SALTs operating in communities throughout Queensland. Each SALT was comprised of local leaders who were passionate about enabling more of the light of Christ to shine in their community. They were typically comprised of local Churches of Christ ministers, Elders and care service managers, but also increasingly local community representatives were also coming on board. For example, in two cases the local Shire mayors became members of the SALT for their community. Each SALT gathered together to research their region, in terms of current missional activity and also the opportunities for future mission. They each devised a Mission Action Strategy for their region. Mission Action Strategies were developed in conjunction with relevant specialist areas (for example, building development, finance, or government), provided with assistance of the Churches of Christ in Queensland Executive Team.

Many new Kingdom Communities (as described in chapter 5) have been established. Some look like local faith communities, as we have typically known them, coming together in fellowship to worship on Sunday and sharing Communion. Some look like men's sheds. Some look like cafes on main streets, such as the Atherton Access Place described in the Introduction. Some have even been new intensive family support centres established in conjunction with the State Government. More recently two new social and affordable housing complexes (with ninety new units in total) were constructed in two different communities to provide much needed accommodation for the socially disadvantaged and homeless, together with four new integrated campuses and faith communities to provide for seniors in their communities.

Each of these has come about through being identified by the relevant SALT as a much needed way of bringing more of the light of Christ into their community. Each has been designed with holistic outcomes in mind considering the physical, mental, emotional and spiritual needs of the community. Each is being built so as to provide a place where people might meet Jesus and access something of the kingdom of God. Each Kingdom Community is intended to be a tangible expression of the gospel.

The shape and form of each Kingdom Community emerges from local leaders meeting together over time to really do the hard work of understanding their community. They are committed to learn what is most needed and what might be done together. The greatest needs cannot always be met, but inevitably as the SALT members have prayed, researched and enquired about their vision, a door has opened to make a difference in some way.

It is not an unrealistic process either. The Mission Action Strategy that underpins each project has to be financially sustainable. The building or purchase of new campuses has generally been financed by Churches of Christ in Queensland through investments and donations, with payback being provided by Local, State and Federal government funding to provide needed care services in the community.

After six years, ten Mission Action Partners across the State were able to be funded through community support to work with the SALTs and key community stakeholders. Each of the MAPs is a trained, endorsed minister with apostolic gifting. Their job is to facilitate the forwarding of the mission by leading and implementing the Mission Action Strategy of the SALT.

Becoming a Learning Organisation

In addition to Action Learning, a second key framework that shaped Churches of Christ in Queensland's leadership thinking around identity and mission strategy was the body of work on leadership action and organisational learning by Chris Argyris.[3] Argyris was Professor Emeritus at Harvard Business School until his death in 2013. He was known as one of the founders of organisational development in addition to his seminal work on developing learning organisations.

Argyris, along with Donald Schön, argued that people have mental maps that guide them on how to act in various situations. This affects the way they plan, implement and review their actions. It is these maps that guide actions rather than the theories they espouse. Their research found that most people are not aware of the maps or theories they do use and there is commonly a split between people's espoused theory and how they actually act. They comment,

"When someone is asked how he would behave under certain circumstances, the answer he usually gives is his espoused theory of

---

[3] Chris Argyris, *Knowledge for Action: A Guide to Overcoming Barriers to Organizational Change*, San Francisco: Jossey Bass, 1993.

action for that situation. This is the theory of action to which he gives allegiance, and which, upon request, he communicates to others. However, the theory that actually governs his actions is his theory-in-use". [4]

For Argyris and Schön, learning involves the detection and correction of error. When something goes wrong or is not working, most people look for another way that will address and work within their governing variables. In other words, goals, plans, rules and values are operationalised rather than questioned. People follow the tried and true ways they have learned. This is what Argyris and Schön called *single-loop learning*.

Charles Schultz captured the phenomenon well in one of his well known 'Peanuts' cartoons. Charlie asks Linus and Snoopy, "What are you guys doing?" They look up and explain that, "We're helping Lucy plant her garden ... first we spaded it ... now we're planting it." Linus then adds, "Actually, we just do what we're told." Charlie then asks, "Well it looks nice ... what are you planting?" They answer, "French Fries." The garden is filled with half planted, cold French Fries! It's funny, but we do the same thing too often.

An alternative response to *single-loop learning*, is to question the assumptions and governing variables themselves. This is what they describe as *double-loop learning*. Such learning is riskier and more difficult, but if managed well, leads to a change of the governing variables and shifts the way in which strategies and consequences are framed and intended. *Single-loop learning* is present when goals, values, frameworks, and the range of options in the way we do things, are taken for granted. The emphasis is on technique and making them more efficient. Any reflection is directed towards making the strategy being used more effective. The questions are, how can we fix this? How can we do it better? *Double-loop learning*, in contrast, involves questioning the role of the framing and learning systems which underlie the goals and strategies. Instead of doing things right, the question becomes, are we doing the right things?

---

[4] Argyris & Schön, *Theory in Practice. Increasing Professional Effectiveness*, 6-7. The gendered language is reflective of the date of authorship.

The underlying theory, supported by decades of empirical research, is that the reasoning processes employed by individuals in organisations inhibit the exchange of relevant information in ways that make *double-loop learning* difficult and all but impossible in situations where much is at stake. This creates a dilemma, as these are the very organisational situations in which *double-loop learning* is most needed.

Argyris' conclusions seem to coalesce with Thomas Kuhn, who popularised the term 'paradigm shift' in his book *The Structure of Scientific Revolution*.[5] Kuhn indicated that even in the scientific field, a paradigm shift has all the hallmarks of what religion calls a major conversion. Those who hold to the old paradigm will defend it as being the truth, or right way, and will ignore and even not see evidence to the contrary. Kuhn said that paradigm shifts become necessary when the plausibility structure of the previous paradigm becomes so full of holes and patchwork fixes that a complete overhaul, which once looked utterly threatening, now becomes a lifeline.

The paradigms of the past century on church and denominational life (as explored earlier in this book) have shaped our understandings of our operating systems and models. This is why many ministers and denominational executives are asking how many people are attending in our buildings, rather than what it means to be followers of Jesus and agents of the kingdom of God. This is central to our rediscovery and development of the concept of Kingdom Communities.

Churches of Christ in Queensland

As outlined earlier, Churches of Christ in Queensland's situation in 2008/9 had become dire, and its viability was at stake. As well as fighting internally, they existed within the wider context of Australians' declining involvement and interest in Christianity. All mainline denominations have been witnessing a declining trend in church attendances (except where there is migration) and even Pentecostal churches have plateaued. More specific detail about this data was covered in chapter one.

---

[5] Thomas Kuhn, *The Structure of Scientific Revolution*, Chicago: University of Chicago Press, 2012.

Churches of Christ local churches were similarly operating in this wider context as a visit to any of them demonstrated. In many churches, the stress of declining numbers and finances, coupled with distrust of the Conference State Office and the silo of Care Services, produced an environment where people had retreated into their bunkers. Independent, *single-loop learning* was largely the only way of operating.

In meetings with local church leaders, Dean heard examples over and over of *single-loop learning* strategies. Typical responses were to see if they could fix the problem of declining membership and Sunday numbers by changing the style of the worship services; or by implementing a wonderful new programme; or by making the sermons more topical; or by making the services more seeker-sensitive; or by improving the signage; or by improving the newsletter or website; or by developing better greeters; or by improving the pastoral care follow up; or by developing their social media presence; or by fixing the building; or by finding a new (younger?) minister, among other ideas.

Single-loop learning is bound by a given 'box' mind set. If the box doesn't work, then we change things in the box. The box itself is never questioned. In the case of advancing the gospel, the box that has developed over a long period of time, that is often understood as the only way of doing this, is church services. Hence, if Sunday numbers and finances are not going well, churches look for better ways of doing and promoting the service rather than exploring alternative ways to advance the kingdom.

All of the strategies mentioned above have merit and have been implemented with enthusiasm in many churches with varying degrees of success. However, the problem of overall declining numbers, abandonment by the younger generations and loss of adherence to Christianity in Australia has continued downwards. Even as more and more local churches struggle and close, much energy is spent on techniques and tactics of getting people into the building, rather than going to them, wherever they are.

Dean snapped a photo of a grand church building he came across in Scotland. It had a large sign out the front promoting a new organ. Of all the things a church could promote to their community about who they are and what they are on about, presumably the leaders thought advertising the new organ would encourage people to come to their church service. Many churches may not use a shiny, new, expensive organ but they do fall for similar tactics.

Double-loop learning actually questions 'the box' itself. It asks; what assumptions are being made about the shape and size of the box in which we are operating? If things are not working the way they should, it asks whether or not the box itself is the problem. In the church context, local churches have looked for other ways of connecting outside of the Sunday morning service box. However, the aim is usually centred with getting people onto their property or into their programs, usually then with the hope of getting them onto their property and into their existing worship services. Worship attendance is by and large the most valued metric that church leaders speak. For example, in recent interview as a part of the opening of a new worship centre, a minister said to a regional newspaper, "Primarily it's about who we are and how we want to function and work together throughout the week, especially for our Sunday services, which are our largest gathering." This a very common sentiment.

The following model was framed from the research of Argyris with later thinking from Romme and Witteloostuiin.[6] It incorporates a further level, called (unsurprisingly) *triple-loop learning*. *Triple-loop learning* goes deeper again than single and *double-loop learning*, bypassing goals and strategies and begins with the question of identity. This includes questions like, who are we? Why do we exist? What do we stand for? What is God saying to us today? Has our context changed and what does that say we should be doing given who God has called us to be?

This means that, instead of fixing things in the box (single-loop) or climbing out of the box to reshape or move it (double-loop), we start with who we are and why we exist, and then design and build a box (or maybe not a box, maybe something very different to a box) from scratch that will best accommodate our mission and context today (triple-loop). As outlined earlier, in the Churches of Christ in Queensland case study,

---

[6] See A. Georges, L. Romme, & Arjen van Witteloostuijn, "Circular organizing and *triple-loop learning*," Journal of Organisational Change Management, Vol. 12, Iss 5, 1999, 439-454.

Dean discovered when he commenced in 2010 that there were two valid stories that people were operating with about identity, or who they really were. Those two stories were essentially the mental maps that had led to how people were behaving and feeling.

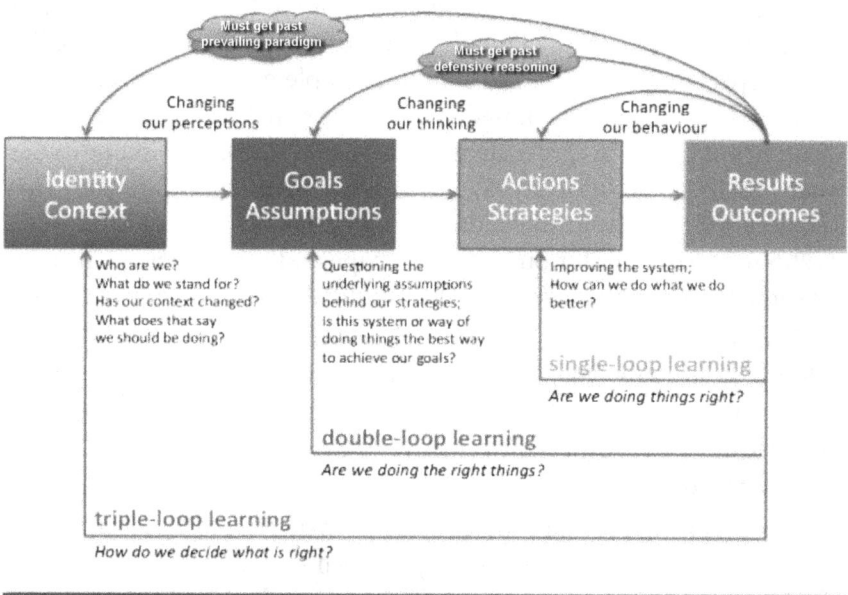

Figure 6.6 – Individual and organisational Learning: triple-loop learning

The discussions with local community leaders who made special comments about how much they appreciated what the Church was doing in their community, challenged the mental map that many in Churches of Christ were holding about what constituted being a church. In effect, this forced *double-loop learning* consideration by asking; what does it mean to be a Church of Christ?

Churches of Christ in Queensland found themselves in triple-loop territory through the framing of the idea of Kingdom Communities. As described earlier, the term Kingdom Community came from searching for new language that would bypass the mental maps (the prevailing box) of being a church or being a care service. Instead of Churches of Christ's identity being seventy churches and lots of care sites running services, they could become two hundred places where the kingdom of God was being expressed in some way.

Framing the new possibility that every place could become a Kingdom Community sent the staff and leadership on a journey back to basics. Jesus talked about the kingdom of God and the kingdom of heaven far more than the church, as we explored in chapter two. The four gospels only mention the church a couple of times, whereas Jesus talked at length about the kingdom. They wrestled with the question; if Churches of Christ in Queensland re-imagined Kingdom Communities, what did the Bible have to say about what these could be like? They asked; if we go back to the source of Christianity, what did that show us about possibilities for our identity, shape and function as a Christian movement today? They were very profound, Action Learning questions.

Grappling with these questions required an understanding of the cultural context of Queensland in the twenty-first century, as well as the people within Churches of Christ who were resistant to change. The senior leaders were especially sensitive to the church practises that were seen as part of their identity and culture.

The graph at the start of chapter Five (**figure 5.1**), showed the declining results from the changing modern ministry context in which Churches of Christ was operating. That context had been changing for the previous fifty years with declining church membership and changing demographic patterns due to migration, individualism and mobility. So, while it was exciting for Churches of Christ leaders to freshly imagine lots of new places where people could access the kingdom of God, they also knew that in practice it would be tough, especially when most Australians don't really care.

It is certainly a truism that people dislike change, especially to practises that are a part of their identity and culture. Yet, the history of progress is a story of individuals being brave enough to climb outside of the prevailing 'box' in search of a solution to a major problem. Seeing that the box itself is the problem can be very daunting. And as history has shown us, the church, like many other institutions and regimes, has resisted questioning and defended its mental maps. Sometimes it has been with blunt tools like bullying, excommunication or even death. Leaders of institutions are generally positive about *single-loop learning* and improving what they are doing. Higher level leaders will engage in *double-loop learning* discussions about why they are doing what they do. However, few people appreciate leaders who challenge practices that threaten part of the organisation's identity. Defensiveness, rationalisation, resistance, and fighting perceived threats tend to be the escalating responses towards such change agents.

Transition is always painful, confusing, messy and sometimes even bloody. The story of Exodus is a classic account of God's people in the wilderness for forty years and the struggles of Moses and others in shaping a new 'map' to take the people to the promised land. The journey took decades and was variously embraced and resisted. There were moments when the people returned to worshipping old idols and they even cried out for Egypt, where they were in slavery.[7]

Without a desert or slavery, there were some similarities within Churches of Christ in Queensland and the story of the Israelites exodus. There was widespread agreement that they needed to leave 'Egypt' and the change in the constitution at the end of 2009 (after years of conflict and reviews), was met with some excitement. The election of a new Council who appointed a new Board with a new CEO demonstrated belief and resolve, albeit still cautious in many quarters, that they might move ahead to 'better land.' There was a common intent to regain a sense of being a unified, missional movement of God's people again.

Others thought the new changes meant that things would be 'fixed' and that the new leadership would bring the care services to heel, while others thought that the priority would be to strengthen the local churches by resourcing them better to do what they have always done. Both expectations were examples of *single-loop learning*. For some, who had already been trying to experiment with fresh ways of being church, as well as for Care leaders who were striving to demonstrate that they were in fact delivering the gospel, there was a hope that the new leadership would expand the space to legitimize what they were doing – in other words, *double-loop learning*. For some there was a simple wish

---

[7] William Bridges, *Transitions: Making Sense of Life's Changes*, Cambridge: Perseus Books, 2004. Bridges has researched and written much about the cycle of endings, transitions and new beginnings.

that the fighting would end, that everyone would just play nicely, and they could get back to each group's separate purposes.

However, across the wider denomination, there were enough leaders who were so dissatisfied with how things had deteriorated, they were willing to grapple with *triple-loop learning* questions. These were the people who asked; if we are to be truly Churches of Christ, what does that say we should be doing? Ironically, the Restoration Movement, from which Churches of Christ was birthed, arose as a result of leaders like Barton Stone and Alexander Campbell, asking similar triple-loop questions. Their questions were about what it meant to be a faithful community of God's people on the frontiers of America a couple of centuries ago. They too climbed out of the prevailing 'box' of theology and church practice by leaving their denominationalism and its ingrained practices so as to dedicate themselves to questions of how. These questions were centred upon a search for the original intentions of Jesus and how the body of Christ could be restored. Their intent was to organise an association of people seeking to grow as a faith community based on the Bible and the simplicity of the early church. This included ideas about the ministry of all believers, weekly Communion, baptism through immersion and congregational autonomy.

This meant that, in a concerted effort to take Churches of Christ in Queensland back to first principles, questions had to be asked like; 'If we are to truly become Churches of Christ, how can we best express this in the Australian context? What is the best way we can forward the good news of Jesus Christ today in Australia?' We have written this book because we think that the answers are becoming clearer for the Australian church because of the deep grappling of local leaders in communities across Queensland (as well as the many other contexts we are acknowledging) who have sought ways to see how they might best enable the light of Christ to shine further in their community.

Bringing the Kingdom in Roma

Another of Dean's early meetings was with the Minister of Roma Church of Christ. It had around ninety folk who met on a Sunday morning. Roma is a community of around 7000 people, six hours drive west of Brisbane. It is the centre of a rich pastoral and wheat-growing district that has had boom and bust cycles associated with mining in recent years. The two of them had been discussing the church and ministry in the community and as they stood outside the front of the main building, Dean asked if there was anything the Conference State office could do to help the church in their mission of bringing more of the light of Christ into their community?

The minister pointed to a duplex house on the property next door to the church and commented that it was owned by Churches of Christ in Queensland Care. He said he didn't know what Care used it for but there were often young guys partying on the weekend and they would leave empty alcohol bottles in the front yard. As Dean looked, he saw that the yard and nature strip abutting the church were unkempt. It was not a good look for people coming to church on Sunday morning. The minister said that he had made enquiries to head office in recent years but they had gone nowhere.

Dean undertook to find out more and promised to get back to him. When he got back to his office he convened a meeting of relevant people from property and development, finance and mission. He asked about the Roma situation. As it turned out, Churches of Christ Care had purchased the property next door to the church with the aim of providing some affordable housing. This had not occurred, and it was being rented to a mining company who used it to accommodate trainers when they flew in to train their mining workers in the region. At the time, Care received around $2500 per month rental income for the arrangement. They reflected that the situation was not very missional when looked at through a lens of bringing more of the light of Christ into the Roma community.

After some research, it was discovered that Roma was the main regional health centre and when someone was admitted to hospital from outlying areas, accompanying relatives struggled to find accommodation. The mining boom resulted in motel and rental properties generally being full and the costs were prohibitive for many struggling families. There were growing incidences of families sleeping in their car at a time when they already had a lot of stress associated with family health issues and finances. A number of church members really wanted to try and do something about this concern. The Church put a proposal to Dean offering volunteers to paint and fit out the property to make it suitable for families. They even offered to coordinate bookings and pastorally care for those staying overnight.

Dean suggested that Care terminate the lease with the mining company for the property and allow the church to use the duplex house to bring some uplift to the community situation. This suggestion was met with strong resistance. The argument was that the asset was owned by Care, a Public Benevolent Institution (PBI), which meant that the approximate $30,000 income per annum must remain within the PBI. In other words, allowing the church to use the asset freely would be a breach of PBI legislation and it would be a loss of $30,000 to Care.

Churches of Christ Care was then turning over one hundred million dollars annually and Dean argued that they could afford to sacrifice $30,000 per annum for this mission which was, in fact, consistent with the original use intended by Care (for example, affordable accommodation). Additionally, he argued, the use of the asset to provide much needed housing was entirely consistent with the PBI Objects of Care. The church voluntarily coordinating the use of this PBI asset was not in breach of the PBI constitution. The instruction was given to terminate the lease and advise the church that the head office would work with them to provide much needed accommodation for people who had a child family member in hospital. The church was naturally very pleased with the outcome and was able to practise as a Kingdom Community in a particular area of need.

With the benefit of hindsight, this seems like a straightforward decision. Yet at the time it was not a simple decision. It was an example of how entrenched thinking had become. When the decision was made, Dean could see in their eyes how several of those present were unhappy. They were likely thinking that they had this newcomer from interstate who didn't understand PBIs and was going to favour the churches. Under the new structure though, both the churches and Care operations were to work together to shine the light of Christ (and there was no inappropriate misuse of PBI rules). So, there was nowhere to go other than to implement the decision. This, and many similar decisions in the early years, made through the lens of mission, gradually shifted the understanding and culture so that everything would be examined through the new lens of enabling more of the light of Christ to shine in each community.

Kingdom Community for the Aged

For some years Churches of Christ had run the Moonah Park nursing home in the Brisbane suburb of Mitchelton. Moonah Park provided quality care to frail and elderly residents. With the new mission of bringing more of the light of Christ into communities through integration and connectedness across Churches of Christ areas, discussions turned to this important care facility. Through the work of a SALT and an undergirding philosophy of becoming a Kingdom Community, a much bigger plan was envisioned for the centre in the Mitchelton community.

Adjoining properties were acquired, and successful submissions made to the Federal and State Governments for capital funding to provide much needed social and affordable housing for seniors in the area. The aim was to create an integrated campus that provided a range of senior living accommodation, care services and community space, allowing tenants to seamlessly access the various services available onsite. Additionally, the vision was articulated to create a centre that intentionally developed and promoted the physical, mental, emotional and spiritual wellbeing of all residents, staff and volunteers.

By 2014, the Churches of Christ Mitchelton Campus had a redeveloped sixty suite aged care facility, a thirty-six place Centre for Excellence in Dementia Care, fourteen retirement village apartments, forty-nine community housing units, a large community centre and outdoor covered BBQ space, a community garden, and many associated services. Managers and staff were committed to the aim of bringing the light of Christ to everyone involved in the Mitchelton campus as well as the wider community. Regular worship services, prayer groups and other community activities were organised alongside the best of clinical care and support. Two ministers/chaplains were employed as part of the staff and volunteers working on the campus.

The transformation of Moonah Park aged care facility into the much larger and integrated seniors' community and Kingdom Community was an ongoing development project over the several years. Various awards have flowed in recognition of the integrated community concept, design and quality of care. The innovation and forethought behind the development led to Churches of Christ's integrated community at Mitchelton being named Queensland's Leading Housing Solution at the 2012 Australian Housing Institute Awards. A new worship service that was designed specifically for those with Dementia at Mitchelton was awarded the national Pastoral and Spiritual Care of Older People award by Meaningful Ageing Australia. Both of the national Seniors Industry Associations have recognised the quality of care with Best-in-Queensland Awards. Following the success of the Mitchelton integrated community, new Kingdom Communities are being developed in Warwick, Meridan, Boonah, Acacia Ridge, Kallangur, Stanthorpe, Cardwell and Blackall.

The design is that they will each be communities that care for the aged and provide affordable housing for the poor, together with a community centre, a community chaplain, and support services that also reach out into the wider community. Each will see the birth of a new Kingdom Community in the centre of each development, providing a vibrant place where people can access the kingdom of God.

In the past two chapters we have explored what has been an extraordinary journey of kingdom life and growth across Queensland as almost two hundred new Kingdom Communities have commenced.[8] It was built on the theory and contextual reflection of the first two chapters and case studies from Brazil (chapter three, Base Ecclesial Communities) and in Australia, Thailand and New Zealand (chapter four, Urban Neighbours of Hope). In the Introduction we shared some case studies from quite different contexts that each have resulted in Kingdom Communities springing up, like mustard seeds. Where more than two of God's people have commenced regularly to gather together to shine the light of Christ in local communities or networks through faith hope and love. We turn now to some of the leadership shifts that are required as well as possible practises for Kingdom Communities.

---

[8] In 2009/10 there were 207 Kingdom Communities and in 2016/17 there were 398 Kingdom Communities registered in Churches of Christ in Queensland. Source: Churches of Christ in Queensland Annual Reports, see Figure 5.2

CHAPTER SEVEN

Leadershifts

"You can't change the fruit without changing the root."
Stephen R. Covey.

"So, Christ himself gave the apostles, the prophets, the evangelists, the pastors and teachers, to equip his people for works of service, so that the body of Christ may be built up until we all reach unity in the faith and in the knowledge of the Son of God and become mature, attaining to the whole measure of the fullness of Christ."
Ephesians 4:11-13

Andrew can still vividly remember the first time he went to a non-English speaking country. He was a young adult and it was his first trip overseas. After twenty-four hours in a jet he finally arrived at Charles de Gaulle Airport in Paris. He was jet-lagged, excited and on his own. The aim was to get to a hotel near Ile de la Cite where his uncle and a colleague were staying. From there the three of them would explore Paris. He just had to get himself to the hotel. Getting off the plane and through customs seemed easy enough. He simply followed the person ahead of him. Eventually, with his passport stamped he walked through the glass doors and was in France on his own.

All of the signage was in French, which given that he was in Paris was to be expected! That was the moment that he kicked himself for not paying attention more in French classes at school! To make matters worse his poor attempts at French only brought out the famous Parisian arrogance in people when asked for help. He really was on his own. So, he took a deep breath and bought a ticket for a bus that said, Avenue de l'Opera and hoped that it meant the famous Paris Opera House. On the bus he followed the map as he travelled along and despite a moment or two of breaking out in a cold sweat when they drove to another airport, surely enough he had picked the right bus and it eventually deposited him outside the Opera House. His next adventure was to figure out the Paris Metro (the underground train system), which fortunately was colour-coded. Finally, he arrived at the right hotel, met his uncle and the real adventure of exploring Paris began.

That is a common experience for any of us who have travelled to a foreign, non-English speaking city for the first time. Most of us have had wide and varied experiences in facing situations that have demanded a radical reorientation that began with feelings of being unequipped for the challenge. During the (long) process of writing this book, Dean went through a life-threatening diagnosis, treatment and recovery that required far more from him and his wife, Janette, than they ever expected. We think of friends who have suddenly lost a loved one; or found themselves in a second marriage and had to incorporate their partner's children into a blended family; or aid and development workers who have had to live through civil unrest in a strange land; or colleagues who have had to escape their homeland as a refugee for a safer land where they could live unhindered; or friends who have faced sudden, unplanned retrenchment and had to walk out of the building only with a box of possessions and a cab-charge ticket, not even being permitted to say goodbye to colleagues.

Such situations present us with complex, emotionally demanding, adaptive challenges. They are a part of life but that does not make them easy. It is human nature to look for shortcuts and easy solutions to get out of some situations but in ones like those we have described a person, family or community is faced with a really tough challenge that has no easy way out. It requires us to adapt to the changed circumstances and make permanent changes.

Throughout our combined years in and around Australian churches we have found, on the whole, that when it comes to embracing change, churches are just like the people who comprise them. If they can recalibrate around a change without directly facing it or changing themselves then they will. This applies in areas of finance, pastoral transitions, properties and changes to programs. However, sometimes things are even more challenging and threaten the sense of unity or existence and require more significant change. These challenges can be in regard to a theological position, pastoral responses to contemporary issues, failings in leadership, style of worship services or models of governance. It is usually on these matters, that denominational guidance or external consultants are brought in (often too late in the piece). Sometimes these crises result in people leaving the church or sadly, even splits of the congregation or denomination. Most concern a collision of one, two or more core issues including culture, leadership, values, governance, integrity, theology or unity.

This book is concerned with far more than skill issues or technical challenges. We are addressing a kingdom response to the profound changes that have transformed Australian society. We are the ones who find ourselves in a strange country, tired, confused and without correct language. Ours is a moment of time filled with rapid, discontinuous and unpredictable change. Many churches really are stuck (see chapter one) in quicksand and it is clear that they are well into their last generation unless something changes. We also see all too often the tremendous efforts churches will go to in order to avoid double and triple look learning (see chapter six).

Shipwrecked

Our colleague, Stephen Curkpatrick teaches a popular course titled *Memory, Word and Identity in Acts*. It follows Luke's Acts of the Apostles, over the course of a semester. It is always interesting to see the same early pattern of class members, who start perplexed by the nature of the growth, development and spread of the early church. They tend to come to the course with a mystical and romantic view of Acts. Like it was a fairy tale filled with miraculous growth, the occasional, courageous hero and heroine and massive numbers of conversions that result in significant growing churches (make no mistake, these things are all there but nothing like a fairy tale and nothing like modern church practice in Australia).[1] Finally, just as students expect a happy ending, Luke concludes his Luke/Acts account troublingly. He tells the account of a shipwreck. On a boat headed for Italy, Paul and some other prisoners are struck by a cyclone, which threatens their lives. The story is found in Acts 27.

---

[1] Alan Kreider, *The change of conversion and the origin of Christendom*, Harrisberg, PA: Trinity Press, 1999, explores the journey of the early church from Acts of the Apostles through to Christendom and notes the changing patterns of behaviour, belief and belonging. It is a fascinating read and exposes the profound differences between early church practices and modern Australian church life.

After fourteen days of fighting the storm and throwing nonessential items overboard, the crew runs out of technical answers. They do not know what to do. The water is becoming shallow with successive depth soundings. Paul reassures the captain and crew that the ship might not survive but that no lives will be lost. Interestingly, in the storm they have a final meal together for physical and spiritual sustenance in a clear act of memory of the Lord's Supper. Then they run the ship onto a beach to try to get to shore. It gets stuck on a sandbar and starts to break up. Everyone is required to swim to shore and those who cannot swim grab whatever floats to try to make it. In all, each of the 276 aboard makes it safely to shore – but the ship is smashed up.

The image of a shipwreck may not satisfy our modern sensibilities for a 'happy ever after' ending, but that is how the text goes. The big, safe boat is smashed to pieces and everyone clings to whatever floats to get themselves to shore. With the waves crashing upon the breaking-up ship, Luke's message rings clear. The church is not, firstly, about the growth of a large, competent and complex institution. Remember at the time Luke wrote Acts that Christians faced persecution, rumours and misunderstanding, they had no buildings, no clergy, no congregations or denominations and in this story, Paul is literally a prisoner in chains for the gospel. Luke was making many points here, but one is obvious: the story of the early church does not end with a big, well-resourced ship led by a capable captain. We are left with small, nimble and often-powerless people and groups, who are, themselves, often fractured by life's circumstances and dependent on the hospitality of others. It is in powerlessness and hospitality that the reign of God's kingdom becomes reality.

The end of Acts has been the testimony of countless Christians over the ages and still is today throughout the majority world church. In fact, more Christians are persecuted and suffer than ever. This is a salient point for us to come to grips with. As Westerners, we so are dependent on our own competence and ability. Many in the Western church still treat the majority world church as if we have the answers, as our colonising mindset continues. Yet, really, we are the ones who have much to learn.

Andrew can remember being at Oliver Tambo Airport, in Johannesburg on his way home from time in Lusaka, Zambia. He had enjoyed a wonderful time, being introduced to amazing and beautiful people while listening to their stories. In one slum in Lusaka a group of us were moved by the resilience of a local congregation who could not even afford a roof for their building and also by our translator who, herself, was living with HIV due to a straying husband. She had pioneered a ministry to other women in the same situation. In village after village we were struck by the growth and adaptive creativity achieved by local Christians so as to live out the gospel locally and meaningfully.

Sitting at the airport and reflecting on this visit, Andrew was watching the many other cultures in the terminal café while waiting for the next flight. He noticed a large group of Western Christians who were obviously on a short-term mission trip. They were obvious because they all were wearing the same tee shirts, which proudly proclaimed, "X Church Mission trip – bringing light to the darkness". Andrew wondered if they were going to learn much from their trip or whether they would be too busy imparting their own cultural values? It is impossible to learn much when we believe we already know the answers.

Western Christians are very good at telling others what to do and calling it proclamation. We have less developed skills like deep listening in our own context. We miss out on so much by talking about ourselves rather than listening deeply and understanding our neighbours and communities. For church leaders the challenge becomes ever harder because so much time, energy and focus is required to keep things at church going. There is rarely time to really sit back and – from the balcony – get some perspective about what God is up to in our community.

If we are to embark on a serious and contextual journey of entering into our neighbourhoods and listening to what God is doing and calling us to participate in, we might be surprised at how little ends up in formal church activities. The use of SALTs by Churches of Christ in Queensland to pioneer Kingdom Communities as a response to community need (as told in chapters five and six) demonstrates the potential of research and listening. When Andrew was a local church pastor he tried to understand the local community that existed outside the physical walls of the church.

He would often get down to the church very early on Sunday mornings to get the pew heaters warm for the older members of the church. They were old gas heaters that required a few hours to warm up. That gave him some time to have a last read through the message and also to pray over the day's activities. About two hours before the service was due to start he would find everything completed and had only one final ingredient to add for the sermon to improve: good coffee!

So, he walked across the road from the church to a market that was held every Sunday. He would wander up and down the market aisles and bump into people and enjoy the market atmosphere. Experience had taught him where the best coffee was to be found until it was time to get back across the road to the church. As he would near the church building the sounds of the rehearsal could be faintly heard. He would then have a chat with the people on the hospitality roster who were getting the building ready, especially for visitors who might come.

As minister, the rest of the morning would follow its usual blur of activities and conversations until he found himself locking the doors and going home for a late lunch. The church was filled with great people of different ages and cultures. It felt like a giant family. Coming from the market to the church, Andrew would try to search for some meaningful points of connection between the regulars at the market and the regulars at the church, but it never quite happened. No one knew how. Sometimes setting up a stall in the market was suggested but no one could see how that would really translate to the growth of service. Today, both communities still continue alongside each other with almost no connection.

So, what can be learnt by this apparent polarity between the church and the market?

First, any presence by Christians in the market was supported and welcomed by the church – but it never lasted. This was because the ultimate metric used by the church was how many people came on a Sunday. Any missional presence in the market was supported, if it resulted in people coming across the road, onto the church property and into the church building. No one could figure out how to get people to cross the road and into the church, despite better signage, Christmas presentations and many programs. So, the market was rejected as a fertile place for mission. The church members didn't seem prepared to ask, 'What was God doing in the market and how could they partner, there? In our view, this was not asked because of the deeply ingrained view that the real goal and success of a church is all about attendances on Sunday, and that the kingdom of God is only where the church is visibly present.

One of the great contemporary challenges for church leadership is how to encourage, develop and motivate church members to, metaphorically, cross the road and develop a Kingdom Community there. Like Paul and his fellow passengers, who lay scattered across that Maltese beach, Christians ought to be far more intentionally immersed into local communities like mustard seeds, or yeast, or salt or light. William Temple famously said that, "The church is the only society that exists for the benefit of those who are not its members." Is that honestly the case in modern church life?

Church growth theory has caused the opposite, through teaching church leaders that the growth of institutional church is their primary goal. As a result, all sorts of books, study tours, conferences and leadership programs have been created to pass on lessons about how to grow churches. It is very similar to how to grow a business. Of course, doing church well is certainly better than doing church poorly. However, the inherent goal in building a business is the finding and keeping of customers who will pay for what you are offering. Whilst some of the principles are certainly transferrable, this consumerism model of growth and its inherent assumptions have not changed the five-decade long pattern of church decline in Australia. It also seems to have produced an unconscious 'theory-in-use' that the kingdom of God is only where the church happens to be within their community.

Second, a fair percentage of active participants in Andrew's church had no real interest in a presence in the market because they did not live in the local area. When you live and attend to local issues and events you tend to become concerned for the welfare of those that participate and share in the experience. The fact that many church members lived beyond walking distance from the church was a deterrent to a local focus.

This was a part of Andrew's problem that led him to leave the church! Andrew's family lived as close to that church as they could afford, but housing prices and the absence of a manse required them to live further away, in a different suburb. The flow on effects meant that their children would go to different schools, they shopped in a different supermarket and they voted in a different electorate. There is no magic rule, but every non-local action adds up and the result was another church where over fifty percent of the congregation commuted to the suburb for worship and fellowship, and then left.

Leadershifts

Many committed, faithful, godly people who have followed a call into pastoral leadership, experience the relentless demands and expectations for corporate leadership and growth, conflict management, branding expertise, up front style, performance excellence and the ability to abate another exodus to the bigger church up the road. Meanwhile at the bigger church up the road, the leadership is experiencing the same pressures and more often. It is a giant food chain. Pressures like these are the natural outcome of the corporate institution that the modern local church has become in pursuit of unquestioned growth in a declining market, rather than kingdom activity. Among many theologically reflective leaders with whom Dean and Andrew talk, there is a deep, gnawing sense that something is terribly wrong. They are increasingly not able to be what they were called to be. More and more effort is required in areas that are, at their core, not centred on partnership with God.

In many churches it feels like the course has already been set and that the prayers prayed are focused on asking for God to bless what they are about do. The deeply prevailing paradigm of what a church is means there is little space to ask what God is doing and how we can serve and partner. They are going to do what they have planned to do anyway. It is a reflection of the colonising impulse set deep within Western culture. Because we believe we know, we seek to build and plant our predetermined models.

The result is that churches set a strategic plan and go about trying to achieve it without seeking and discerning the patterns of creation and renewal that are already occurring in the local area.

There are major shifts required in leadership perspective and activity if we are going to practise a deeper sensitivity to the creative work of God. It is simply not fruitful for the church to continue to charge in with good plans from a 'we know best' perspective. Many churches are preaching that Jesus is the answer when they have not listened for the question.[2] We might know Jesus through a life-changing, personal and revelatory experience, however that does not give us a monopoly on discerning what God is up to nor is it necessarily where our communities' needs lie.

Jesus taught about the importance of putting the needs of others before our own. Trying to plant and invigorate predetermined models of church without deeply listening to, and understanding our neighbours, whom Christ has taught us to love, reflects a focus on ourselves. Listening with a heart of compassion and seeing with fresh eyes what is needed to bring light and life to people, will lead us to new possibilities for being God's church in communities.

In this section we will examine some of the shifts required so that leadership can become more attuned to what God might be up to in context. If we are to faithfully contextualise local and networked Kingdom Communities, then these are the sorts of shifts that leadership will need to undergo. In essence these are shifts *from* focusing on growing congregational numbers *to* forwarding the three essentials that Jesus taught: loving God with our whole heart, mind, soul and strength; loving our neighbour as ourselves; and, living the way of life Jesus showed us, teaching others and baptising them into Jesus' Way.

As we have discussed earlier, our mental maps shape what we see, how we behave and what we measure ourselves against. The overriding shift is about moving the mental map that most ministers and Elders have grown up with; we are winning if Sunday morning numbers and financial giving are going up, and we are failing if they are going down.

---

2 We are reminded that Jesus usually asked questions or told parables rather than telling answers, even when asked for answers. This link records 135 of the questions Jesus asked, https://mondaymorningreview.wordpress.com/2010/05/14/137questionsjesusasked/

The shift that needs to occur is about how leaders see themselves and their primary mission – which we argue (above) are the three Jesus essentials – and how they measure themselves and those they are called to lead, against these.

Don't get us wrong though; numbers are inevitably important and are generally the main way we measure progress and success in most fields of endeavour. There is accountability with metrics, but it is crucial that the right objectives are measured. We will say it again: growing Sunday services are certainly preferable to dying Sunday services; but, the primary purpose of a Christian leader must be the development of disciples around the three essentials.

Seven Leadershifts

1. *From* a focus on attracting attendees into a local congregation *to* equipping people for service in Kingdom Communities.

It is understandable that modern church life is vastly different to early church life, given the centuries, cultures, countries, oceans, discoveries, empires and movements that separate us. Yet the early Christians should also be a great inspiration and encouragement for us, in these times that we are called to live and minister to one another. We are well guided if we pay close attention to their *raison d'être*, because despite the changes required for contextualisation, their mission is still our mission – being witnesses and citizens of the kingdom of God.

When viewed through this lens, the modern focus on the growth of corporate churches is strange, if things stop at that point. The early church generally met in secret or privately, had no staff, no large attendances, no band, no website, no denominations, no Bibles and no separate buildings. They did not occupy themselves with the creation of methods and tactics designed to attract people into attendance. Their focus was about how to follow the Way of Christ. Leaders of their ekklesia were committed to establishing and following practises that formed better and more faithful followers of Jesus. The quality and characteristics of disciples, and the community in which they were a part, was what became so attractive. They were neighbours and friends who lived out what St Francis is famously attributed as saying, "Preach the gospel always, use words only if you must."

If we are to reclaim a New Testament focus in attending to our local neighbourhoods and communities, we will simply have to cease trying to extricate people from these communities. In fact, we will turn things around and do all we can to support Christians living their faith out locally in Kingdom Communities, not as isolated missionaries but as vibrant and caring little groups of followers of the Way. Remember, Jesus called us to love our neighbour. This is also the best method of discipleship and the only domain where it is really tested.

It is a common experience that within three years of conversion a new Christian will have severed most of their meaningful friendships with non-Christians. On one level this is understandable as the new Christian seeks to grow and be with others who share their passion and joy. However, missiologically it is obviously disastrous and in terms of discipleship it creates a polarity where there is a subtle message that God disciples through Christian activities only.

Throughout this book we have presented many different case studies of different Kingdom Communities, where a group of two or more of God's people are following agreed practices so as to shine the light of Christ through faith, hope and love. Some are very small and respond to a specific context, like Urban Neighbours of Hope. Others have become quite substantial in terms of numbers and budget, like Cornerstone Christian College in Busselton or some of the Aged Care Centres in Queensland. The point is not the size, it is the kingdom of God.

This presents local churches with some practical identity, structure and program issues. Church activities can no longer be only centred upon attractional, Sunday activities or simply getting more people onto the property. Rather, congregations could become a network of dispersed Kingdom Communities. Perhaps this will lead to some church networks that organise a monthly or quarterly major gathering instead of the usual weekly services. Perhaps they will prefer that Kingdom Communities take priority for breaking bread and praying together? It is sensible that some activities like children, youth and certain specialised programs are centralised, which could become another Kingdom Community.

Just this past Easter, Andrew and Kim dropped their children off at their church youth group Easter camp. From the Friday to the Monday they camped in tents, sat around the campfire, enjoyed reflective worship services, went on walks, played games and did the things that young people have been doing on camps for generations. On other weeks they meet on Friday nights to worship or to do fun activities. They pray for each other and encourage each other in following Christ. Dean and Andrew can think of no better starting point for any congregation than to develop a Kingdom Community among local young people.

The biblical idea of ekklesia is not about gathering people in rows on a Sunday and listening to an expert person up the front or in the production of excellent performances. The New Testament idea of ekklesia is a group of committed people who gather regularly, break bread, discern the activity of God and encourage one another as followers in the way of Christ. Then, as they do these things, their fruitfulness becomes evident and the kingdom light is shone in many and varying dark places that need light.

Modern church growth theory has trapped too many church leaders into thinking that increasing their church attendance is their highest goal. Others are busy trying to keep up with things to do as well as spending valuable time on committees and endless meetings. The relentless cycle of church-centred busyness stops most church leaders from ever stepping back and assessing the effectiveness of it all in respect to *missio Dei* (the mission of God). If we step back and honestly assess all of the activity; small groups, rehearsals, rosters, meetings and programs that are internal to the church, we might be surprised at how little time active church involvement actually allows people to love their neighbours and attend to the local neighbourhood.

Jesus never grew a large or mega followership; indeed, large crowds were fickle to him. We should study how far things in the modern church have strayed from the rhythms and practices of the early church, who were only ever as big as a house could accommodate – forty at the most.

While the weekly worship service for many is a meaningful act of gathering together, it is a very different exercise compared with how Christians met in the first century. Early Christian churches met in

Chapter Seven: Leadershifts

homes, which are far more intimate settings than modern churches can ever be. Hospitality was central to the life of the community. The place of the home was far more connected to the normality of everyday life. Sacred space for early Christians was not in a building constructed for large gatherings overseen by professional clergy but in fellowship in homes among people who were connected with daily life.

Whenever we visit a church we are reminded of the huge difference between a first century ekklesia and today's typical congregation. Many churches are tough places to break into for first time visitors. Sometimes the church has a spot where people can greet one another or 'pass the peace'. This is often where visitors (especially the introverts) sit isolated, while the church family greets one another. It is one thing to be welcomed at the door by a member of the 'hospitality' team who are rostered to greet newcomers. It is another thing to receive hospitality freely from the heart. The difference often comes to a head at the Lord's Supper. Often when we hold the elements of a small, broken-off bit of cracker and a really tiny plastic glass of grape juice, we think of how different this memory-action was in the early church. Here we are helped by Robert Banks.

Through a fictional character named Publius, Banks describes a typical meeting of early Christians in *Going to church in the first century*.[3] In this easy to read and fascinating booklet, Banks describes the streets, houses, dangers, customs, egalitarianism and simple greetings that made early Christians so radically different to other religions. As the evening among followers progressed, a homemade meal was brought to that table. The group stopped, and the host described the meaning of the Lord's Supper, prayed and broke the loaf of bread into, 'substantial portions'[4] and passed it among the guests. Later in the evening after most of the meal had been eaten, the conversation was again interrupted by the host who had all the cups refilled. He then took his cup in both hands and invited the room to drink together and take all that had been discussed to heart.[5]

---

[3] Robert Banks, *Going to Church in the First Century*, Jacksonville: Seed Sowers, 1980.
[4] Robert Banks, *Going to Church in the First Century*, 21.
[5] Robert Banks, *Going to Church in the First Century*, 35.

The earliest churches had no public meetings. There was no signage, no building and no easy way to find a local gathering of Christians. They effectively operated as an underground network and news was spread relationally. Attendance at a local church meeting was often dangerous for all concerned. The idea of public, advertised meetings was unimaginable for the first three hundred years of Christianity like it is in parts of the world today. Christians had to be cautious and suspicious about newcomers as they might be spies from the state or religious authorities.

Occasionally however, a neighbour became inquisitive about the changed conduct that had occurred in their neighbours and wanted some of what they saw. The neighbour's ethics, morals and high regard for human flourishing looked attractive. The book of Acts (Acts 2:47) records that many early Christians were looked upon with respect and favour by their community. At times when an enquirer displayed sufficient interest, the Christian didn't invite them to a church service, as that was still too dangerous. They needed a little more vetting. So, they talked further with them and if the enquiry seemed genuine they would invite another Christian to meet with them and see if they seemed safe and genuine. The aim was never to invite people to a church service. Inquiry about the Christian faith deserved far more respect through meals, conversations and Bible studies. Attendance at a worship service was something that only started once someone came to faith and was baptised.

Christianity shouldn't be a religion at its core. Certainly not like other religious faiths are practised. Society and some churches call it a religion but really it is a transformational faith through encounter with the Risen Lord Jesus that calls us to a communal life in our pursuit of him and his kingdom. The effects of Cox's *Age of Belief* are what have led us to call it a religion. Australian society (as discussed in chapter one) is hungry for spirituality but is turning its back on institutional religion. As we seek to partner with what God is up to in the world, we have a choice: keep trying to represent Jesus through religious institutions that aim to get people into a religious building as the primary method of evangelism or to humbly enter neighbourhoods and communities as servants and witnesses of Jesus' kingdom, and see where that adventure takes us.

A wonderful example is found in the following story. Several years ago, the Urban Neighbours of Hope, Springvale team had been assisting the Burmese refugee community in their integration to Australia. In that time, they had assisted with housing, advocacy, language, tutoring and developing relationships across the wider Burmese community. Being refugees with horrid past encounters, some community members found settling down and living their new lives in a strange culture very difficult. The local UNOH members, living by their well-developed practices, were aware of these challenges and in partnership with the local Burmese community suggested that a restaurant could be developed. The purpose of this restaurant was firstly for employment creation, empowerment and belonging among the Burmese community. However, advocacy of the Burmese cause was also high on their agenda. The restaurant ran for a few years and then moved into a catering business. It was a social enterprise that was also a wonderful story of the sort of thing that can happen when God's people attend to the neighbourhood.

When we reduce the imagination and focus of God's people to activities within the existing walls of the Christian church we sever the limitless possibilities of real and genuine demonstration of the kingdom of God. The examples of UNOH used throughout this book are constant encouragements to us of what a small and locally focused group of Christians can produce when they intentionally listen and look for the signs of God at work. From making bus shelters and renewing local parks, igniting small business enterprises, opening social enterprise cafes and the invitation of small intentional communities in local areas there is no shortage of what can start when we release people into mission and service in the neighbourhood.

There is a fable told about school. One year the school Principal, in discussion with the staff, developed a theme for the entire year. The theme was titled, 'The Ocean' and the entire curriculum from kindergarten to year twelve studied the usual subjects, but they were all designed around the sea. English classes studied books set on or under the ocean. History and geography classes studied the globe from the perspective of the sea and explorers. Even mathematics classes were adapted.

As an extra point of engaged learning, all of the technical classes adapted to the theme by building a boat. A retired boat builder was contracted to guide the learning and week by week the plans turned from design to construction. There was great excitement and investment by all the students and staff in the project and slowly the boat started to look like an actual object that could carry people on the water.

As the year passed the boat came near to completion. All the students gathered on the last day of school for the boat launch at a local boat ramp. It was a tremendous day filled with celebration and Mrs Kafoops (a greatly loved and retired teacher) was asked back to christen the boat, which was named in her honour. That summer some of the students freely gave their summer holidays to attend to the last details to finalise the boat.

The boat was a total win. As time passed in subsequent years the students often talked about the 'year of the boat' as it came to be known. Some of them would often walk down to the jetty where it was moored to look at it and remember the part that they helped construct. School reunions were great times to talk about it. The boat was a real source of unity and memory.

One day, at a school reunion someone asked if anyone had actually sailed on the boat? No one knew anyone who had. Enquiries were made but no one could find a person who had actually taken the boat out of the harbour. Soon discussions generated towards activism. There was a growing sense that the boat should be sailed, at least once. The issue was raised at a school Board meeting and a committee was established to conduct a risk analysis. A consultant was engaged to bring expertise to the matter.

Eventually the matter was settled. Two decisions were made. The first decision was that the boat was never to leave the jetty. It was deemed to be too great a risk and the possibility of accident or loss of the boat not worth the risk. The second decision was to establish a committee to preserve the boat and oversee its maintenance and possibly write a history, including the names of all who helped build it. The two decisions were unanimous.

Chapter Seven: Leadershifts

It is a fable that carried a point with a bit of a sting. Churches, denominations, care agencies, seminaries and Christian gatherings can become like the boat. There is singing and emulation of traditional customs and activities but the essence and reality of shining the light of Christ in the community can be talked about but rarely actually, meaningfully achieved, certainly when compared to the effort put in for attracting people to come into the building. Excuses are often made but if a boat never leaves the harbour what is the point of its existence?

Demographers and statisticians tell us that a regular church attendee is now someone who turns up once a month or more. We'd hate to think how our sporting clubs survived if that was the level of support expected. We have both known ministers who counted the numbers of people in attendance at worship services every week as if it meant something. More than one minister has told us that attendance numbers show if God is blessing their church!

We are reminded of the words of Lesslie Newbigin,

> "We do not find Paul concerning himself with the size of churches or with questions about their growth. His primary concern is with their faithfulness, with the integrity of their witness ... There is a deep concern for the integrity of the Christian witness, but there is no evidence for anxiety about or enthusiasm for rapid growth. In no sense does the triumph of God's reign seem to depend on the growth of the church."[6]

While a gathering of the faithful is a heart-warming activity, we question how much kingdom light is really shone by lots of people sitting in rows singing songs and receiving warm platitudes – unless they then 'Go' (Matt 28:18-20). Some do but lots don't. Frances Chan was founding minister of a five thousand strong megachurch in California. One day the coin dropped, and he realised that five thousand people were coming to watch him use his gifts. As minister, his job was to see the five thousand people use their own gifts. He resigned as minister and eventually set up a discipleship making ministry of Kingdom Communities, which as they multiply, will number well in excess of anything a megachurch could

---

[6] Lesslie Newbigin, *The Open Secret: An Introduction to the Theology of Mission*, Grand Rapids: Eerdmans, 1995, 125.

house. Better still, each group is now activated in shining the light of Christ and seeing each member use their gifts with far less use of resources.

In the following chapter we will develop the idea of spiritual practices in more detail. For now, we note the shift for churches from being large enterprises where few people use their gifts to lots of small Kingdom Communities where many more people are engaged. That has always been where and how Christian formation and discipleship is best achieved. We note that this does not necessarily imply that each minister should resign and follow the methods and model of Frances Chan, although it is a good challenge. New Hope Baptist Church in Melbourne's eastern suburbs is an example where their resources are being turned into a training and support base for one hundred and fifty Kingdom Communities and growing.

2. *From* centralised 'hub and spokes' structured congregations *to* a 'distributed network' of Kingdom Communities supported by a local congregation

The difference between a hub and spokes model and a distributed network were explored in chapter three. This is where we need to be a little sensitive. The current model of church has an inherent conflict of interest. Clergy inevitably have a vested interest in maintaining the hub and spokes model, as it justifies their existence and provides meaning and income. It is also such a dominant model that it has become the default of almost all Western churches. It is worth noting that in times past in some churches there was no appointed minister (or priest) as all members were considered ministers. In Dean and Andrew's tradition (Churches of Christ) until only about fifty years ago, if churches employed anyone it was a gifted 'evangelist,' who engaged in intentional mission and evangelism. The modern, professional minister tends to have a far more internal and centralised focus that is generally required to be directed to the benefit of the church that employs him or her. This is explored further in leadershift 4.

In Indonesia, Christian churches have small and nimble training colleges that have a primary priority for developing leaders who can live in and establish local, contextual Christian communities. As a part of their college training, students go to villages in twos where they start a Kingdom Community. They cannot even pass their degree until they have successfully started a Kingdom Community and developed the leaders to a point where they can return to college to complete their studies. The aim is not to plant a church where they as the planter/minister stay with everything centralised around them. Once established, these leaders must develop the local people to take charge of the Kingdom Community in their village because they are going to move on back to college and then probably another village. That's how their distributed network grows and spreads.

However, please note that there are experienced regional coordinators and training colleges who guide, resource and support this work. A careful reader will note that we are not proposing a model that is a radically, laissez-faire distributed network model of Kingdom Communities. Our understanding of the early church was that it was indeed a network of autonomous house churches. Many would have been linked in and accountable to wider networks, while the pastoral epistles demonstrate that others became heretical or simply went badly off the rails. There were many tests and challenges to negotiate as the earliest 'ekklesias' commenced life and sought occasional guidance from apostolic leaders (or were given it without invitation if necessary!)

Our aim is not to throw out the baby with the bathwater. We live in a society that expects higher standards of leadership and governance in community settings, particularly from religious bodies. Christians should set the standard in this area, not adhere to the lowest common denominator. Therefore, some Kingdom Communities may freely want to drift off on their own, to pursue their own vision that is not what we envisage as the gold standard. Across Churches of Christ in Queensland, as the Kingdom Communities grew, there were clear lines of accountability, minimum standards, alignment, leadership qualification and branding (to name a few key areas). In Indonesia it is the same, although formed in a different context. Urban Neighbours of Hope similarly work at standards, practices and criteria for association under their banner.

Maybe Andrew's daughter's netball club is a good model to use as an illustration On any Saturday at the local netball facility there are ten courts filled with hundreds of netballers. The youngest start earliest and throughout the day the competition ages get older. Andrew's daughter plays in one team from one club. That is her primary netball community with whom she plays and trains. The club is small, yet she doesn't even know most of the girls on the older teams who play a few hours later. She knows that they too, play for the club and wear the same smart, violet coloured uniforms but that is about all, unless there is a teammate's older sister on another team. Her primary community and place of focus is her team, as it should be. However, across the club and the wider competition are a whole set of rules and standards that range from umpires, uniforms, playing rules, representative teams, coaching standards, duty-of-care standards, wet weather policies, and so on. Each team is not a radical, laissez-faire team. To play for the club and the competition is to agree to abide by certain principles and standards.

Each Kingdom Community must naturally develop its own system of oversight and coordination that incorporates an eldership type function. We anticipate that this will often be done in partnership with a congregation or denomination. Size matters here as a small, neighbourhood Kingdom Community can share responsibilities more easily, whereas a degree of structure is inevitably needed in a larger setting like a school or aged care centre. Obviously, the group should adapt necessary structural changes as growth and changes occur.

The key shift we see for a congregation is that if it adopts this model, its primary concern becomes about the heath, vitality and effectiveness of Kingdom Communities (which could function in a thousand different modes and locations), not about how to attract people on Sundays to worship services. A denomination will also change focus from the number of attendees in congregation worship services to the number of active Kingdom Communities in each congregational network and the number of active participants in each Kingdom Community.

3. *From* pastorally focused clergy *to* gifted (often bi-vocational) leaders focused on encouragement, development and equipping all of God's people as ministers through Action Learning teams and Kingdom Communities

Many local churches are confused in their understanding and function of leadership. This paralysis in leadership means that churches usually are not equipped to lead out of the situation in which they are stuck. Current models of governance have inbuilt defaults, which keep churches stuck, often rationalising that at least they are still alive and caring for those in their system. Pastoral care is very important and has a central ongoing role for caring ministry, but is not the primary or only mission of the church.

Things have also changed in society. Decades ago, a local minister was generally a well respected member of the community who even wore a special uniform, so they could be identified. As we have seen in chapter one, community opinion of clergy is now at very low levels with no sign of change in the foreseeable future. We have inherited a professional model of clergy developed through the centuries as Protestant movements adapted the model of priest to pastor-teacher. The titles of Pastor and minister are problematic. Pastor represents the gifts of pastoral care and teaching, which do not encompass the greatly needed gifts of evangelist, prophet and apostle. Minister suggests that the individual who carries the title does the ministry and everyone else in the church is not a minister, which is the wrong message to communicate, biblically.

The current model of professional minister also seems to have an inbuilt and discriminatory code against women. In the two movements in which Andrew has been an ordained minister (Churches of Christ and Baptist), women have been ordained for decades. Both movements are proud of their generally non-discriminatory appearance. Yet, in both of these movements there are no female senior ministers of large churches anywhere in Australia.[7] Most Church Boards are still dominated by men.

---

[7] There are two spouses who are co-Senior Ministers with their husbands (they are the elected co-Senior Minister) yet there are no female only Senior Ministers of large churches across Australia that we know of in these two denominations. Even if there were several

The DNA of most church leadership is established before the church even begins. Consider the model and practice of church planting. In Australia, many church plants are very expensive and, in terms of the return on each dollar invested, are a pretty poor use of funds. If you consider the cost in years of theological study prior to ordination and accreditation of the church planter, the cost of purchasing land, the amount of money required to pay a church planter and the other associated expenses required for branding and office hire it usually amounts to several hundreds of thousands of dollars before a church has even commenced. It is no wonder that church planting is not being widely pursued in many denominations, which is, historically speaking, staggering for evangelically oriented denominations.

In order to become viable, the new church plant then has to be able to pay its planter/minister. Maybe a mother church or the denomination helps with initial funding but as that scales back the new church must ultimately pay its minister. This usually becomes the subtle initial focus of the church and while initiatives into the community are also planned, everything usually falls over if the minister cannot be supported. If 'successful' this means we now have another church whose primary priority is the payment of its minister, and if they are paying him or her then they have to produce some results, which are usually measured in terms of the growth of the church attendance. The quickest way to fix that problem is to produce a service that attracts other Christians. If the church plant grows, more specialised staff are added, and the result is another local church reliant on clergy who are overseen by Elders or a church board. This is typical of most church plants and forms the future structure of the church, its clergy and mission for the rest of its life. Having described this pattern, both of us have ministered in a local context and we feel the need to acknowledge the many ministers who yearn to be more widely engaged in mission, but are constrained to produce activities oriented towards attendance results by the Church Board to whom they are accountable – and who have the power to fire them.

---

more, which we trust will eventually occur, they would still be vastly outnumbered by the large number of male Senior Ministers.

Intertwined with the problematic areas of leadership for churches and church plants there is yet another area of great tension in church leadership. It is in the area of governance. In recent years we have lost count of the number of churches that have broken down in this area resulting in a major setback for the church and its leaders. The core issue is usually about where the authority lies for the oversight of the church; with the minister or the Elders? The pattern is that usually the Elders give the minister enough rope and then pull it hard when a problem emerges. Time and again good people (both Elders and minister) hurt each other because of this tension. Somehow the current system does not usually enable mutuality and deep relational investment in one another's giftedness.

In the early church, the leaders of local ekklesia (Kingdom Community) were both male and female. Paul lists some of them from the church in Rome in Romans chapter 16 and there are other references throughout his epistles. These leaders were immersed in their local community and practised ministry as and where it arose. The Elders were located in Kingdom Communities as there was nowhere else to be situated. They didn't employ someone to do the ministry. They also functioned as an apostolic team. Some were evangelists or prophets or teachers or pastors and some had apostolic gifts that served whole systems and networks. A few were full-time on faith support (1 Cor 9:3-14) but the majority had bi-vocational ministries where the church might provide an honorarium for time not spent at work (1 Tim 5:17-20), if needed. Paul was the most famous example of this (Acts 18:3).

The shift being explored here is towards a team of appropriately gifted people giving whatever gifts, time and expertise they have to offer in ministry and mission through training, encouragement and development of leaders of Kingdom Communities. The resulting oversight becomes an apostolic team of gifted people; apostles, prophets, evangelists, pastors and teachers.

4. *From* the provision of buildings, resources and personnel that are geared for attendance to the provision and coordination of resources that support Kingdom Community presence and mission in local communities in networks

Over fifty percent of church buildings lie empty for most of the week. Huge funds are directed in furnishing auditoriums that hold large numbers of people, yet are only used for a couple of hours each week. Imagine what could be achieved if community kitchens, training rooms, employment creation spaces, childcare facilities, sports facilities, labyrinths and prayer gardens, contemplation spaces, artist studios, low cost professional business centres, neighbourhood houses and job creation programs continued to flourish on more church owned facilities for the benefit of local needs through lots of diverse Kingdom Communities.

North Fitzroy Community Church in inner-Melbourne had the common church problem of a relatively large auditorium space compared to the rest of the church facilities. Steve, then the minister, had been listening deeply throughout the local community and identified that the church could offer space for local artists. Being in the inner-north, the community in North Fitzroy had very little space for artists who worked from home to be able to work in a community space in an environment shared with other creative types. As a result, 'The North Collective' was established. The church also established community arts grants to support local artists.

Kardinia Christian Church in Geelong, Victoria, thrives in a very different context. Kardinia is a large, suburban, multi-campus church led by Leonie and Rick Wright. The team at Kardinia also listened to their local needs and discovered a lack of childcare facilities. So, in 2006 they established Kardinia Childcare and Kindergarten on adjoining land. The need for childcare was real and today the centre has grown to become one of the biggest and best centres in Victoria. The values of the church are modelled through caring and professional staff and close connections with other church members and staff. Kardinia Childcare and Kindergarten is a wonderful example of Kingdom Community.

Rivers Church of Christ in Kallangur, Queensland, is a true light for many hundreds of families in their community. Church members have created another Kingdom Community that gathers every Thursday morning on their site. "Moreton Bay Community Matters" provides boxes of food sourced from a huge community garden that has been developed on the church site as well as local providers who donate surplus and left-over goods. Haydn, a community chaplain, and a team of volunteers coordinate the morning. People come for the food, which is available for a nominal contribution, but also for a coffee and a chat in the warmth of the community. Connections are made, people help out each other, prayers are offered for those who want them, and a sense of belonging and hope has developed for many who are doing it tough in that community. Dean's wife, Janette, who is a psychologist, is also a familiar presence there providing encouragement and counselling as required.

5. *From* local church-centred conversations and metrics *to* deep listening and Action Learning in local communities

Andrew can remember once being at a really boring barbeque. It is pretty hard to make a barbeque excruciating, but this one did it! Eight people sat down to a lovely meal and proceeded onto typical conversations about weather, sports, common connections and local issues. The children had self-organised into a game of hide and seek so the adults sat around the table to relax. Seated around the table were an electrician, a doctor, a criminal lawyer, a paramedic, a triathlete, a dietitian, a builder and Andrew (sounds like the start of a joke!). One of the couple's present were new migrants. It was one of those times where Andrew was able to sit back, relax and listen to the interesting conversations that would surface throughout the discussions.

Then the problem emerged. The host, who had invited the guests, was greatly enthused about a recent overseas trip that he had been on and insisted on talking about it way too much. Most of the group had not been to the country that he had visited so there was a degree of initial interest, but not for two hours! For the rest of the evening no matter what was being discussed, the topic was continually brought back to his travels. For example, at one-point people were listening to the triathlete share a little about the Hawaiian triathlon as he had placed very highly three times (if you don't know, that is a really big deal). Yet, somehow the conversation was dragged back to the host's experience of Hawaii.

It could have been a great barbeque and the chance to make some new friends, but no one had the opportunity, because the host was only interested in his world. Andrew noticed people yawning and glimpsing at their watches to see when it was a suitable time to politely make an excuse and leave. Churches can also be like this. The people in them spend so much time and energy within the church that they often forget to show any interest in people outside the church walls. The whole Christian community becomes an echo-chamber.

Church leaders can be worse. If you have ever been to a church ministers' conference you will know the scene. There is a pecking order around leaders with the biggest churches. The speakers tend to be from bigger churches because they are assumed to be successful ministers and therefore it is expected that they will have some insights and advice to guide others present. Often the speakers are from America (showcasing the latest trend) because it is assumed that what occurs across the Pacific will easily translate to Australian culture (it doesn't). Usually the speakers are male.

Of course, there is nothing wrong with successful church leaders, Americans, or males speaking. There is lots of wisdom to be gained from listening to the experiences and learnings of others. But, and this is a big but, too often, they are the only voices that we end up hearing. This practice is also a recipe for colonising preferred models rather than seeking an understanding of what God is up to in local contexts. The host at the barbeque thought all was going well when actually everyone else was looking at watches and wondering when it was possible to escape.

Healthy, attentive leadership opens deep, listening conversations with neighbours, community leaders, those who are at the front line of service provision, and voices that are often unheard. These were the voices that Jesus often allowed to 'interrupt' his ministry. Dean has unpacked how Churches of Christ in Queensland transformed their whole system to research and respond to places of darkness in local communities through Action Learning in chapter six. Whenever Dean and his executive staff were in a local community setting they sought out community leaders and simply asked what is going on and how can they help? There is nothing stopping any local church starting their own 'SALT' immediately.[8]

6. From denominational franchises *to* a movement of Kingdom Communities and networks

In chapter two we briefly traced the rise of the modern denomination in Australia. We explored how the congregational model, based on medieval village life, had followed migration into the cities and was now in demise because of mobility, competition, modern fluid networked life and the rise of mega-churches who prefer to advance their own brand and don't need a denomination's brand. We also scoped how the modern denomination had become the 'head office' for smaller congregations and assisted with pastoral movements, business administration, insurance, specific ministry supports (Christian Education, children, youth, women, and so on,) and was generally led by skilled ministers who had been promoted into denominational leadership. Most denominations facilitate a model of congregation that is homogeneous across its system.

We are still convinced that denominations have a vital role to play in the future of the Australian Christian movement. However, the shift that denominations need to make is significant. They no longer can manage an existing, diminishing congregational model in one silo, while in other silos, the business, education and care operations manage with different plans and agendas. As Paul spells out in 1 Corinthians 12, we need to think and work as one integrated Body. The paradox is that all need to be empowered and to have life and their own shape in their local communities; yet there must be one coordinating structure with one mission (which we suggest is bringing the light of Christ into communities), and one agreed plan for the best use of major resources

---

[8] See Alan Roxburgh, *Introducing the Missional Church: What it is, Why it matters, How to become one*, Grand Rapids: Baker, 2009; *Missional Map Making: Skills for Leading in Times of Transition*, San Francisco: Jossey-Bass, 2010, 125-188. Alan Roxburgh & Fred Romanuk, *Missional Action Teams: A Workbook for Participants*, Vancouver: Missional Leadership Institute, 2003.

across the denomination to forward the mission. In Paul's metaphor, the eye is designed to see, and the ear to hear. They have different functions, but are part of the one Body. The desire of some denominational leaders to have one preferred, franchise model of congregation no longer works. The future of denominations lies in a multiplicity of expressions that ultimately are each Kingdom Communities. Some Kingdom Communities will be coordinated through a local congregation. Some will be sparked via specialist care agencies. Some will be birthed by denominational leaders facilitating Action Learning teams of local leaders in local communities who are passionate about seeing more of the light of Christ in their community. Each model needs to shift from growth for growth's sake, to local expressions of two or more of God's people who follow regular practises so as to shine the light of Christ through faith, hope and love.

Kingdom Communities seem to spring up in three natural avenues. *Firstly*, congregations can encourage them either through the identification, permission giving, training and sending of two or more people to areas of response (for example, youth, young adults, neighbourhoods, community need, and so on.). They can also come about through the careful implementation of Action Learning teams. In Churches of Christ Queensland, these groups were called SALTS (see chapter six) and through research and listening to the local community some wonderful Kingdom Communities came about as a response to the findings of these groups.

Secondly, denominations can enable new Kingdom Communities to be created. This is usually best done through an Action Learning process where needs can be gauged. However, it is also common for enthusiastic individuals to approach denominations directly for spiritual cover and support for a new area where a Kingdom Community could be established. God has moved them in some way and they feel called to action. Denominations also have the opportunity to re-missionalise their care and service departments through Kingdom Communities. Aged care, child care, social work, camping and other charitable areas within denominational operations can and should all be vitally connected to the work of the kingdom. They are not ends in themselves.

Finally, Kingdom Communities can spring up through two or more people who have responded and don't really fit into a church or denominational structure. The following story is a wonderful story of a minister who 'got it'. Bill had always had a great passion for supporting disabled people. He grew up with a brother who had a permanent disability, and this probably influenced him in his selection to complete a degree in disability studies at university. He knew that with a little bit of assistance, disabilities could often be overcome. He loved his area of work and had often talked with his minister about ways that the church could better integrate disabled people.

Bill met Karen and eventually they married. His enthusiasm for disabled people had a great influence on her and they worked together to integrate disabled people in their church. Their minister was quite supportive of any initiatives that they took but they were constantly concerned that disabled people were properly integrated. While the church leadership was positive in theory about disability there was little real work done in this area apart from buildings following appropriate standards. Bill knew that unless their minister had a real heart for this area, the ministry would only be surface deep.

The church was going through its annual new year drive for people to join small groups and Bill realised that the people he had a heart for would be more of a burden than welcomed in the groups. Besides, going out on a weeknight when you were disabled was a logistical challenge. The result of this was that Bill and Karen decided to start a small group for disabled people and their family and friends. The group met on Sunday afternoons around Communion and a Bible study. It grew like wildfire because it offered mutuality and support to everyone: disabled and able bodied.

Their minister approached them after church one day and asked how the group was going. He was frank and told them that he loved what they were doing but didn't know how to support them. None of the pastoral care and leadership training nights for small group leaders seemed appropriate for the needs of their group. They shared that what they really needed was just prayer, interest and the occasional use of the church hall for special functions. Those things were easily accommodated, and the group continued to grow as word spread about an inclusive community that provided care and support for disabled people. Today there are six of these Kingdom Communities across the city that have each morphed out of the original group. They are each networked with each other and come together quarterly for a joint celebration event. Bill and Karen are still members of the same local congregation, which has been faithful in providing what they needed, but very few of the members of the six Kingdom Communities are members of the congregation. The families need the group as much as the disabled individuals, but no one seems to go the next step and join the congregation.

The interesting thing about Bill and Karen's story is that the unique needs of their ministry ultimately determined that most of their ministry became quite independent of their congregation. A healthy, supportive relationship has been maintained between Bill and Karen and the minister but the groups have become a real distributed network. They do not report into the church hierarchy, and because some groups have spun across the city, there is no geographic connection to their church. In a sense Bill and Karen provide apostolic leadership across the six groups through their founder status and relational style.

The challenge for a local church is what takes priority: being a Kingdom Community or being a church program. The two do not have to be in opposition, however, the priority needs to be resolved. A church program will tend towards a hub and spokes model and new initiatives generally have to be authorised by leadership. A Kingdom Community will tend towards a distributed network where the mission comes from the grassroots.

The story of this distributed network of Kingdom Communities for disabled people and their families has no identification with a denomination. There is no need. Bill and Karen's church is a member of a denomination but that denomination's statistics don't include the expanding network of these Kingdom Communities across the city, yet! To be counted as a member church of the denomination, churches are required to identify with a belief statements, have appropriate denomination branding on all documentation, pay an affiliation fee and have a membership of over twenty members. These Kingdom

Communities are organic, relational and fly under denominational radars. We argue that in such situations, with wonderful kingdom ministry, it is best to let links be built relationally and see whether they intentionally connect to a church denomination or not.

The church in China has presented a similar scenario in recent decades. Missiologists have been staggered to find the actual scale of Christianity, which will result in China being the largest nation of Christians in the world in the next decade or so. The early church displayed the same dynamic and by the arrival of Constantine, Christians were estimated to have been approximately ten to twenty percent of the Roman Empire.

7. **From surface level spirituality *to* deeply rooted spiritual formation through regular practices**

There is a short story at the beginning of Acts chapter nineteen that describes Paul's arrival at Ephesus (see Acts 19:1-7). Upon arrival he found a group of about twelve disciples. The first recorded question that he asked was, "Did you receive the Holy Spirit when you believed?" In essence he was asking if they took God into their mind only, or did they also embrace God with their hearts and become filled with him in their soul? Another way of asking this could be, "Did God get inside you?" They replied, "No, we have not even heard that there is a Holy Spirit."

So Paul asked, "Then what baptism did you receive?"

"John's baptism," they replied.

Paul said, "John's baptism was a baptism of repentance. He told the people to believe in the one coming after him, that is, in Jesus." On hearing this, they were baptized in the name of the Lord Jesus. Paul put his hands on them and the Holy Spirit entered them.

There are many leadershift points to note here. For example, Paul's focus on the spiritual formation of those disciples by asking, "Did you embrace God with your heart? Did God's Holy Spirit get inside you?" Or, the importance of baptism and its context.

Luke (the author of Acts) describes the group that Paul met as disciples. Yet interestingly, they had not, by that stage, heard of, or experienced God being inside them. Presumably, they were trying to practise the Way of Jesus together, which is why Paul identified them as disciples, but his first question was whether they had received the Holy Spirit.

As Christian leaders, we obviously yearn to help people to become followers of Jesus, however, as critical as this is, it doesn't stop there. Paul's view of a maturing disciple involves spiritual formation and the indwelling of the Holy Spirit (Col 1:28-29). As well as leading others, this is of course equally true for ourselves as leaders.

Henri Nouwen said,

"The central question is, are the leaders of the future truly men and women of God, people with an ardent desire to dwell in God's presence, to listen to God's voice, to look at God's beauty, to touch God's incarnate Word and to taste fully God's infinite goodness?"[9]

Action and reflection shape our formation. Steve Drinkall, one of Churches of Christ in Queensland's key mission leaders, developed a great engagement practice to help people to simply start connecting with others in their community. This practice is being used by many leaders involved in the mission of bringing the Light of Christ into communities. Steve called the practice, To whom are you sent? It can be memorised by linking the ten points to our ten fingers:

Develop a Rhythm of Prayer in relation to your community:

1. Pray a blessing on this place.
2. Pray that God would help you to see these people the way He sees them.
3. Pray that you would find peaceful and hospitable people with whom you can collaborate.
4. Pray that God would hold back any unseen forces that are negatively affecting this place.
5. Pray that God would grant people an ability to repent and have faith.

---

[9] Henri Nouwen, *In The Name of Jesus: Reflections on Christian Leadership*, New York: Crossroad Publishing Company, 1989.

Chapter Seven: Leadershifts

6. Extend friendship:
7. Learn someone's name.
8. Hear their story.
9. Ask God what is the next right thing to do, to love and serve this person?
10. Do it.
11. Ask, who else can I connect this person to?

A Kingdom Community leader is one who sees discipleship and community as a lifelong journey involving our minds and hearts. It requires a lifetime of learning, understanding, openness and discernment of God's movement and prompting in ourselves and our neighbours. It involves the gifts of the Spirit and Love (1 Cor 12-13). This Leadershift is about leading people into lifelong spiritual formation and maturity, rather than a subliminal model of good attendance and fellowship.

We now turn to the glue that holds it all together. The practises and rhythms that sustain a Kingdom Community.

CHAPTER EIGHT

Practises of Kingdom Communities

"Practice does not make perfect. Practice makes permanent. Repeat the same mistakes over and over, and you don't get any closer to Carnegie Hall."

Sarah Kay (poet)

"Whatever you have learned or received or heard from me or seen in me—put it into practice. And the God of peace will be with you."

Philippians 4:9

Human beings haven't changed in their deep needs for clean water, food, air, shelter, safety, love, belonging and self-esteem, yet ours is an age of rapid, discontinuous change, spiritual questioning, anxiety, individualism and consumerism. People long for a meaningful purpose to their life but there is profound dysfunction in the search for spiritual depth and community connectedness. People find themselves increasingly alienated, directionless, and hungry – even in church life. Indeed, large numbers are leaving church life but keeping their faith, as noted earlier in Alan Jamison's work.

Impulse drives much of modern Western culture. People dip in and out of activities and relationships are often driven by a consumerist sense of need for image, feeling, or want. For example, just look at Facebook. Australian Bureau of Statistics data shows the average weekday time devoted to 'social and community interaction' has fallen from ninety-two minutes to thirty-six minutes for women since 1992. For men, it has fallen from seventy-three minutes to twenty-eight minutes. The design of suburbs and neighbourhoods facilitates this dehumanising process. The car provides mobility and frees people to drive for whatever or whoever meets their wants immediately, as does mobile technology. Local suburban neighbourhoods promise good lifestyles yet fewer people really live connected lives.

Church life is sadly often no different from this pattern. Local churches contend for survival and watch as their internal systems struggle because of a scarcity of committed people and resources to support them. Ministers, most of whom entered their role with a sense of call to a vocation, are expected to become chief executive officers of small businesses and all that this entails. Meanwhile, within a twenty-minute drive or so waits a megachurch that promises people what they want. We know too many people who have attended a church for years and hardly know more than a few people in the congregation – and have never had a meal at someone's home. This is the world in which we live.

Somehow, there needs to be a better way that brings wholeness and unity to desperate, alienated, and lonely people who do not necessarily even know the state of their condition. Dorothy C. Bass says there is a rejection of, "The separation of spirituality from action, of theory from practice, and of theology from real life."[1]

Alasdair MacIntyre in *After Virtue: A Study in Moral Theology*,[2] provides a critique of modernity, which he terms the 'Enlightenment Project'. MacIntyre argues that many significant Enlightenment and post-Enlightenment moral philosophers, including Kierkegaard, Marx, Kant, and Hume, failed in their project because they were all victims of the historical era in which they wrote. Among many things, MacIntyre offers a critique and way forward for the circumstances of our cultural context. Churches are deeply shaped by these influences of modernity. Consequently, they struggle to comprehend any other imagination or rhythm for ministry. We need to explore practises in life that can guide us to authentically and to meaningfully become a sign, instrument, and foretaste of the kingdom of God.

MacIntyre teaches us that practices are the only way of embedding people's highest internal meanings. This connection of practises as an expression of meaning represents the unifying themes in his work. For MacIntyre, the abstract must be grounded in the local and particular. Practises are not perfected but are pursued regularly so as to enable continuous reflection, learning, and improvement. MacIntyre says, "In

---

[1] Dorothy Bass, (ed.), *Practicing our Faith: A Way of Life for Searching People*, San Francisco: Jossey-Bass, 1997, iii.
[2] Alasdair MacIntyre, *After Virtue: A study in Moral Theology*, Notre Dame: Univerity of Notre Dame Press, 1997.

heroic society, character of the relevant kind can only be exhibited in a succession of incidents and the succession itself must exemplify certain patterns."[3]

The idea of practises is well known to anyone who has learned a musical instrument or played a sport. It assumes that regular participation helps bring about improvement. Improvement may also be enhanced through theory, mentoring, teaching, and coaching. However, MacIntyre argues that it is the actual act of regular participation that is the sign of an individual's commitment. MacIntyre argues the need for practise rather than romantic intention. Ruth Haley Barton is another author who has written about the importance of sacred rhythms or practises.[4] These are voices that we think deserve amplification.

It is the intention of this book to connect theory and practise. We do not intend that the practises described in this chapter be taken out of their theoretical context. They are one method of formation that reflects a pattern of formation through practises.[5] It is our argument that practises must be enmeshed into the rhythm of a Kingdom Community. Too often catechesis (what is often called religious education) is a cerebral and doctrinal program rather than something enmeshed into our daily walk and practise. For example, *The Evangelical Dictionary of Theology* provides a typical definition of the way that catechesis is often kept in the abstract domain without any grounding in the local and particular. It defines catechesis as, "A popular manual of instruction in Christian beliefs, normally in question and answer form."[6]

Therefore, formation into the Way of Jesus is best achieved through Christian practises. There are individual practises such as reading the scriptures, meditation, prayer and private retreats and there are

---

[3] MacIntyre, After Virtue, 125.
[4] Ruth Hayley Barton, Sacred Rhythms: Arranging our lives for Spiritual Transformation, Grand Rapids: InterVarsity Press, 2006.
[5] See Diana Butler-Bass, *The Practicing congregation: Imagining a new old church*, Herndon: Alban Institute, 2004, for development of practices within the life of a congregation or Kingdom Community.
[6] Elwell, Walter, A., (ed.)., *Evangelical Dictionary of Theology*, Grand Rapids: Baker, 1984, David Wright, "Catechisms".

collective practises.⁷ These collective practises are intended to be pursued in the fellowship of other Christians within the context of a local and particular community or neighbourhood – in the life of a Kingdom Community. The definition of these practises is taken from *Practicing Our Faith: A Way of Life for a Searching People* as, "Things Christian people do together over time in response to and in the light of God's active presence for the life of the world."⁸

Introducing: Behaviour & Belonging

Continuing with what we developed in chapters one and two, Alan Kreider, in *The Change of Conversion and the Origin of Christendom*, summarises the situation for the church in Western culture,

"Throughout most of the West, Christendom is in a state of decrepitude if not decomposition. In many countries shoppers flood the malls on Sundays, while Sunday morning has become a special time for sporting events. And people vote with their feet. In most Western societies, polls show that a majority of people believe in some sort of God, but church attendance has become a counterpastural activity ... Many Western Christians have succumbed to a nostalgic prescription for the future in which God, working through revival or renewal or evangelisation will once again bring about a world that Christians can rule. It is likely that many Westerners will resist this, as they resist Christianity in general, because they associate it with things that authority figures have forced them to say or do. Because of Christendom, when Christianity is mentioned they will experience boredom or revulsion."⁹

Therefore, in a fashion similar to Macintyre's (who went back to Aristotelian practises as a way of moving beyond the debris of the 'Enlightenment Project'), Kreider visits the early church for insight about how the Church can faithfully live under the reign of God today. It is in this research that Kreider explains the behaviour, belonging, and belief trialogue we have briefly mentioned previously. He then draws three

---

7 See for example, The Spiritual Practices of St Ignatius Loyola, https://www.ignatianspirituality.com/ignatian-prayer/the-spiritual-exercises
8 Bass, (ed.)., *Practicing our faith*, 5.
9 Kreider, *Change of Conversion*, 99-100.

'clues' (Kreider's term) for followers of Jesus in a post-Christendom era. These three clues are all concerned with the nature of spiritual formation.

Firstly, Kreider teaches that local churches need to become communities who have a deep appropriation for the counter-narrative of God as perfectly self-disclosed in the son, Jesus. As this process goes on, churches become aware of the competing narratives and messages in their context and can maintain a filtering process with regard to which ones bring freedom (light) and which ones bring bondage (darkness). He notes,

> "Thinking missiologically, they asked in case after case whether a given practice was life-giving or whether it led to bondage ... And at least some of the catechesis of early Christianity were aimed at forming communities of free people in which the addictions of that blighted pagan society were being addressed and overcome."[10]

The discipline of Spiritual Direction uses terms such as life-giving versus life-sapping, and freedom versus being bound. The Quakers, who are known for their discernment practises, encourage people to 'place each path near the heart' and see which one brings consolation or desolation.

Secondly, Kreider unpacks the need for a conversion that transforms behaviour as well as belief and experience. He notes that pre-Christendom conversion involved change in each of these three areas and describes how this changed as Christendom emerged. The shift in the fourth and fifth centuries was that instruction gave attention to correct belief, and concern for behaviour atrophied. This concurs with Cox's theory of the *Age of Belief* as explained in the Introduction. He summarises,

> "The early Christians led us to reconsider the balance of ingredients in conversion. They wrote relatively little about experience; there is no extensive literature of inferiority before Augustine. They did of course emphasise right belief; already in Justin and Irenaeus this is very evident. But the emphasis in the early Christian liturgies of the believer's sense of belonging – their affinity and allegiance – seems extreme to us. Even stranger to us is the Apostolic Tradition's focus upon transformed behaviour as the heart of catechism."[11]

---

10 Kreider, *Change of Conversion*, 103.
11 Kreider, *Change of Conversion*, 103.

Finally, Kreider comments about the formative power of the formational practises. Early documents in the Church's history suggest that catechesis took years of mentoring under the guidance of an approved sponsor, and powerful things occurred in the life of the initiate during this process. Today when people are converted, emphasis is upon inner experience and cognitive belief. In the early church, conversion was a result of a lengthy process and was ultimately celebrated by baptism. Kreider notes, "The teaching and example of the catechists and sponsors and the practical involvement of the catechumens concentrated on transforming the catechumen's behaviours in ways consonant with the church's understanding of truth."[12]

So, empowered by Kreider's analysis of what brought real, enduring, fruitful formation, we seek to present some basic practises that can re-emphasise behaviour and belonging as a counter-balance to the already existing emphasis of belief in modern church life. We are not questioning the importance of belief, but we are seeking to reintroduce behaviour and belonging as parts of basic Christian formation. This is similar to the era Cox introduces us to in the Ages of Faith and the Spirit. Therefore, we describe four practices around which Kingdom Communities can be aligned.

As we do so we want to identify three influences on the modern mindset that shapes our bias. *Firstly*, thinkers such as Descartes, Kant, and Newton developed an intellectual foundation that thrived for four hundred years, of which we are recipients. This foundation was centred on a dualism between knowledge and the physical realm. Stanley Grenz wrote,

"The modern, post-Enlightenment mind assumes that knowledge is certain, objective and good. It presupposes that the rational, dispassionate self can obtain such knowledge. It presupposes that the knowing self, peers at the mechanistic world as a neutral observer armed with the scientific method. The modern knower engages in the knowing process believing that knowledge inevitably leads to progress and that science coupled with education will free humankind from

---

[12] Kreider, *Change of Conversion*, 104. Catechists are teachers of the faith and catechumens are new converts under instruction.

our vulnerability to nature and all forms of social bondage."[13]

Secondly, (as noted by Grenz) particularly through the contribution of Isaac Newton, humans have an imagination of the universe as a machine. It follows logically that the human mind, through scientific method, is able to explain the workings of the universe in an attempt to ultimately conquer it. "The modern human can appropriately be categorised as Descartes' autonomous, rational substance encountering Newton's mechanistic world."[14]

Newton's metaphor for the world was a machine. It is this mechanistic idea that has brought tremendous influence upon human organisations. The Industrial Revolution reorganised societies. However, the imagination for social systems changed, also, because of Newton. Churches, like other social organisations, have adopted this imagination, often with modernist reasons for how mission can be done better with greater productivity and effectiveness. Few, however, have ever stopped to ask what effect this is having upon the faithfulness of the community they are designed to organise.

This is perhaps because of the *third* dominant influence of modernity that forms our modern imaginations, namely that the world (including humans) can best be understood by breaking everything down into the smallest possible components for study and domination. Francis Bacon perhaps best summarised this method through which modernity operates. Consequently, he is known as the father of modernity. Bacon devised the method of breaking things into their smallest parts in order to conquer. His widely known method for conquering nature, was through "wrestling it to the ground".

This readiness to conquer through division and a mechanical imagination, shaped generations of factory and management organisation and production, and has consumed and formed the Western church's imagination for self-organising and mission. Consequently, it has also had a huge effect on methods of Christian formation and often has turned formation simply into programs for information transfer.

---

[13] Stanley Grenz, *A Primer on Postmodernism*, Grand Rapids: William B. Eerdmans, 1996, 81.
[14] Brian Carrell, *Moving between the Times: Modernity and Postmodernity*: A Christian View, Auckland: Deepsight Trust, 1998, 35.

The effects of these forces upon modern church life have been profound on belief, belonging and behaviour. *Belief* has become a privatised system of information that affects the subjective realm of the modernist duality. There is little or no place for holistic catechesis between beliefs and what people know as objective truth. Put more plainly, when most Christians confess, 'Jesus is Lord', they mean it personally. They often don't appreciate that the claim is over the whole world.

The area of *belonging* has also been profoundly affected by modernity. Seeing people as individual, replaceable parts of a machine has become a reality in the modern corporatised church. In the workforce they are known as Human Resources. People think that they belong, but they do not know each other. They meet only in between pews for an hour or so each week and rarely have a meal together in someone's home. Because of modernity, churches have come to accept that such isolation is normal or excuse it because of busyness.

Grenz summarises,

> "The ideals of the thinking self, knowing itself and of the mechanistic universe opened the way for the modern explosion of knowledge under the banner of the Enlightenment project ... [which] in turn, produced the modern technological society of the twentieth century. At the heart of this society is the desire to rationally manage life, on the assumption that scientific advancement and technology provide the means to improving the quality of human life."[15]

Behaviour has been greatly affected by this modernist framework. Too often we sit in a group or a committee where the participants may have very different behaviours or even character in the other forums of society (family, work, church, and so on). Because there is such a great emphasis in belief as the most important element in many modern churches, behavioural modification is often considered unnecessary (or at least secondary) for salvation. We have all seen contradictions in the behaviour of believers perhaps frustratingly when cut off from the selfish driving of someone with a Christian sticker on their car!

---

[15] Grenz, *Primer on Postmodernism*, 81.

Four Practises

We have sought to incorporate all three aspects of Kreider's ingredients of holistic Christian formation (behaviour, belonging and belief) in the design of four practises that could be suitable for a Kingdom Community. These have been developed as a process to help guide members of a Kingdom Community to be formed together, toward holistic Christian expression. There is nothing exceptional about what we present here. As Dorothy Bass has amply demonstrated in *Practicing our faith: A way of life for searching people*, there are a multiplicity of combinations and practises that can guide formation. Christian practises refer to the things that Christians do as a sign of their values and priorities toward becoming like Christ. They are the basic daily practises of how we 'live differently'.

Bass describes some of what distinguishes Christian practises,

"They emerge from engaging the narratives of the congregation's tradition - both the larger Christian tradition and the denominational tradition; they resurrect, re-appropriate, redefine, rework, or recover older Christian practices; they lead to a deeper understanding of congregational identity and vocation; they are relevant in their cultural setting yet are not blurred with the culture; they are spiritually authentic, congruent between inner experience and outer expressions; they provide accountability in the community; they demonstrate seriousness in devotion and commitment; they are shared; they foster community; they "cost something" in terms of Christian discipleship; they are not privatized, but have public expression and consequences."[16]

Practises can be hard work and unpopular in a culture such as ours where autonomy and individual freedom are valued above community, servanthood and discipline. Yet these pressures do not change the reality of the fruitfulness from regular practises. Graham Hill and Grace Ji-Sun Kim note that following practises isn't always easy. They comment, "It's especially hard in modern, liberal-democratic, consumeristic, and individualistic societies. So much so in these societies push back against

---

[16] Bass, (ed)., *Practicing our Faith*, 65-66, summarised.

discipline, accountability, stability and community. But discipleship and community must go hand in hand."[17]

As we have discussed earlier, being near a Kingdom Community assumes the people becoming involved are at least interested in or open to the kingdom of God and living the Way of Jesus. They experience the positive example through the life of the Kingdom Community as the pathway to kingdom life (for example: love of God; love and concern for each other and neighbours; teaching and invitation for them to experience God's reality, and so on). With this dynamic in mind, core members of a Kingdom Community will likely be pursuing individual practises such as reading scripture and praying. The following four practises are collective practises that we suggest as the sort of things that need to be integral to a Kingdom Communities' rhythm.

Practise One:
The Practise of Regular Table Fellowship and Breaking Bread

The place of the meal has largely been lost in church life, indeed in modern life. Families rush about their daily tasks as parents juggle work responsibilities with the needs of their children. Children are almost as busy as their parents. They seem to attend an endless progression of training and coaching sessions. Most church Sunday morning church programs are just as frantic, and apart from the first couple of songs and a small talk, the children are herded out to their own Sunday school lessons.

As a result of such busy activity and over programmed lives, many church children rarely spend relational time with Christian adults other than their parents. Children are also rarely present when the Lord's Supper is celebrated because they are out at Sunday school. They miss seeing the Lord's Supper. Mind you, a small piece of neatly cut white bread or a sliver of a cracker and a tiny plastic cup of grape juice really do not seem adequate symbols of the Last Supper nor of the abundance

---

[17] Graham Hill, & Grace Ji-Sun Kim, *Healing our Broken Humanity: Practices for Revitalizing the Church and renewing the World*, Downers Grove: InterVarsity Press, 2018. Hill and Kim develop nine holistic practices: re-imagine church, renew lament, repent together, relinquish power, restore justice, reactivate hospitality, reinforce agency, reconcile relationships and recover life together.

and life-giving nature of the gospel and life in the kingdom. Somehow the solemn, symbolic and reverential nature of Communion has become removed from daily life and inaccessible to many of those with whom Jesus would spend time.

Therefore, the development of the centring practise of regular table fellowship (a proper meal) and the breaking of bread within this context is a wonderful opportunity for the development of Kingdom Community life and formation. It is around the table that a place is set for each guest and where a sacred space is created. When regular table fellowship is mentioned, this means that there is an intentional space provided for other human beings with whom we share a common concern for life in all its fullness. Daniel Homan and Lonni Collins Pratt observe,

"The table is where you connect and belong. It is a place where the past remains alive in the memory of the very old, and the future sparkles with possibility. It is enchanted. We lean close together, we share a glass, we tell a story. Through this simple human relating, the universe feels as though it is right again."[18]

Tables are one of the most important places of human connection. We are often most fully alive to life when sharing a meal around a table. In her book *Making Room: Recovering Hospitality as a Christian Tradition*, Christine Pohl observed, "A shared meal is the activity most closely tied to the reality of God's kingdom, just as it is the most basic expression of hospitality."[19]

Throughout the Bible God has a way of showing up at tables – in both the Old and New Testaments we find a table: the table of Passover and the table of Communion. New Testament scholar, Tom Wright captured something of this sentiment when he wrote, "When Jesus himself wanted to explain to his disciples what his forthcoming death was all about, he didn't give them a theory, he gave them a meal."[20]

---

[18] Daniel Homan and Lonni Collins Pratt, *Radical Hospitality: Benedict's Way of Love*, Brewster, MA: Paraclete Press, 2002, 108.
[19] Christine Pohl, *Making Room: Recovering Hospitality as a Christian Tradition*, Grand Rapids: Eerdmans, 1999, 30.
[20] Nicholas Thomas Wright, "The Cross and the Caricatures," London: Fulcrum, 2007.

Practise Two:
The Practise of Deep Listening

We are, generally, not good listeners. We are good at offering our opinion, however, few of us genuinely listen to each other, our neighbours, or community narratives. The Christian message taught to us over many decades is partly to blame for this situation. We are often told that that we have a message to proclaim, but rarely are we taught to be still and listen.

When Andrew arrived as minister at his last church, it was trying to emerge from a deeply conflicted situation over worship style and form. Good people from both sides had dug the usual trenches over the 'worship wars'. The argument to hold two separate services based on style (one traditional and one contemporary) could have won the day. As a part of the process of guiding the church towards unity, Andrew asked various people to participate in diverse listening and story-telling groups. They were asked to sit and listen to stories from in their group about their experiences of God and mission. The exercise brought many people together and differences reduced as people saw the significance and meaning that the various experiences had created. Listening to each another softened hearts and enlarged relationships and respect.

That church has come quite a long way over the years, because of that experience and many others since. While there were natural age and cultural differences, the church determined to choose unity and respect rather than division and separation because they listened to each other. The challenge before us in contemporary society, is for us to listen to the world outside the doors of the church. We would do well to heed Henri Nouwen's advice,

> "To listen is very hard, because it asks of us so much interior stability that we no longer need to prove ourselves by speeches, arguments, statements, or declarations. True listeners no longer have an inner need to make their presence known. They are free to receive, to welcome, to accept. Listening is much more than allowing another to talk while waiting for a chance to respond. Listening is paying full attention to others and welcoming them into our very beings. The beauty of listening is that those who are listened to start feeling accepted, start

taking their words more seriously and discovering their own true selves. Listening is a form of spiritual hospitality by which you invite strangers to become friends, to get to know their inner selves more fully, and even to dare to be silent with you."[21]

One specific practice that has been a feature of many indigenous cultures and has been a practice of the Quakers since the seventeenth century are 'Listening Circles'. People sit in a circle and listen deeply to each other, and each person speaks from the heart. The focus is on dialogue – on exploring and learning together through deep listening. The roots of the word *dialogue* come from the Greek words *dia* and *logos*. Dia means 'through' and '*logos*' translates as 'word' or 'meaning'. In essence, in this context a dialogue is a *flow of meaning*. But it is more than this too. William Isaacs in *Dialogue and the Art of Thinking Together* says,

> "In the most ancient meaning of the word, *logos* meant 'to gather together', and suggested an intimate awareness of the relationships among things in the natural world. In that sense, *logos* may be best rendered in English as 'relationship'. The Book of John in the New Testament begins, "In the beginning was the Word (logos)". We could now hear this as, "In the beginning was the Relationship." To take it one step further, dialogue is a conversation in which people think together in relationship. Thinking together implies that you no longer take your own position as final. You relax your grip on certainty and listen to possibilities that result simply from being in relationship with others - possibilities that might not otherwise have occurred. To listen respectfully to others, to cultivate and speak your own voice, to suspend your opinions about others - these bring out the intelligence that lives at the very centre of ourselves - the intelligence that exists when we are alert of possibilities around us and thinking freshly."[22]

The practice of deep listening was marvellously exemplified by one of Churches of Christ in Queensland's Community Chaplains, Haydn. For many months Haydn walked the streets of a suburb north

---

[21] Nouwen, H., *Bread for the Journey: A Daybook of Wisdom and Faith*, New York: Harper Collins, 2009.
[22] William Isaacs, *Dialogue and the Art of Thinking Together*, Cambridge: Currency, 1999.

of Brisbane, connecting with shop owners and regulars, and other on the ground community people. He was supported by a Mission Action Support Team, which included several other ministers who prayed for him and provided encouragement and practical support. By truly listening, relationships developed. A number of new regular meeting groups formed around common need and interest. Through Haydn's gentle leadership these slowly developed into Kingdom Communities comprised mostly of people new to the Way of Jesus.

Dean remembers being invited to participate with one of these groups. A group of around thirty people had become established through Haydn's deep listening to where God might be at work in people. This group met regularly to drum together on large and small bongo drums, and to share and reflect on the word of God, and to pray and care for one another. Everyone sat in a big circle. It began slowly and chaotically but amazingly settled into a flow with everyone somehow immersed in a deeper rhythm. The drumming together went on for a while and then naturally seemed, by unvoiced consensus, to come to a place of stillness. It was a spiritual experience. In this state of sacred stillness, the Bible was read out loud and heard afresh. It is fair to say that this was a different experience and composition of characters to many of the groups with whom Dean would normally meet. Yet there was no doubt, having shared fellowship with the group after 'the service' that there was a Kingdom Community in existence. Hand to Hand and Moreton Bay Community Matters were two other groups that evolved into Kingdom Communities in that region through Haydn and others' deep listening and discerning of where God was prompting people, and allowing the most appropriate form of being in community to coalesce.

Practise Three:
The Practise of Hospitality to the Stranger

Human need for help from others is universal. As hard as a person might try to preserve independence and self-reliance, we can each find ourselves in need at random moments. Throughout history, there have been moments when people were dislocated and in need of hospitality from strangers. Sometimes people have taken them in and helped them, and other times no one has helped them. Perhaps, the anxiety that is rising most in modern society is of the stranger. The less we know our neighbourhood the more the anxiety grows. The stranger has long been a subject of fear throughout history and still is today. Ana Maria Pineda comments, "The stranger seems to portend danger – sometimes of physical harm, but also because the stranger represents the unknown, a challenge to the familiar constructs of our personal world."[23] Jesus' famous story of the Good Samaritan directly speaks to this issue and illustrates what loving our neighbour looks like in practise (Luke 10: 25-37).

In 2011, Queensland was devastated by floods across much of the State. Brisbane was flooded as the Brisbane river burst its banks. Water flowed into the basements and ground floors of many of the city's high-rise office blocks, shutting down electrical switchboards, and consequently all power. Suburbs adjacent to rivers went underwater with hundreds of communities being dispossessed. Fortunately, Dean's home was on high ground, and he and his wife (and dog), along with many others around the State, opened their home to accommodate those who had been forced to leave their own place. A mother and her young daughter ended up staying with them for a couple of months after their home and most of their belongings were destroyed.

It was an emotional time as strangers rallied together to help each other. As the waters began to recede, neighbours who previously hardly knew each other, banded together to help clean out mud and ruined belongings of others who were suffering in their area. Some folk supplied a steady stream of drinks and food to the workers. Some businesses and churches were astounding in their generosity and practical assistance to those in need in their community. The extraordinary circumstances broke down barriers and brought strangers together. Everyone remarked on the amazing volunteer armies that turned up for days on end to help in the many communities affected. They were called affectionately, 'The Mud Army'. Whatever their background or belief, people seemed to sense a united Spirit in what was happening. People who would normally never get involved, felt moved to volunteer. Warmth and welcome abounded, and as often happens in the midst of tragedy, new relationships formed,

---

[23] Bass, (ed.)., *Practicing our Faith*, 31.

neighbourly relationships strengthened, and there were many blessings. Yet, after months of cleanup and rebuilding, people gradually returned to their normal way of behaving, life settled back into its old patterns and the boundaries returned.

The practise of providing Hospitality to the Stranger has the look and feel of people stepping out to help their neighbours during a flood. A Kingdom Community that practises this, strives to be in touch with the Spirit of God and has that orientation to readily extend welcome and love to the stranger in need. In the Christian tradition, offering hospitality is a moral requirement. There is an ever-present expectation that God's people will offer hospitality to the stranger and treat such a one with mercy and justice. This emerges from the hospitality that God has shown the people of God in the first place. Ancient travellers, whether pilgrims or traders, often suffered poorly when they ventured beyond their own provinces. Therefore, since at least the fifth century, Christians have offered international guest houses for travellers. The term for these houses was hospice, from the Latin *hospes*, which means guests. The needs of the lame and ill over time required that these hospices often became the forerunners of modern hospitals. However, the term originally was designed for strangers who were away from home and dependent upon others.

Often a host who initiates hospitality to the stranger soon becomes a recipient of grace and hospitality. This is the circular, mutual nature of this practise. It is, therefore, a step toward the transformation of local communities. Ana Maria Pineda comments,

> "This circle of mutual hospitality can embrace and transform the people who enter it. The early church, which met in houses, grew up turning hosts into guests and guests into hosts. The apostle Paul, whose ministry involved travelling from one house church to another, looked forward to the nourishing hospitality that awaited him in each place, just as the young churches looked forward to the gifts he would bring them."[24]

---

[24] Bass, (ed.)., *Practicing our Faith*, 34.

Chapter Eight: Practises of Kingdom Communities

As Kingdom Communities practise the welcoming of the stranger, the barriers of modern communal life are broken down. The nature of modern, suburban town planning has conditioned people toward privacy, fear of the stranger and a lack of hospitality. These characteristics are the reason the practise of hospitality is suggested here as a practise. It is as fears are overcome and hospitality is offered that, in turn, the giver and community can receive and be transformed.

In his first year in Queensland, Dean recalls meeting with a group of local church Elders to brief them about a new social housing complex that Churches of Christ was opening in their area. They were appreciative of the briefing and Dean suggested that it might be an opportunity for their church to connect with the forty or so new residents. One of the Elders put forward the idea of slipping Bible tracts under the doors. Another built on this and suggested a copy of their church newsletter be put in each letterbox, as this had the time of their Sunday services and contact details if anyone wanted to come along. No one advanced any strategy of actually meeting the people and welcoming them. The mindset was similar to the situation that Andrew described at his Church running alongside the market across the road.

Churches of Christ put forward a persuasive case to the Queensland State Government for the funding of a chaplain to work with the social housing residents. Data was available on the rate and number of incidences that occur on average in public housing complexes. The government was persuaded to trial a community chaplain on the basis that they would more than pay for themselves through the reduction of incidences and requirements for Housing Department personnel to intervene. This is indeed what happened, and Churches of Christ were able to move forward in appointing community chaplains to work with other social housing complexes. How did the chaplain, who was a stranger to the new residents (who were strangers to each other) proceed? He put on a barbeque on the lawns next door to the units and invited each of the residents. More than half came along to check it out and have a sausage. He followed this up by visiting each unit to simply say, "G'day" and to let them know that he was their chaplain. Many didn't even know what that meant. So, a conversation evolved around this. Some invited him in for a cuppa. He listened deeply and so community began. Within a year, a prayer group had formed through people wanting prayer and wanting to pray for and bless others in need. Reading of scripture evolved through a desire to understand more. And there was great celebration at the first baptism – an emotional event for a lady who had suffered much over her life journey. Today a Kingdom Community exists in this housing complex. It is beautiful.

Practise Four:
The Practise of Discernment

Discernment creates the capacity to see. To discern is to see through to the essence of a matter. Discernment distinguishes the real from the phony, the true from the false, the good from the evil, and the path toward God from the path away from God. There are at least four occasions recorded in the book of Acts when we can see the Church seeking to discern God's will (Acts 1:12–26; 6:1–7; 11:1–18; and 15). Members of the New Testament church believed that God would guide individuals and communities; they expected to be led by the Spirit (Galatians 5:18, Romans 8:14).

The practise of discernment or finding God's will together is one that is often raised by leaders. The question of what God might want us to do often surfaces during times of transition. For example, when a new direction is being sought for the church, or when the church building is no longer fit for purpose, or a minister finishes their ministry term.

In chapter nine of the Book of Numbers there is a great description of God's people knowing and following God's will,

> "When the Cloud lifted above the Tent, the People of Israel marched out; and when the Cloud descended the people camped. The People of Israel marched at God's command and they camped at his command. As long as the Cloud was over The Dwelling, they camped." (Num 9:17-18 ESV)

We wish it was always so clear. Unfortunately, it is a rare occurrence these days when life's major decisions are made in the company of other people. Unless there is illness or retrenchment or some other form of unplanned calamity, many people make their biggest decisions independently, often without family input. This independence is the way we in the West are conditioned, and many would argue it is our right in a free society. This individualism makes us weak at collectively discerning God's actions and the things in which God might be calling us to participate. Luke Timothy Johnson describes some qualities of discernment,

"Discernment enables humans to perceive their characteristically ambiguous experience as revelatory and to articulate such experiences in a narrative of faith. Discernment enables others to hear such narratives as the articulation of faith and as having revelatory significance. Discernment enables communities to listen to such gathering narratives for the word of God that they might express. Discernment enables communities, finally, to decide for God."[25]

There can be problems with discernment as a practice. It can empower the spiritually manipulative to attempt to control; it can be vague; it is not always correct; it can often miss signs of emergence because of centuries of tradition; and it is slow and messy. However, discernment is necessary and, when done with time and reflection, can be a rich practise in the formation of followers of Christ.

Johnson offers the following criteria for a group discernment process. *Firstly*, he suggests that any group discernment process must have the aim to edify. His argument is based on Paul's writings, which he summarises as follows; "Paul therefore speaks of edification as that expression of the mind of Christ (1 Cor 2:16) in which each person looks not to his or her own interests but to the interests of others."[26] He continues, "Indeed, the entire language of our own age, to the extent it speaks of the rights of individuals or groups as absolute and nonnegotiable demands requiring recognition by every assembly, must be recognised as deriving from a spirit of the world and not of God."[27]

Secondly, Johnson argues that discernment primarily has concern for the whole group of believers rather than just the individual's needs or wants. Therefore, if a group member requests something, the group

---
[25] Luke Timothy Johnson, *Scripture and Discernment: Decision making in the Church*, Nashville: Abingdon, 1983, 109.
[26] Johnson, *Scripture and Discernment*, 116.
[27] Johnson, *Scripture and Discernment*, 132.

should ask questions like, 'Does this build up the whole body or is this a request of self-interest?' The purpose for a discernment process is in asking how the group can be distinguished from those outside it.

Finally, Johnson concludes that discernment within a group should be a process of disarmament. It should seek to develop unity rather than dualism. It should seek to reduce competition, oppression, hatred, envy, and fear, rather than promote them. It should lead to diversity of membership and giftedness.

"Outside in the world, background and pedigree and wealth and social status and ambition and power call the tune. In the church, another measure is to apply, one in which gender, social status, and race are not to matter either negatively or positively, one in which lowly-mindedness seeks to serve the interests of others, one in which the temple of God is built up in love. This indeed is a daunting standard. But the subject is not getting along in the world. The subject is building up God's people in holiness."[28]

Ruth Hayley Barton describes a helpful and practical process for Kingdom Community discernment.[29]

- Clarify the question for discernment. What starts off as a question about a new building project or strategy might deepen into a question about mission and values, and whether we are pushing our own agenda or whether God is really opening up new opportunities. Our discussions in chapter 6 about *single-*, *double-*, and *triple-loop learning* can be useful tools to assist in clarifying the question for discernment.

- Involve the right people. A prerequisite for community discernment is that the individuals involved are committed to collectively seek God's will in relation to the question at hand, have some experience at spiritual discernment, and some knowledge of the area to be discerned. In this respect it is similar to the make up of the Strategic Action Leadership Teams (SALTs) described in chapter six.

---

[28] Johnson, *Scripture and Discernment*, 132.
[29] Ruth Hayley Barton, *Strengthening the Soul of Your Leadership: Seeking God in the Crucible of Ministry*, Downers Grove: IVP Books, 2008, 197-207.

- Pray without ceasing. Hayley Barton suggests several kinds of praying: prayer that acknowledges our dependence on God; prayer that we would be indifferent to ego, prestige, comfort, and all things but the will of God; and prayer for wisdom. Dean and Andrew cannot emphasise enough the importance of constant prayer as an essential ingredient for discernment, and for the health of any Kingdom Community.
- Listen on many levels. This is our second practise described above.
- Select an option that seems consistent with what God is doing amongst us. God will already be prompting and moving people. Look for the green shoots of new life and energy.
- Seek inner confirmation. This is where everyone steps back and individually sits with the preferred option and asks God for confirmation. Another angle on this is the saying: let's sleep on it and see if it still feels right in the morning.
- Agree together. Dean recalls an occasion when there was a major issue and decision to be made about direction at Churches of Christ in Queensland. The stakes were high. His team gathered what information they could to inform the decision, there was discussion, good listening and collective prayer. It was agreed that each person would individually pray and mull it over, and that they would meet again in three days' time. They convened and amazingly two of the team had had similar dreams about the way forward. They shared these and there was a strong coalescing around what to do. Dean recalls the feeling at the time was that described by the leaders in Acts 15:28, "It seemed good to the Holy Spirit and to us."
- Do the will of God as we have come to understand it.

Discernment, or finding God's will together, is an important practice within Kingdom Communities. Precisely as these words are being written, Andrew can hear the sounds of saxophone practice going on upstairs from one of his children. Squeaks and mistakes are mixed with the occasional run of well-played notes, as the instrument is slowly mastered, and the apprentice is formed into a better saxophone player. Practise makes perfect they say! The practises outlined in this chapter are intended to function in a similar fashion.

We have imagined a Kingdom Community rooting itself in regular (weekly) table fellowship and Breaking of Bread (Practise One). Like an anchor in a safe harbour, this practice is bedrock for the group. Over the meal together they practise deep listening (Practise Two) to the stories shared across the table and from throughout the week. Sometimes the stories will have come from the Practise of Hospitality to the Stranger (Practise Three) and other times from the many interactions and reactions to life in the neighbourhood. Then, as the group hear the layers of stories and interactions around the table, they discern (Practise Four) what God might be doing, saying or calling for their participation. Over weeks, months and years the pursuit of these practises will form them in local kingdom ministry.

The four practises we have discussed are, in our view, arguably integral to a healthy Kingdom Community. However, we stress that they cannot be compulsory. Indeed, practises are likely to differ in form and degree between established and emerging Kingdom Communities. If you are a part of a Kingdom Community, there is a wonderful opportunity for the group to discuss what might be useful practises that form members and the group towards shining the light of Christ through faith, hope and love. The practises in an Aged Care or Housing setting may be different from a school or a neighbourhood – or they might not be![30]

---

[30] Alan Roxburgh, *Joining God, Remaking Church, Changing the World*. Roxburgh outlines five practices: Listening, Discerning, Testing and Experimenting, Reflecting and Deciding. They are similar to what we have outlined and come from many conversations spent together. Michael Frost, *Surprise the world: Five habits of highly missional people*, Colorado Springs: NavPress, 2016. Frost outlines the five practices used in his church: Small Boat Big Sea. The five practices explained are: Bless, Eat, Listen, Learn and Sent. They are very contextual to Kingdom Community practices in Australia.

Chapter Nine

Frequently Asked Questions.

The following questions have arisen over time from many people and places. These are the ones that seem to keep coming back to us. We have tried to answer them in a general sense in the book as well as here, but we caution that every circumstance is unique and deserves its own considered answer, if that was possible.

What is the definition of a Kingdom Community and are they real?

A Kingdom Community is a community of two or more followers of Christ who together commit to regularly pursue practises that bring the light of Christ into communities through faith, hope and love. In Churches of Christ in Queensland they are called 'Kingdom Access Places'. In Churches of Christ in Victoria and Tasmania, the phrase 'Communities of Hope and Compassion' has been created so as to enable these groups the possibility to flourish. At New Hope Baptist Church, in Blackburn North, they are called 'Communities of Hope'. Urban Neighbours of Hope still operate in Australia, New Zealand and Thailand. Base Ecclesial Communities have been going in Brazil (and elsewhere) for over seventy years. Sure, they are real.

Our simple definition brings together the principles found in Matthew 18:20; 22:34-40; 28:18-20; John 8:12; 1 Corinthians 13:13; Colossians 1:28-29; Ephesians 4:11-13 and countless others that emphasise the following commitments:

- They meet regularly and include care, prayer, Bible study and mission.
- They practise hospitality within their community and among strangers.
- They attend locally, listen deeply and discern together what the Spirit is calling them to do in response.
- They break bread together, usually over a meal when they meet.

- They are committed to real unity among all Christians in their city and universally.
- They develop an agreed rhythm and set of practices.
- They act justly, love mercy and walk humbly with God (Micah 6:8). They love God and one another.

In recent decades there has been a rediscovery of house churches across Australia[1], with notable work written by Robert Banks.[2] Also, as mentioned in this book, the Forge Mission Training Network[3] taught and advocated for experiments where small, intentional, missional communities could contextually model Christian witness outside the bounds of the traditional local church. Being prophetic and, for some, radical, Forge tended to polarise traditional church leaders, however the legacy of publications, experiments and its ongoing and growing influence across North America, especially through the leadership of Alan Hirsch and Michael Frost ensures that the work is ongoing. There are many elements from Forge's legacy that are adaptable to the future growth of Kingdom Communities, especially if assisted by Leonardo Boff's sage advice to reduce conflict with the traditional local church.

Throughout this book several stories have been included to intentionally point to real life examples. In the case of Queensland, Kingdom Access Places have the following elements:

- Twelve or more people who connect with an identifiable rhythm and regularity,
- At least three people who would self-identify as members of the Church of Christ Mission Workforce,
- The group is designed to give people in the community access to the kingdom of God – "there is a danger they will meet Jesus",
- The group has some definable and nameable leadership and governance, and

---

[1] See for example, oikos.org.au
[2] See Robert Banks, *Going to church in the First Century*, Parramatta: Hexagon Press, 1980, and *Paul's idea of community: The Early House Churches in the Cultural Setting*, Grand Rapids: Baker, 1994, and *The Church Comes Home*, Peabody: Hendrickson, 1998.
[3] See forge.org.au

Chapter Nine: Frequently Asked Questions.

- The group has traceable links for Churches of Christ Queensland.

Churches of Christ Victoria/Tasmania call these groups Communities of Hope and Compassion. They describe a group is a community of hope and compassion if it:

- Is becoming an 'order of local missionaries; confident of affirming and translating the story of God's salvation through Jesus Christ in a variety of ways and contexts.
- Gathers and grows disciples of Jesus, who are becoming lifelong learners with a developing spiritual maturity, evidenced by the fruit and gifts of the Spirit, each seeking to operate within the fivefold ministry pattern of Apostle, Prophet, Evangelist and Pastor/Teacher of Ephesians 4.
- Sees worship, prayer and learning as expressions of a gathering and sent Community, propelling people outwards to a watching and waiting world.
- Centres its life on the Bible and in particular the New Testament; reading it and discerning from it a picture of God's kingdom, the salvation story, and transforming spiritual practices.
- Invites accountability to one another; demonstrating the fruit of time spent in supporting and watching over one another in love.
- Knows it is an incomplete expression of the reign of God and is committed to the journey of seeking and discerning a fuller and fresher expression of Christian witness, unity and life.
- Welcomes the stranger, demonstrating hospitality and its message of grace and generosity.
- Has mission as its priority and actively engages all those who are yet to belong.
- Seeks to name where God is at work in their neighbourhood and to join with him there, exhibiting an observable and graceful influence and impact.
- Engages its neighbourhood, by being an incarnational 'contrast' community, and a witness, sign and foretaste of the kingdom.

- Practises justice and reconciliation as signposts of the kingdom; revealed by a diversity of age, gender, race, ability and socio-economic identity.[4]

A third example of Local Ecclesial Communities being encouraged, sent and multiplied is from a local church. New Hope Baptist Church in North Blackburn has identified a strategy of developing Communities of Hope. They currently number 150 such groups that range across numerous cultures, languages and ages. New Hope Senior Pastor Allan Demond sees Communities of Hope as a strategic means to extend the kingdom and enable expressions of leadership not possible in a church based only on congregations. Demond says,

"Communities of Hope are open and people who don't know Jesus are welcome to join them. They are communities shaped by Jesus' values and his mission. They are led by a follower of Jesus and they are committed to making more followers. They are places where people can explore and eventually encounter Jesus and dedicate their life to him. Some Communities of Hope are as small as three people and others are made up of hundreds and may even contain other sub-communities within them. These Communities of Hope are healthy when they make disciples – when they help people find the Jesus-path to hope."[5]

Where should a local church start if it wanted to advance Kingdom Communities?

We suggest you start with what you have. Most churches already have some small groups or ministries that are genuinely local in their focus (for example: playgroups, midweek Bible studies, meals-on-wheels or social welfare programs). The key shifts that these groups may need to undertake will concern their identity, practises and leadership. Remember that one of the significant transitions that groups need to undergo is often from a hub and spokes model to a distributed network. A Kingdom Community is not just a program of the church, it will become the community of primary connection for most of its members.

---

[4] Churches of Christ in Vic/Tas, "Renewal Challenge FAQ's", May 2015.
[5] https://www.newhope.net.au/vision

Chapter Nine: Frequently Asked Questions.

The transition is somewhat similar as the transition that young adults go through as they move towards maturity. One of the functions of adolescence is the cutting of parental controls and cords as the maturing young adult takes responsibility for themselves. This can be daunting for any parent but is the only known path to maturity. Accordingly, the parent is often affirming the young adult, checking in on the wisdom of certain decisions and trying to ensure that there are other helpful and wise resources available (other adults, mature friends and positive community groups, for instance) and there to help when needed.

It is the nature of groups and programs in a hub and spokes model to always report up or in and seek resources and feedback from the central, administering authority (in this case the church hierarchy). In a corresponding fashion the central authority will often delegate resources and personnel to grow the spokes in terms of what it requires. This means that often the central authority will behave in a 'top-down' manner and attempt to direct the nodes towards whatever is within its strategic plan or leadership priorities. Tension arises when the central authority is out of touch with the spokes. Strategic plans fail when the spokes are not able to provide feedback soundings from the grassroots to the centre or when the central authority simply fails to respond to the grassroots.

A distributed network will be far more agile and independently geared. By definition it isn't particularly seeking guidance or direction from the central hierarchy and won't look naturally to that authority for strategy. Rather a distributed network seeks what it needs to grow, adapt and prosper from wherever that can be found (within the Kingdom Community, from other Kingdom Communities, external resources and particularly what is already present within the local community). Most Kingdom Communities in a distributed network will always take any resources offered but we suggest caution. Remember that you are trying to encourage maturity of the Kingdom Community, not dependence.

If a local church makes an intentional decision to transition in this direction, then everything in the church will eventually be affected, so take your time and be thorough in your research. The *first* area that you are seeking to change is the local group's identity. They need to become far more of a caring and practising community than many church small groups often become. They may or may not 'check in' to the church leadership and programs. This needs to be determined from the outset.

The *second* area to encourage is the Kingdom Community's focus. Kingdom Communities generally need to be local. Members within a node should live in close proximity and each should be willing to commit to the local area as discussed in chapter four. There are excellent resources that provide thoughtful and practical methodology as to how to go about this. Michael Frost explores five practises that his church 'Small Boat Big Sea' has used for years, which have caught on across parts of the Western world.[6] Alan Roxburgh also outlines five alternative practises with useful practise guides.[7] We have developed four possible practises in chapter eight.

Third, the nodes need to have clearly identified leadership. Obviously a very small Kingdom Community has little need for formally designated leadership roles as there is greater capacity for relational decision making. If two or three neighbours covenant together in a neighbourhood there is little need for much structure – just the practises. However, as a Kingdom Community grows larger, it faces a decision of multiplying into smaller Kingdom Communities, or in the case of a school, developing a formal structure.

So, with all that being said, we would start with an Action Learning team. This is what was called a SALT in Queensland. A group of people could be called together to assess local areas of darkness or need and possible responses. A new Kingdom Community could be in the process of being birthed.

How does a network of Kingdom Communities grow?

A small Kingdom Community started in a local neighbourhood may be able to stay together for many years. If someone has a big enough back room, garage or yard, then the group can grow to a reasonable

---

[6] Michael Frost, *Surprise the world: Five habits of highly missional people*, Colorado Springs: NavPress, 2016. The five practices explained are: bless, eat, listen, earn and sent.
[7] Alan Roxburgh, *Joining God, Remaking Church, Changing the World*. The five practices are: listening, discerning, testing and experimenting, reflecting and deciding.

size without dividing. The early churches that grew often were limited by the capacity of a house where people met. In the good fortune that a Kingdom Community of local neighbours grows to a point where there is no house to fit everyone, a choice can be made about dividing up. If a Kingdom Community gets too big, then the dynamics will change to a point where things start to look like a local church. When that happens, you know that it is time to do something.

Because we live in a highly mobile society, it is likely that members of a Kingdom Community who have been positively formed through the community will want to start another when they move. This is often how the early church also spread. This should be a core outcome of any healthy discipleship and formation process. If they begin a new Kingdom Community where they move, there is every possibility that the groups can stay interconnected. The same sense of sending should apply to members who start a Kingdom Community in their professional or leisure networks. This could happen in the workplace, sporting clubs, computer gaming groups, and so on.

Does church size have any influence on ability to transition toward a model of Kingdom Communities?

There are advantages and disadvantages in every church size. The bigger the church the greater the resources (people and facilities) but bigger churches tend to also be top-down, program oriented and regional in composition, which can confuse the focus on local neighbourhoods. Big churches provide wonderful opportunities for networking, showcasing and connecting people and ideas and can also help provide useful training and motivation. Often bigger churches emphasise their small groups as their primary building blocks, places of connection and pastoral care, so the step towards Kingdom Communities is foreseeable but not always easy and the two can be confused in that context. A Kingdom Community is far more than a typical church small group. The key point of differentiation between the two will be the degree of whether a distributed network or hub and spokes model is employed.

The determining issue in whether a big church takes the step towards a distributed network is about power and control. There is tremendous kudos in some pastoral networks for leaders of large churches. Giving away that kudos and influence will require leaders with a kingdom eye and healthy dissatisfaction with the status quo, as will giving away the power that comes from being at the helm in the centre of a hub and spokes model. Large churches also tend to have already broken away from pastoral care dependent models of ministry from paid staff, which is an added advantage.

Smaller churches are, by nature, generally more predisposed to local proximity than their bigger siblings but also tend to have stronger pastoral links with a traditional minister. This understanding of clergy needs to be undone if the local church can move forward. An overemphasis on a centralised minister will never release nodes from unhealthy co-dependence. Smaller churches need to learn that just because they are local and identify with a suburb does not mean that they are necessarily attentive to the local neighbourhood. Indeed, if they are concerned and attentive in the local neighbourhood they will be far less concerned with their denominational identity or traditions, preferring rather to attend to the local patterns and rhythms.

Are church buildings and properties needed?

Yes and no. It is hard to answer a question like this for every context, however there are some principles that might apply. Most Kingdom Communities in most Australian contexts will not need any church buildings. Homes, cafes, community halls and local parks will be preferable and more 'accessible' than church buildings for many Aussies. However, this is not always the case. The movement in recent years towards community choirs is a case in point. Churches have struggled to maintain choirs in a traditional liturgical sense in recent decades. Yet, now they are a wonderful possibility for diverse gender, age and ethnicities to come together to sing. A church building could be ideal for this sort of activity.

The general principle that we would apply is how many hours per week is a church building needed? If the auditorium is only required for under, say, twenty hours each week[8] then basic stewardship questions need to be asked. It becomes hard to justify multi-millions of dollars being tied up in church assets that are rarely used. There are some churches in capital cities with a weekly attendance of only a few people who frequent the building for about an hour per week. If the building is worth ten million dollars (which with increasing land values is often the case) that means that a local church could be costing over $500,000 per worshipper. That could be used far more effectively in mission.

There are many possibilities where a Kingdom Community may need dedicated buildings. However, most are not specifically for religious purposes. Examples could include schools, hospitals, refuges, dance studios, sports facilities, homes for refugees (rented or owned), opportunity shops, welfare programs, cooking schools, art studios, among others.

Taking a step back from these very important stewardship issues, many Kingdom Communities will not need buildings other than private homes. The nature of the majority of these communities are small, dispersed and situated very locally. This also enables effective mission in the inner city where property costs are usually prohibitive, and the standard outer-suburban church car park and large scale land usage is not possible.

Are you saying that the role of a traditional local minister is gone?

The beauty of Leonardo Boff's *Ecclesiogenesis* is that nothing has to die for Base Ecclesial Communities to grow. Base Ecclesial Communities still hold an important place for priests although, in the 1980s when it was written, there were few available, especially for the poor. In Australia we too are headed for a shortage of traditional quality generalist ministers in most Protestant denominations. There are several reasons for this: there are fewer churches that can afford them; they are getting more expensive as cost of living increases in Australia; there are more ministers out of ministry than in ministry in Australia due to the stress of the job; society trusts of traditional clergy

---

[8] Some would argue for a far higher amount of hours per week to justify a church auditorium - say forty.

are at record lows and accordingly fewer people are presenting for this pathway at theological colleges; most people in church ministry are now in specialised roles; and, younger people increasingly are not choosing this pathway, especially for a whole lifetime (they aren't choosing any career for a lifetime!).

The generalist minister may not be completely gone but it is possibly near its use-by date, as a model. We have no reason for concern here (although we do agonise with those who are mid-career and have been formed for this vocation alone). There is nothing particularly biblical about this role, nor is there any particular biblical argument for ordination, which doesn't make it wrong – just not essential. Andrew was at an ordination service recently and after the service he intentionally asked each of the ten newly-minted ordinands what ordination meant theologically. Few could provide an answer. The closest answer was something like, "I guess it means that I am recognised by my denomination." We would argue that is the function of accreditation, not necessarily ordination, especially in any movement that stresses the priesthood of all believers.

Increasingly, the criteria, skills and gifts required for minister endorsement and ordination has been towards teaching, administration and pastoral care (Pastors and Teachers). This is a part of a move towards the minister becoming a 'professional'. A consequence has been that those with apostolic, prophetic and evangelistic gifts (Apostles, Prophets and Evangelists) have often not been able to fit within the rigid structures and positions available. We have one colleague who could not be ordained by his denomination because he was an evangelist and they would only ordain him if he was a pastor in a church!

In a time of rapid discontinuous change and the decline of current models we are faced with the need for broader vision, theological reflection, imagination, new possibilities, a bit of a shake up and a deep engagement with culture. Apostles, Prophets and Evangelists offer these sorts of capacities of which we are so in need. There will always be a place for other leadership gifts, but we must learn to enable more Apostles, Prophets and Evangelists to emerge through our systems or we will continue to lose too much.

Chapter Nine: Frequently Asked Questions.

If you were a local minister or church leader where would you begin?

We suggest these steps:
1. Read *Kingdom Communities: Shining the light of Christ through faith, hope and love*, as a team (ministry team or church Elders). We acknowledge that we have a conflict of interest in suggesting our own book but we can suggest no other resource like this that will develop solid theological and theoretical foundations for the journey ahead (that's why we wrote it!). Some people are natural readers while others really have to be pushed. Perhaps reading a chapter a week (or fortnight or month) and then discussing and reflecting as a group will allow sufficient time for most of the team to come along on the journey.

2. Start to build in practises and a narrative of Kingdom Communities as a way of life and formation throughout the church. This can be as a whole congregation or in the various small groups and ministry areas. Encourage individual practises and collective practises using all avenues of influence to shape the culture around Kingdom Community practises over a twelve-month period. With clear intentionality, commence building into the congregation a narrative of Kingdom Communities (what they are, case studies, possible areas to commence one, and so on), while implementing the four community practises that we have outlined (or design your own).

3. Analyse the dominant leadership behaviours in the church. What is being communicated through the example of those in leadership? Ask, are we capping God's potential through stifling imagination or fanning the flames of the Holy Spirit through a culture of risk and enterprise?

4. Determine what will be measured. This is what people will focus on. Look at what is measured and report on this internally and to the congregation. We suggest that things like baptisms, numbers of Kingdom Communities, people being trained for leadership and numbers of regular community contacts. Highlight the number of people being connected with (not just those attending worship). Highlight and honour the people who are being 'sent'

from the church – for example, measure the numbers involved in ministry that is engaging with people outside of the church boundaries, as well as those within. Also, start measuring and feeding back to the congregation how well they are progressing with the individual and collective practises.

5. Commence a process of church wide research and listening to the local community to find out what is going on. What, and where are the major areas of darkness? Where is God already at work in the community? Where is the energy?[9] Where are our current islands of strength? Where is the life in our church at the moment?

6. Through the church leadership and governance processes, determine a response that the church is going to make through the initiation of what could become a new Kingdom Community. Discern the response collectively. Do the hard work of listening deeply. Are there individuals in the church who are being prompted by God? Is there a theme? Pray for and look for a coalescing of thought and feeling about a particular area that could enable more of the Light of Christ to be shining. Consult with specialists who can help shape the directions you are discerning (for example, community development, property, finance, government relations, and so on). We have a colleague who was removed from his ministry position because he did many of these things and initiated some wonderful community responses – but it was without the support and 'buy in' of the church. It is better to move slowly and be together than splinter too quickly. Be wise.

---

[9] Andre Van Eymeren, *Building Communities of the Kingdom: How to work with others to build great spaces and places*, Morning Star: Melbourne, 2017. Van Eymeren has written a useful book that uses a well-developed tool of Asset Based Community Development to help identify local areas of darkness and energy.

CONCLUSION

And Finally…

"A person who walks in purpose doesn't have to chase people or opportunities. Their light causes people and opportunities to pursue them."

Common Proverb

"You are the light of the world. A town built on a hill cannot be hidden. Neither do people light a lamp and put it under a bowl. Instead they put it on its stand, and it gives light to everyone in the house. In the same way, let your light shine before others, that they may see your good deeds and glorify your Father in heaven."

Matthew 5:14-16

If you have ever had to travel, you will know the importance of good curtains, especially when you are trying to sleep in a different time zone. If you travel in a westerly direction it becomes relevant when your body clock sometimes wakes up too early. The quality of the curtains is crucial when you lay awake at three in the morning telling your body to go back to sleep. Really good curtains block out external light. Whereas, a tiny lack of overlap in the join of the curtains or a slight gap at ceiling lets in a stunning amount of light from the street. Curtains are even more critical if you have travelled east.

Light conquers darkness. A gap in the curtains, the digital clock-radio, the tiny green dot on the smoke alarm or the corridor light squeezing in under the hotel door all prove that. You can't use this metaphor in reverse though. Darkness doesn't conquer light. To make a room completely dark takes a good amount of planning and thought. And even if you successfully darken a room, a mobile phone just has to ring for more light to come.

The Bible says the same things about Jesus and the kingdom he established on earth. John commences his gospel, "In him was life, and the life was the light of humanity. The light shines in the darkness, and the darkness has not overcome it" (John 1:4-5). The testimony of the Easter events sealed the matter. After Jesus was dead and buried in the tomb, his followers went away to mourn. Yet, on the Easter Sunday morning the women were the first ones called to preach eternity's greatest message of hope: the light had come back from the darkness and conquered death itself. Death could not keep Jesus down or therefore blot out the light.

At the head of each chapter we have used a meaningful quotation and Bible passage that (hopefully) has whet your appetite for the proceeding chapter. The Bible passage above from Matthew's gospel reminds us that we are indeed stewards of the light and we are not to put it under a bed or hide it away. No way! Those of us who know the Light are responsible for finding meaningful and appropriate ways of making it available and accessible to others, especially those who are in darkness and need it most.

We have endeavoured to present the idea, theology and reality of Kingdom Communities throughout this book. We have seen too many effective Kingdom Communities (many hundreds of them now) to not write this book. Wherever we look we see them, just like when you spot the same make of car as the one you drive. We have also bumped into too many bounded congregations, denominations and care agencies, where the light has not been shone nearly as brightly as it could be. It has been, in effect, smothered or placed under a bowl because the institution insisted on doing things the way they have always been done (maybe with technical and tactical improvisation), regardless of the cultural changes surrounding it.

We can make no apology for the adventure towards which this book may call you. We too are on that path and understand how inconvenient and yet meaningful and exciting it can become. For us it has been a bit like the difference between a morgue and a birthing ward at a hospital. One is quiet, cold, orderly, predictable, carries no expectation and is manageable – the morgue. The other often has emergencies, lots of blood, outrageous expectations, panic, screams, the unknown, is hard to manage, is painful but brings new life.

We wrote this book with a desire to open greater possibilities for local congregations, denominations, Christian care agencies, seminaries, schools, groups and individuals who don't seem to fit in the typical church. We are convinced that local congregations have so much to offer. The combined synergy of all the gifts and skills of congregants can result in wonderful kingdom possibilities in many areas of the community if people are empowered, trained and released through Kingdom Communities. They can focus on whatever God opens them to: families, children, youth, young adults, prisoners, frail aged, lonely, addicts, women, men, professionals, unemployed, the environment, First Australians, sports, creative, drugs, homelessness, students, among others. But mostly in local neighbourhoods with neighbours where more than two followers of Christ who are committed to the regular pursuit of basic practises for the purpose of shining the light of Christ through faith, hope and love. That is the normative, historical, biblical and basic pattern of ekklesia.

Denominations too have been within our sights as we have watched the impossible loads they often carry. Dean knows only too well the pressures and expectations that denominations and judicatories carry as a passing model fails to connect with the emerging generations of Westerners and care agencies, and the congregational arm struggle for common mission and purpose. Maintaining churches and their personnel is hard enough without all the other added pressures, compliance and crises. We rarely see a happy bishop or denominational executive – there is too much to carry in overburdened systems and an old model. So, we hope we have shone some light for the crucial role this level of church governance can contribute in the *missio Dei*.

Care agencies (including the many Christian para-church groups) have so much to contribute. If the value of personnel, assets, expertise, networks and influence from this sector was realised fully for the kingdom, the mind boggles. What if more Christian hospitals, educational institutions, aged care, human services, welfare, camping and chaplaincy services were supported by and very intentional in contributing to the formation of Kingdom Communities more – both within and without their boundaries? Their access and potential to shine light into the darkness of society is second to none and embodies holistic Christianity.

Seminaries are greatly needed in the task ahead. While old *Age of Belief* frameworks pass away, critical new methods are required that develop praxis and excellent pedagogy for mission in the *Age of the Spirit* and through Kingdom Communities. A major shift for seminaries will be away from pastor-teacher minister formation to the diverse leadership categories for many people who will be bi-vocational. A shift will also be required towards a broader application of theological education for the whole enterprise of God in the world, not just the traditional, institutional church. Spiritual formation based around practises that flow through Kingdom Communities will become essential.

However, there is another group who have been on our hearts as we wrote. It is the many thousands of people who love Jesus but who have given up on the institutional church. For one reason or another they just can no longer do it. Yet their spiritual life is eager, and their love of Christ is pure. These are the folks who Alan Jamieson awakened us to; the ones who have left the building but kept their faith. Rowland Croucher also opened our eyes to the many good people who loved God and followed his call into pastoral ministry and then got devoured or broken. There is another way, and we hope we have rekindled the dream for these good folk.

A couple of years ago, Andrew was boarding a plane from Melbourne to Adelaide. It was at gate ten in the Qantas domestic terminal – the memory is still so clear. With boarding pass in hand, he was following a young woman to be checked onto the plane. She had a violin hung over her shoulder and was just about to pass the air stewardess when she was pulled back.

"Madam, I am afraid that violin is oversized, and I'll have to put it underneath with the luggage."

The young woman, quietly spoken, was barely audible from a metre behind as she replied, "I have a very special violin which I need to carry with me on board. I'm not permitted to release it to someone else."

Andrew, who had been waiting for his boarding pass to be scanned in that haze typical of travellers, slowly became awakened to a developing scene. The slightly officious stewardess tightened her stance, "I am afraid that you will not be permitted to board with that violin young lady."

"You don't understand. This is a very important violin and I can't let anyone else handle it. It is very precious. I even have a letter from the insurance company that proves it," the passenger said.

"Well then you have a choice. You will have to not board or put the violin underneath but at the moment you are causing a scene and holding up the queue."

Being almost in the conversation and sensing the distress in the passenger (triggered by the officious nature of the stewardess) and with the final half dozen passengers also watching, another passenger asked, "What kind of violin is it?"

The young woman turned with a desperate, pleading look on her face and replied, "It's a Stradivarius. I'm meant to play it tonight in Adelaide and I am not permitted to let anyone else handle it. There will be security in Adelaide to meet me."

Immediately, Andrew understood that it was a violin easily worth over five million dollars. It was the rarest and the best violin available and probably was about three hundred years old. It appeared some of the other passengers also knew what a Stradivarius was and the stewardess, aware that this was genuine, could see that she was losing the demarcation battle. She called her boss and to cut a tense story short, the violin travelled with the young lady, who must have been one of Australia's elite violinists.

Antonio Stradivari (1644 - 1737) was a master violin maker who ran a music shop in Cremona, Italy. Being a master, he trained younger apprentices and effectively ran a violin making school through his working life. He used proven techniques to make the violins but also knew where to source the special timber. The best timber came from a certain species of tree, which grew at a certain elevation on a certain side of the mountain. His apprentices learned from a master and the violins were sought from across the globe.

Brian McLaren tells the story of the Stradivarius school, which lasted after Antonio had died. Eventually the source of wood ran out and so the school slowly diminished. The violin makers kept their craft but not with the same timber. Decades later it was discovered that a village in the location of the depleted timber had constructed all their houses with the very same timber. The floorboards and the ceilings were constructed with the exact timber needed to make a proper Stradivarius violin. The villagers were offered a tidy sum of money to replace the floorboards and ceilings of their houses, which meant that there was a new supply of the wood.

Once the timber had been taken from the houses and piled up, the challenge came of how to sort the timber. There were only a couple of master violin makers alive who knew how to properly sort it. They were called up to the village with some young apprentices who were given the task of learning how to sort the timber. What occurred next was fascinating and caused Michael Polanyi to reflect on the process of formation in his seminal book, *Personal Knowledge*.[1] No words were spoken as the masters sat with one plank of wood at a time, tapping, weighing, feeling, listening to the resin and even spitting on each plank as it was sorted. The apprentices simply watched, gradually deducting what was useful wood and what was ruined. There were no power point presentations; no lectures; no motivational speeches nor were any words necessary. By the end of the process the apprentices could emulate their masters and knew exactly what they were looking for too.

Today there are only about five hundred Stradivarius violins known to be in existence and Andrew was fortunate to get within a metre of one that almost didn't make a flight from Melbourne to Adelaide. It was a memorable experience that reinforced the ongoing value of Antonio Stradivari's master craft, hundreds of years later. It was through the development of certain, repeated practises that great Stradivarius apprentices were formed.

Kingdom Communities too can only achieve their fully formed purpose as useful tools in the missio Dei if we apply ourselves also to practises that help us attend, listen, discern and become sensitive to the activity

---

[1] Michael Polanyi, *Personal Knowledge: Towards a Post-Critical Philosophy*, Chicago: University of Chicago Press, 1958. Polanyi was a Hungarian-British polymath who contributed to chemistry, economics and philosophy.

of God, as well as disturbed by the need of the world. They are not a quick fix or solution to modern church decline. They are not programs either. They are patterns for communities attentive to the kingdom, which therefore makes their form flexible, but they seem always to be categorised as more than two followers of Christ who are committed to the regular pursuit of basic practises for the purpose of shining the light of Christ through faith, hope and love.

We have sought to develop the possibility and reality of Kingdom Communities historically, theologically, through case studies, in a diverse range of contexts, across a denominational system as well as in isolated circumstances. We have also tried to open up some of the useful methodologies that can assist their emergence and ongoing effectiveness, particularly Action Learning (SALTs); *Single, double* and *triple-loop learning*; Deep Listening; leadershifts; and practises. The world needs light.

Alan Roxburgh introduced the work of Edith and Victor Turner over twenty years ago to those of us concerned with the engagement of gospel, culture and ekklesia through the publication of *The Missionary Congregation, Leadership, and Liminality*.[2] Victor and Edith Turner were British cultural Anthropologists who lived much of their lives in Zambia (which was then named Northern Rhodesia) among the Ndembu people. It was there that they studied culture, customs and rites of passage. As a part of their learning about the rites of passage, they applied a theory (developed by Arnold van Gennep) of three stages of liminality: pre, liminal and post.

Liminality is a state that an individual or group of people can experience when there is significant transition. If we use the simple example of crossing a road, liminality is the point when you are well past making the decision to cross the road, in fact you are so far across the road you cannot go back and must continue across to the other side. The journey is not complete but it is well underway. We each have liminal experiences in life (for example, between primary school and high school, between jobs or when tentatively entering a new relationship

---

2 Alan J. Roxburgh., *The Missionary Congregation, Leadership, and Liminality*. Harrisburg, PA: Trinity Press International, 1997.

or departing a long standing one) and therefore we can appreciate how disorienting things can be for what Victor Turner called, 'in betwixt and between'.

Turner's understanding of liminality was in regard to the rites of passage of the young men of the Ndembu tribes. These were young people who moved between childhood and manhood through a convergence of puberty, testing, story-telling and initiation. The process involved a pre-liminal phase (when they were still regarded as children and belonged with then women and girls); a liminal phase (when they were ripped from that place of comfort and security), and a post-liminal phase when they again understood their place among the tribe, but now as men.

The Turners discovered that an essential outcome, central to the whole process, was that the young men transitioned as a cohort into manhood and therefore could not go back to become children again. They had become men. It was not a transition to be completed alone. The whole liminal phase was shared by all who were of similar age and whatever obstacle that was thrown against them (often intentionally as part of the process by the older men) was done so that they could bond together. The key lesson was that the best chance of survival for each emerging man and the tribe they defended, was through sticking together and helping each other. This outcome was called *communitas*.

Communitas is a word very similar to community yet the two words usually carry entirely different qualities of experience, especially in modern life. We often hear churches describe themselves as communities and some even add this word to their name to emphasise the point. However, the idea behind communitas goes far further than most people experience in the average church – though it certainly does and can happen there. Communitas refers to the experience of a cohort who have undergone an often-traumatic transition, together. It can be experienced by a sporting team that achieves a significant achievement together, a company that endures hardship and restructure or a Kingdom Community that forms its own practises and identity over time. Importantly, only those in a cohort, who stick through the ups and downs of the journey, are the ones who are formed and shaped by the experience. Thus they find themselves bound by communitas, which can really only be known in its fullest degree by others who have had the same experience.

We see many examples in the Old Testament where the people of God endured a liminal space, sometimes for decades in the desert or exile, and emerged bonded by communitas. We can see many moments where a group of early Christ followers experienced communitas in the New Testament. In times of persecution and danger, the group no doubt experienced liminality followed by communitas. In liminal moments of theological reflection and uncertainty where what God was doing was unknown and Councils or discernment were required, communitas was an outcome. Throughout the history of the church this phenomenon has reoccurred. Indeed we venture to say that liminality and communitas are regular marks of the activity of God and the formation of his followers and should be normative. They don't come easily but they do form God's people.

Throughout this book, each case study presented has carried the challenge of a liminal space, which has defined real and genuine communitas (in a men's shed, among a team of suburban grandparents called to a ministry among prostitutes, in the founding of a school or among poor, rural Brazilian people, for instance). It has been experienced because the journey was done together by more than two followers of Christ who are committed to the regular pursuit of basic practises for the purpose of shining the light of Christ through faith, hope and love. All of the Kingdom Communities, whose stories we have told, contain this rich experience. Actually, it is hard to see how disciples can be formed without liminality and communitas, which after all are how God and life tend to bring maturity.

And finally ... we tell an intentionally simple case study, to complete the circle where we began. An older couple retired to Queensland from Victoria where they had been involved in serving within their church for decades. Upon arriving at the Sunshine Coast, they heard about Coffee Chaplaincy – a group of Christian volunteers offering coffee, warmth and a listening ear from a coffee cart in the community. Although the older couple felt overwhelmed and underprepared, they stepped out and joined the team. They reflected that their life within their church had been good but always with the other church members. They had never done something like this – stepping out engaging with the community in service.

Since then, their eyes have been opened to where, and how, Jesus is active in the wider world. They have joined a Kingdom Community that has formed around the visiting coffee cart and associated chaplaincy, as various needs arise because they deliberately put themselves into a place of use to God. Volunteers, regulars and new people connect, and their stories are gradually told as they are listened to, loved, prayed for and uplifted. The couple themselves are alive with so many stories of lives touched and possibilities for enabling the light of Christ to be shining more in individuals and families in their community. They feel blessed and now describe themselves, in what was meant to be retirement, as passionate local missionaries. They are alive to Christ more than ever. They now know that the harvest is really, really ripe.

Time and again, we see similar stories taking place. When people break out of a religious framework, join a team and engage in 'people to people' care, their theology and worldview often changes. We pray that Kingdom Communities truly enable the light of Christ to shine through faith, hope and love. After all, Paul said, "Three things will last forever—faith, hope, and love—and the greatest of these is love" (1Cor 13:13).

Bibliography

Argyris, C. *Knowledge for Action: A Guide to Overcoming Barriers to Organizational Change*, San Francisco: Jossey Bass, 1993.

Argyris, C., & Schön, D.A. *Theory in Practice. Increasing Professional Effectiveness*, San Francisco: Jossey-Bass, 1974.

Banks, R., *Going to Church in the First Century*, Jacksonville: Seed Sowers, 1980.

Banks, R., *Paul's Idea of Community: The Early House Churches in the Cultural Setting*, Grand Rapids: Baker, 1994.

Banks, R., *The Church Comes Home*, Peabody: Hendrickson, 1998.

Barker, A., *Making Poverty Personal: Taking the Poor as Seriously as the Bible Does*, Grand Rapids: Baker Books, 2009.

Barreiro, A., *Basic Ecclesial Communities: The Evangelization of the Poor*, New York: Orbis, 1984.

Barton, R.H., *Sacred Rhythms: Arranging our lives for Spiritual Transformation*, Grand Rapids: InterVarsity Press, 2006.

Barton, R.H., *Strengthening the Soul of Your Leadership: Seeking God in the Crucible of Ministry*, Downers Grove: IVP Books, 2008.

Bass, D.C., (ed.), *Practicing our Faith: A Way of Life for Searching People*, San Francisco: Jossey-Bass, 1997.

Boff, L., *Ecclesiogenesis: The Base Communities Reinvent the Church*, New York: Orbis, 1986.

Boff, L., *The Maternal Face of God: The Feminine and Its Religious Expressions*, New York: Harper/Collins Publishers, 1989.

Brafman, O. & Beckstrom, R.A. *The Starfish and the Spider: The Unstoppable Power of Leaderless Organizations*, New York: Penguin Putnam, 2011.

Bridges, W., *Transitions: Making Sense of Life's Changes*, Cambridge: Perseus Books, 2004.

Butler-Bass, D. *The Practicing Congregation: Imagining a New Old Church*, Herndon: Alban Institute, 2004.

Carrell, B., *Moving between the Times: Modernity and Postmodernity: A Christian View*, Auckland: Deepsight Trust, 1998.

Carver, J. *Boards that make a Difference: A New Design for Leadership in Non-Profit and Public Organizations*, San Francisco: John Wiley, 2006.

Chadwick, H. *The Early Church: The Story of Emergent Christianity from the Apostolic Age to the Dividing of the Ways between the Greek East and the Latin West*, London: Penguin, 1993.

Congar, Yves., *Power and Poverty in the Church*, Baltimore: Helicon Press, 1964.

Covey, Stephen, R., *The Seven Habits of Highly Effective People: Restoring the Character Ethic*, New York: Rosetta LLC, 1989.

Cox, H., *The Future of Faith*, New York: Harper One, 2009.

Crowley, F., *A Documentary History of Australia: Colonial Australia*, Melbourne: Nelson, 1980.

Dotlich, D.L., & Noel, J.L., *Action Learning: How the World's Top Companies are Re-creating their Leaders and Themselves*, San Francisco: Jossey-Bass, 1998.

Elwell, Walter A., (ed.)., *Evangelical Dictionary of Theology*, Grand Rapids: Baker, 1984, Wright, David F., "Catechesis".

Elwell, Walter A., (ed.)., *Evangelical Dictionary of Theology: Volume 2*, Grand Rapids: Baker, 1988, Ladd, George E., "Kingdom of God (Heaven)".

Frost, M., Exiles: *Living Missionally in a Post-Christian Culture*, Massachusetts: Hendrickson, 2006.

Frost, M., *Surprise the World: Five Habits of Highly Missional People*, Colorado Springs: NavPress, 2016.

Frost, M. & Hirsch, A. *The Shaping of Things to Come: Innovation and Mission for the 21st Century Church*, Grand Rapids: Hendrickson, 2003.

Gladwell, M., *The Tipping Point: How Little Things Can Make a Big Difference*, London: Abacus, 2002.

Grenz, S.J., *A Primer on Postmodernism*, Grand Rapids: William B. Eerdmans, 1996.

Heifetz, R., & Linsky, M., *Leadership on the Line: Staying Alive Through the Dangers of Leading*, Boston, Harvard Business School Press, 2002.

Heifetz, R., *Leadership without Easy Answers*, London: Belknap Press, 1994.

Heifetz, R., Grashow, A., & Linsky, M., *The Practice of Adaptive Leadership: Tools and Tactics for Changing your Organization and the World*, Boston: Harvard Business School Press, 2009.

Hellerman, J.H., *When the Church was a Family: Recapturing Jesus' Vision for Authentic Christian Community*, Nashville: B & H Publishing, 2009.

Hill, G., *GlobalChurch: Reshaping Our Conversations, Renewing Our Mission, Revitalizing Our Churches*, Downers Grove: IVP Academic, 2016.

Hill, G., & Kim, G.J.S., *Healing our Broken Humanity: Practices for Revitalizing the Church and renewing the World*, Downers Grove: InterVarsity Press, 2018.

Hirsch, A. & Ferguson, D., *On the Verge: A Journey into the Apostolic Future if the Church*, Grand Rapids: Zondervan, 2011.

Hirsch, A., *The Forgotten Ways: Reactivating the Missional Church*, Grand Rapids: Brazos, 2006.

Holt, S.C., *God Next Door: Spirituality and Mission in the Neighbourhood*, Melbourne: Acorn, 2007.

Homan, D., & Collins Pratt, L., *Radical Hospitality: Benedict's Way of Love*, Brewster, MA: Paraclete Press, 2002.

Hughes, P.J., Fraser, M., & Reid, S., *Australia's Religious Communities: Facts and Figures from the 2011 Australian Census and other Sources*, Nunawading: Church Research Association, 2012.

Isaacs, W., *Dialogue and the Art of Thinking Together*, Cambridge: Currency, 1999.

Jamieson, A., *A Churchless Faith: Faith Journeys beyond Churches*, London: SPCK, 2000.

Jamieson, A., MacIntosh, J., & Thompson, A., *Five years on: Continuing Faith Journeys of those who left the Church*, Wellington: Portland Research Trust, 2006.

Johnson, L.T., *Scripture and Discernment: Decision making in the Church*, Nashville: Abingdon, 1983.

Kreider, A., *The Change of Conversion and the Origin of Christendom*, Harrisberg, PA: Trinity Press, 1999.

Kuhn, T., *The Structure of Scientific Revolution*, Chicago: University of Chicago Press, 2012.

Laloux, F. *Reinventing Organizations: A Guide to Creating Organizations Inspired by the Next stage of Human Consciousness*, Brussels: Nelson Parker, 2014.

Mackay, H., *Beyond Belief: How we find Meaning, with or without Religion*, Sydney: Pan Macmillan, 2016.

Mackay, H., *The Art of Belonging: It's not where you live, it's how you live*, Sydney: Pan Macmillan, 2014.

Mackay, H., *The Good Life: What makes a life worth living?* Sydney: Pan Macmillan, 2013.

MacIntyre, A., *After Virtue: A Study in Moral Theology*, Notre Dame: University of Notre Dame Press, 1997.

Malina, B., *Christian Origins and Cultural Anthropology*, Atlanta: John Knox, 1986.

Morris, R., *Scoping Study: Impact of Fly-in-fly-out/ Drive-in-drive-out work practices on Local Government*, Sydney: Australian Centre of Excellence for Local Government, 2012.

Newbigin, L., *A Word in Season: Perspectives on Christian World Missions*, Grand Rapids: Eerdmans, 1994.

Newbigin, L., *The Open Secret: An introduction to the theology of mission*, Grand Rapids: Eerdmans, 1995.

Nouwen, H., *Bread for the Journey: A Daybook of Wisdom and Faith*, New York: Harper Collins, 2009.

Nouwen, H., *In The Name of Jesus: Reflections on Christian Leadership*, New York: Crossroad Publishing Company, 1989.

Nyhuis, R.J., *Pentecostal Ministry Formation within Christian Revival Churches (CRC) in Australia: a History, Case Study and Vision*, Melbourne: University of Divinity - Doctor of Philosophy, 2018.

Peterson, E., *The Message: The Bible in Contemporary language*, Colorado Springs: NavPress, 2002.

Pohl, C., *Making Room: Recovering Hospitality as a Christian Tradition*, Grand Rapids: Eerdmans, 1999.

Polanyi, M. *Personal Knowledge: Towards a Post-Critical Philosophy*, Chicago: University of Chicago Press, 1958.

Revans, R., *ABC of Action Learning*, Surrey: Gower Publishing, 2011.

Risson, G., & Brown, C., *The Church from the Paddock: A History of Churches of Christ in Queensland 1883 – 2013*, Second Edition, Kenmore: Churches of Christ in Queensland, 2016.

Rogers, E.M., *Diffusion of Innovations*, New York: Free Press, 2003.

Rohr, R., *Everything Belongs: The gift of contemplative prayer*, New York: Crossroad, 2003.

Rohr, R., *Falling Upward: A spirituality for the Two Halves of Life*, Hoboken: Wiley and Sons, 2011.

Romme, G.L., & van Witteloostuijn, A., "Circular organizing and triple-loop learning," *Journal of Organisational Change Management*, (Vol. 12, Iss 5, 1999).

Rothwell, W.J., *The Action Learning Guidebook: A real-time strategy for problem solving, training design, and employee development*, San Francisco: Jossey-Bass Pfeiffer, 1999.

Roxburgh, A.J., *Introducing the Missional Church: What it is, Why it matters, How to become one*, Grand Rapids: Baker, 2009.

Roxburgh, A.J., *Joining God, Remaking Church, Changing the World: The New Shape of the Church in Our Time*, New York: Morehouse, 2015.

Roxburgh, A.J., *Missional: Joining God in the Neighbourhood*, Grand Rapids: Baker, 2011.

Roxburgh, A.J., *Missional Map Making: Skills for Leading in Times of Transition*, San Francisco: Jossey-Bass, 2010.

Roxburgh, A.J., *Structured for Mission: Renewing the Culture of the Church*, Downers Grove: IVP, 2015.

Roxburgh, A.J., *The Missionary Congregation, Leadership, and Liminality.* Harrisburg, PA: Trinity Press International, 1997.

Roxburgh, A.J., & Romanuk, F., *Missional Action Teams: A Workbook for Participants*, Vancouver: Missional Leadership Institute, 2003.

Schwartz, C.A., *Natural Church Development: Eight Essential Qualities of Healthy Churches*, Mt Gravatt East: Direction Ministry Resources, 1996.

Sparks, P., Soerens, T., & Friessen, D.J., *The New Parish: How Neighbourhood Churches are Transforming Mission, Discipleship and Community*, Downers Grove: IVP Books, 2014.

Suter, K.D., *The future of the Uniting Church in Australia: The Application of Scenario Planning to the Creation of four 'Futures' for the Uniting Church in Australia*, Sydney: University of Sydney – Doctor of Philosophy, 2013.

Turnbull, C., *A Concise History of Australia*, Melbourne: Currey O'Neil, 1983.

Turner, E., *Communitas: The Anthropology of Collective Joy*, New York: Palgrave Macmillan, 2001.

Van Eymeren, A., *Building Communities of the Kingdom: How to work with others to build great spaces and places*, Morning Star: Melbourne, 2017.

Wright, N.T., *Simply Christian*, New York: Harper One, 2006.

Wright, N.T., "The Cross and the Caricatures," London: Fulcrum, 2007.

Zaffron, S., & Logan, D., *The Three Laws of Performance: Rewriting the Future of your Organization and your Life*, San Francisco: Jossey-Bass, 2009.

Acknowledgements

Thanks...

No book is written without the support of many people, nor does it develop in isolation from a concept and move towards fruition without even more participants. We name here those closest to this project, fully aware of all the others who have offered invaluable help at many points along the wild and testing journey. We are not being insincere in saying thank-you to the many unnamed folk who have played a pivotal part in our lives and thoughts as we have brought this to fruition - you know who you are and we trust you share in the joy of this project and the advance of the Kingdom it is intended to serve. Seeds for this book were sown many years ago in both Andrew and Dean and more acutely started to sprout shoots from 2010 when Dean commenced as CEO of Churches of Christ in Queensland and Andrew as Principal at Stirling College – University of Divinity. From separate parts of Australia and in very different contexts, our observations, learning, testing and imagination have been sparked and sharpened by the potential and reality of Kingdom Communities. We are grateful to Morning Star Publishing for committing to this project as publishers and especially to our editor, Amanda McKenna who has been so knowledgeable, accurate and professional.

Andrew wishes to specifically record his thanks to the wonderful learning community that is Stirling College. There is no other seminary like it – the Christological commitment; the beauty of its campus; the generous orthodoxy of its diverse community; the brilliance of collegiate membership in the ecumenical and constantly evolving University of Divinity; the investment and care of over a century of alumni and supporters; the extraordinary research and learning that flows into papers, articles, books, people and Kingdom Communities; and the extraordinary Board, staff, faculty and students who make it what it is. Special thanks to my two Board chairs over the journey, John Sharpe and Lynette Leach, who have been constant and tireless in their support of the college's mission and quality as well as the completion of this book.

The bulk of Andrew's writing for this manuscript was completed in Busselton, Western Australia, while on sabbatical, generously provided by the Stirling College Board. Andrew and his family were virtually adopted by the beautiful people of Cornerstone Church of Christ and Cornerstone Christian school, especially the Atkinsons, Riches, Reids and Sykes families as well as Gary Maynard, Jo Needham and Brittany Haythornthwaite. This book was written with a photo of Ringwood Church of Christ in Andrew's phone. Ringwood is a dynamic, creative and generous community of Christ's people who are always attempting to make space in their busy lives for the pursuit of God expressed as love in action in the community. Our faith is orthodox but our methods may not be! At every point this book had to pass the test of building up and helping communities such as Ringwood in the challenging reality of local ministry. Some individuals also have been exceptional encouragers on the journey and Andrew wishes to thank these folk for assistance in enabling this book to come to fruition: Sarah Bacaller, Merryl Blair, John Bond, Josh Bond, Mark Lau Branson, Paul and Amanda Cameron, Sam Curkpatrick, Stephen Curkpatrick, Colleen Davies, Rohan Dredge, Greg Elsdon, Michael Frost, Darryl Gardiner, Graham Hill, Alan Hirsch, Amit Khaira, Rick Lewis, Brian Macallan, Penny Martin, Tim McCowan, Lauren Miko, Alan Niven, Mark Riessen, Angela Sawyer, Peter Sherlock, Theresa Taylor, Chris Turner, Belinda Waterhouse, Tania Watson, John Williamson, Arthur Wouters and Caroline Young. Also my thanks to the team at Churches of Christ in Queensland in the years of this book's focus, in particular Tim McMenamin, Steve Drinkall, Gerry Weatherall, Desley Millwood, David Swain, Donna Savill, and Gary Edwards who live this stuff and enabled generous, open access and friendship. I wish to especially acknowledge the UNOH teams in Melbourne, Auckland, Sydney, Wellington and Bangkok who live out this stuff so well that we built a whole chapter about their incredible work – the best is yet to come! Alan Roxburgh has been a source of constant encouragement and through The Missional Network enables thoughtful, reflective and grounded conversation from theorists and practitioners. His foreword is a generous example of his ongoing leadership and laying down of the challenge before us all about discerning what God is up to. The opportunity of co-authoring this book with a super-skilled and thoughtful leader and friend who has actually implemented this material and proved that it really is happening across a whole system has been a joy - thanks Dean and also to Janette who has supported, verified and tested this along the way. Finally and appropriately, huge thanks to my best friend and wife Kim, along with James and Ellie who have lived and breathed this book and allowed dad to go away far too often as stories were sought, bits were read and pieces were tested.

As well as the hundreds of front line leaders who contributed to the transformation and integration of Churches of Christ in Queensland and Care during his tenure as CEO from 2010-2017, Dean wishes to thank those who he worked most closely with during these years: David Swain who was Chief Operating Officer, and Gerry Weatherall, Chief Mission Development Officer – both key colleagues in the development and implementation of our movement ideas; Desley Millwood, our Communications Director who coordinated and promoted the new mission narrative everywhere; Tim McMenamin, missional leader and champion of the Strategic Action Leadership Teams, together with Steve Drinkall, gifted frontier leader; Steve Slade, Company Secretary and "consigliere"; Trent Dean, who kept us honest and safe as Head of Assurance services; Peter Cranna, our Chief Financial Officer, followed by Michael Brand who both ensured we were being truly good stewards of all of Churches of Christ's assets. Frances Paterson-Fleider, Bryan Mason, Kim Teudt, and Jane Carter all played key leadership roles in forwarding the light of Christ in communities. Dean also wants to acknowledge Gary Edwards as Chair of the Board and Greg Runge as Chair of Council for their significant roles in engaging and aligning our stakeholders around the new vision, mission strategies and possibilities for the future. Additionally, Dean wishes to thank his wife Janette, a Mission Action Partner on the front line, for her constant love and feedback on how well we were actually doing; his good friend Brian Donovan for his leadership coaching and encouragement; Keith Farmer for his mentoring and wise counsel, and Spiritual Directors George Warren and Bruce Warwick for their companionship, wisdom and prayer over many years. Dean's contribution to this manuscript was written over six months as he recovered from treatment for Acute Myeloid Leukaemia. One of the blessings of this difficult time, was the opportunity to reflect deeply on the matters we discuss in this book. I (Dean) am deeply thankful to everyone who has travelled with me on the journey - hopefully you will be able to read the strands of your influence in this book. And, lastly, a very big thank you to my co-author Andrew for your friendship, encouragement in what we were trying to do, and invitation to join you in the writing of this book.

www.ingramcontent.com/pod-product-compliance
Lightning Source LLC
Chambersburg PA
CBHW060351190426
43201CB00044B/1992